THE ESSENTIAL WRITINGS OF BERNARD COOKE

College of the Holy Cross Archives. Used with permission.

THE ESSENTIAL WRITINGS OF
Bernard Cooke

A Narrative Theology of Church, Sacrament, and Ministry

Bernard Cooke
with
Bruce T. Morrill

FOREWORD BY
Elizabeth A. Johnson

Paulist Press
New York / Mahwah, NJ

Acknowledgments of permissions to reprint copyright material are listed under the appropriate entries in Abbreviations and Acknowledgments of Works Cited.

Cover design by Joe Gallagher
Book design by Lynn Else

Library of Congress Cataloging-in-Publication Data

Names: Cooke, Bernard J., 1922– author.
Title: The essential writings of Bernard Cooke : a narrative theology of church, sacrament, and ministry / Bernard Cooke, with Bruce T. Morrill ; foreword by Elizabeth A. Johnson.
Description: New York : Paulist Press, 2016. | Includes bibliographical references and index.
Identifiers: LCCN 2015033776 (print) | LCCN 2015044215 (ebook) | ISBN 9780809149759 (pbk. : alk. paper) | ISBN 9781587685880 (ebook)
Subjects: LCSH: Catholic Church—Doctrines. | Cooke, Bernard J., 1922–
Classification: LCC BX1751.3 .C6557 2016 (print) | LCC BX1751.3 (ebook) | DDC 230/.2—dc23
LC record available at http://lccn.loc.gov/2015033776

Published by Paulist Press
997 Macarthur Boulevard
Mahwah, New Jersey 07430

www.paulistpress.com

Printed and bound in the
United States of America

Contents

Contents

Foreword

By all accounts, American Catholic theology began to come of age in the mid-twentieth century. Among the notable figures of that period and beyond, Bernard Cooke stands tall not only for a highly original body of writings spanning more than a half-century but also for his visionary leadership at both the academic and popular levels. Just as the Second Vatican Council was getting underway, Cooke founded a PhD program specifically for lay theologians at Marquette University that from the start, not only welcomed but promoted women as teachers and scholars. During that decade, Cooke was a bit of a "rock star" on the Catholic religious educational scene, lecturing to crowded auditoriums of nuns and other laypeople and producing accessible books conveying a practical theology based on the vision of Vatican II. With his departure from the Jesuits and subsequent marriage, however, came his loss of both a prominent university platform for his scholarship and diocesan and other church-based venues for his popular presentations.

The Catholic Church and the theological academy, of course, continued to evolve through the 1970s, as did Cooke's research and writing about church and ministry. This proved to be groundbreaking work that returned him to the national stage in the early 1980s. At that time, I was completing my own graduate studies in theology at the Catholic University of America. As I entered the world of professional theology, I began attending the annual meetings of the Catholic Theological Society of America (CTSA). Its founding members had all been priests, and membership was only slowly beginning to shift to include qualified persons who were not ordained. This move was not without friction, as academic rather than ecclesial rules of procedure required clergy to cede dominance and share leadership with lay members.

A sea of men in black topped with Roman collars—such is the memory I have of my earliest attendance at CTSA meetings; only about 5 percent of those gathered in the hotel ballroom wore more colorful clothing, let alone skirts. In that setting, controversy swirled over the candidacy of Bernard Cooke for the role of president, the first married man to be so nominated. Some held it was not fitting for someone who had made his life choices to lead the still largely clerical society; others argued that his academic credentials and the quality of his work would make him a superb leader. It was a signal moment in the history of theology in this country when a majority of his peers voted in his favor. Another striking moment came the following year (1983) when, according to the Society's custom, Bernard Cooke delivered the presidential address. For the first time ever, a family was in attendance. His wife, Dr. Pauline Turner, sat attentively in the front row while his young daughter, Kelly, filled with enthusiasm, scampered irrepressibly around taking pictures of him with her Instamatic camera, flashcubes going off to boot. That little scene symbolized to me what a huge change was underway in how Catholic theology was increasingly going to be done—and by whom—and in how it was being transformed from simply an academic exercise into a means of vital contact with problems of today's people.

The hallmark of Bernard Cooke's theology was his insistence on the sacramentality of human lives shared in communities, on the concrete character of living persons and human history as revelatory of the unseen transcendent mystery we call God. He was best known as a sacramental theologian, but the selections from Cooke's many publications that Bruce Morrill has organized into four thematic chapters in this volume treat us to the full scope of his theology. From fundamental theology (the nature of revelation and grace) to Christology and pneumatology to sacraments and, finally, ministry and popular traditions in the Church, Cooke consistently presses a vision of Christian life as grounded in friendship and guided by prophets, nourished essentially by the love of Jesus realized in the Eucharist. Morrill's artful weaving of passages from Cooke's candid memoir throughout the book draws the reader into an intimate narrative theology enabling Cooke to teach afresh in this hopeful new moment for the Church.

Elizabeth A. Johnson

Preface

This book is a highly personal work of theology, and personal in more than one sense. Structurally, it comprises the integration of selected writings from the five decades of publications by the influential American Catholic theologian Bernard Cooke (1922–2013) with excerpts from his unpublished memoir. Interpretation of human experience—individual and communal, contemporary and historical—as sacramentally revelatory of God's active presence to people became the fundamental principle guiding Cooke's lengthy career as a professor and prolific author. Often noted for the lucidity of his academic prose, Cooke in his memoir repeatedly characterizes his as a "down-to-earth" approach to theology. The weaving of his life story with the major themes running through his publications, then, promises a profitable synthesis of his experience-based theology. With the sacramentality of friendship—meaningful relationships of all kinds, including between humans and the divine—constituting the heart of his theology, Cooke's accounts of key relationships and experiences in his own life fittingly elucidate the convictions driving his proposals for renewed living of Christian tradition and the reformed life of the church in our time.

Cooke's theological project, a vocation assigned him as a young Jesuit in the early 1950s, was the development of a "theology of the laity," that is, an original approach to teaching and writing about the content and practice of the faith in an idiom conducive to a rapidly changing American Catholicism. Entrusted by his Midwestern Jesuit superiors to acquire the requisite theological knowledge and pedagogical skills to transform moribund college- and university-level religious education, Cooke returned from doctoral studies at the Institut Catholique de Paris himself intellectually and personally transformed. In late 1957, he arrived at Marquette University not only shaped by newly emerging historical, biblical, and catechetical methodologies but also deeply affected by the persons and, indeed, the fates of the French theologians themselves, many of whom suffered censure only to be vindicated by their roles at Vatican II. His European sojourn included what in his memoir he describes as an even greater influence on his theology: the final year of his Jesuit formation (tertianship) in post–World War II Germany, during which Christology as personal, contemplative, and eucharistic encounter with Jesus became wedded to critical engagement with church and society. The "turn to experience" for Cooke came in the form of a renewal movement in Ignatian spirituality that was under way in certain European quarters, such that when he returned to take up almost immediately the chairmanship of Marquette's theology department, he did so with a passion for helping young men and women appropriate and contribute to the faith in their own context— "down-to-earth" theology.

Cooke's fame was coextensive with his decade of theological leadership at Marquette, where, with limited faculty resources, he revolutionized the undergraduate curriculum while founding a graduate program at the masters and then doctoral levels. With the latter struggling to get underway just as Vatican II convened, Cooke recounts how he turned down more than one bishop's invitation to be a *peritus* at the council—an arresting testament to his humility. He did, nonetheless, serve as a consultant to Cardinal Dearden in Detroit during summers between the Council sessions. Seemingly limitless in energy, Cooke maintained an active role in civic, Catholic, ecumenical, and interreligious affairs in Milwaukee, Detroit, and Chicago, served on national consultations on catechetics and liturgical renewal, participated in ecumenism through bilateral dialogue and journal board memberships, and lectured priests, religious, and laity throughout the United States on the theology of Vatican II, renewal of religious life, the sacraments, and so forth. Internationally, Cooke was involved with the commission drafting the directory on ecumenism (chaired by Cardinal Willebrands), a European conference on renewal of Jesuit spirituality (led by Carlo Martini, later the archbishop of Milan, among others), and lecturing on Vatican II in Japan, Korea, and sub-Saharan African countries. To a steady stream of journal articles and small monographs in 1965 he added his first major book, *Christian Sacraments & Christian Personality*, a standard text for a generation of students, soon followed by a pair of books on revelation, grace, and church.

For all Cooke's enthusiasm for the life of the gospel in the church and for the world, however, by the late 1960s, a deepening alienation from the clerical power structures he encountered in all those arenas—and most fatefully at Marquette itself—led to Cooke's decision to resign from the Jesuits. While his love for the Jesuits made this an agonizing decision, Cooke realized that his work with and research on the laity pulled him to a deepening identification with them as well as to a deepening love for one in particular. After leaving Marquette, he spent a research year at Yale Divinity School, during which he married Pauline Turner, a former colleague at Marquette. In the early years of their marriage, they would welcome the birth of their daughter, Kelly.

Amid the mounting numbers of North American priests and vowed religious departing their ranks, Cooke's move was disheartening and even scandalous to many. His memoir describes his and Pauline's discernment to pursue together a ministry of education, for which the first stage was a joint faculty appointment at the University of Windsor, Ontario, across the bridge from Detroit, where the Catholic theological faculty tapped his expertise in an effort to start a doctoral program. That five-year period included his turning down an invitation from the College of William and Mary to found their religious studies department and the dispiriting episode of being offered a professorship at Santa Clara University only for it to be overturned by the provincial superior of the California Jesuits. With funding for the graduate program at Windsor having never materialized, Cooke, along with a Jewish and a Muslim scholar, became a founding member of the religious studies department at the University of Calgary, where he and Pauline also did catechetical formation work for the Catholic diocese. Still, the couple experienced Canadian life as a sort of exile (his title for that chapter of the memoir), such that when the publication of his magnum opus, *Ministry to Word and Sacraments*, triggered job offers in 1980 from the University of San Francisco, Villanova University, and the College of the Holy Cross, he accepted a professorship at Holy Cross, where he recounts with gratitude a unanimously positive reception by the Jesuits. Beyond the gates of that small undergraduate college his influence resurged through his presidency of the Catholic Theological Society of America, his further publication of journal articles and several books, including his still widely read *Sacraments & Sacramentality*, lecturing nationally in multiple summer ministry and education institutes, service on the editorial boards of major theological journals, and a year's fellowship at the Woodrow Wilson Center for International Scholars in Washington, DC.

Cooke's twelve-year tenure (until retirement at age seventy) at Holy Cross is the point in this brief biography at which the personal character of the present book emerges in a further sense. I was in my senior year majoring in religious studies when Cooke joined the faculty. During the seminar in which he led fifteen of us through a close study of Edward Schillebeeckx's newly released tome, *Christ: The Experience of Jesus as Lord*, he assigned me the discussion and research paper on the Johannine material—portions of which I still tap in my teaching and writing. After my college graduation, Cooke remained a mentor to me, encouraging me to obtain a masters degree in cultural anthropology as a "cutting edge tool" to bring to doctoral studies in sacramental-liturgical theology. That advice alone has proven invaluable ever since. When I eventually joined the faculty at Boston College, I was afforded the opportunity to host Bernard (sometimes with Pauline) for dinner when he offered an annual summer course at the Institute of Religious Education and Pastoral Ministry. He and Pauline pursued some twenty-five further years of teaching, writing, and ministry, mostly in the Southwest, after leaving Holy Cross. While our contact was only occasional—he contributed to a book I edited, we met up at conferences and exchanged consultative emails—I valued him as a model of theology as a vocation, as a comprehensive ministry of teaching, publishing, and pastoral service.

And so it was my turn at humility when several months after Bernard's death on May 31, 2013, his ninety-first birthday, I learned that Pauline had decided legally to entrust me to work with Bernard's personal collection of publications, lectures, and other notes, including a forty thousand-word memoir drafted in his final years, for the purpose of publication. The expressed hope of Pauline and Bernard's closest colleagues was that I might work to bring the material, in some form, into publication. The materials reached me in stages by summer 2014, the beginning of a year's sabbatical leave for me from Vanderbilt Divinity School.

Poring over the pages of the memoir, a draft in need of careful editing, I slowly conceived of a book project: I would integrate portions of the memoir into a thematically organized selection of his writings, with my own analysis weaving biographical and scholarly texts together into a synthesis of Cooke's experience-based theology. By summer's end, I was able to propose the present book to Paulist Press, to whom I am deeply grateful for their favorable decision.

My thanks at Paulist go especially to Academic Editor Nancy de Flon, who has so graciously guided this, my second book with her at the Press. I likewise extend my sincere gratitude to Pauline Turner for her help and encouragement, along with daughter Kelly Turner-Cooke, and their friends Patience and Michael McGuire, who in various ways helped with the project. At Vanderbilt Divinity School, I benefited from the practical and efficient services of Heather Lee, Claire Sauerbrei-Brown, and Marcelle T. Smith. Jonathan Stotts read portions of the manuscript and helped with revising my prose, in places, for clarity. A portion of the fall term of my sabbatical I spent as a visiting fellow at the Katholieke Universiteit Leuven. I am grateful to my host-professor, Joris Geldhof, as well as to the Jesuit Community at Windmolenveldstraat, who provided me such a warm home in Leuven. In spring 2015, I was afforded further ample research and writing time as occupant of the Loyola Chair at Fordham University, where I likewise enjoyed the hospitality of the Jesuit Community.

Bruce T. Morrill, SJ
Vanderbilt University Divinity School
May 23, 2015
Vigil of the Feast of Pentecost

Abbreviations and Acknowledgments of Works Cited

The following texts by Bernard Cooke comprise the published writings reproduced, with permission, in this volume. Excerpts are cited with the following abbreviations.

CSCP   *Christian Sacraments & Christian Personality*. New York: Holt, Rinehart and Winston, 1965.

CTSA   "Jesus of Nazareth, Norm for the Church." *Catholic Theological Society of America Proceedings* 49 (1994): 24–35.

DIA   "Charity and the Eucharist," *Diakonia* 5, no. 4 (1970): 309–25.

DG   *The Distancing of God: The Ambiguity of Symbol in History and Theology*. Copyright © 1990 by Fortress Press, Minneapolis, MN. Reprinted with permission of Fortress Press. All Rights Reserved.

FOP   "Authority and/or Tradition." From *Futuring Our Past: Explorations in the Theology of Tradition*, ed. Orlando O. Espín and Gary Macy. Copyright © 2006 by the Center for the Study of Latino/a Catholicism, University of San Diego. Reprinted with permission of Orbis Books, Maryknoll, New York. All Rights Reserved.

JES   "The Experiential 'Word of God,'" *Journal of Ecumenical Studies* 17, no. 1 (1980): 69–74. Copyright © by Journal of Ecumenical Studies. Used with permission. All Rights Reserved.

JUR   "Fullness of Orders: Theological Reflections," *The Jurist* 41, no. 2 (1980): 405–21. Copyright © by Catholic University Press. Used with permission. All Rights Reserved.

The Essential Writings of Bernard Cooke

MWS *Ministry to Word and Sacraments: History and Theology.* Copyright © 1976/1980 by Fortress Press, Minneapolis, MN. Reprinted with permission of Fortress Press. All Rights Reserved.

PSG *Power and the Spirit of God: Toward an Experience-Based Pneumatology.* New York: Oxford University Press, 2004. Copyright © 2004 by Oxford University Press. Extracts from pp. 168–77, "The Power of Love," reprinted with permission of Oxford University Press. All Rights Reserved.

PT3 "Prophetic Experience as Revelation," *Philosophy and Theology* 1, no. 3 (1987): 214–24. Used with permission. All Rights Reserved.

PT4 "History as Revelation," *Philosophy and Theology* 1, no. 4 (1987): 293–304. Used with permission. All Rights Reserved.

RS *Reconciled Sinners: Healing Human Brokenness.* Mystic, CT: Twenty-Third Publications, 1986.

S&S *Sacraments &Sacramentality*, rev. ed. Copyright ©1994 by Bernard Cooke; Published by Twenty-Third Publications. Used with permission. All Rights Reserved.

Introduction

NARRATIVE ARC OF A THEOLOGY

From the Process of Vatican II to the Papacy of Francis

We are in an era of seismic, epochal change for Christianity and Catholicism—a change of proportions, comparable to that of the medieval period, that will be playing out long into this century, if not into the entire millennium. In these unsettled times, the Church must negotiate its mission and identity amid global, political, ecological, and economic upheavals. Christianity's place in this process of change comprises the fundamental concern of professors and students of theology—for really, why does anybody study, discuss, or write about theology unless they are committed to the mission of the Church, however both *church* and *mission* may be understood? In classrooms and publications, the proper function of academic theology is to serve the primary theology of the Church, namely, the practiced faith of people, as communal bodies—churches or ecclesial communities—and individuals. Baptism, along with the moral doctrine of the common good, proclaims the irreducible yet mutual value of both the individual and the communal. These fundamentals of the tradition, whose source and sustenance lie in Scripture, bespeak a faith revealed through lives and events in history, and for that very reason, the challenge of every generation is to bring that faith to life in their own time.

With the flurry of conferences, publications, and occasionally heated debates marking its recent fiftieth anniversary, the Second Vatican Council undoubtedly stands as the overarching symbol of our period in Christian history. The polarized debate

1

over the interpretation of Vatican II that began shortly before the actual anniversary of the Council's first session pitted neo-conservatives who emphasized the limits of the conciliar documents against progressives who analyzed the council as a process, and received a startling jolt with the election of Pope Francis in 2013. For decades, Vatican authorities had been casting and recasting the parameters of the debate. The strategic symbolism of Francis's immediate words and actions signaled a new vision for the Church. Several commentators characterized Francis in the endearing image of Pope John XXIII, once again opening the windows of the Church into the world, pastorally attentive to the suffering and struggling goodness of people in an era riddled by war, economic inequality, and ethnic-nationalist antipathies. Constantly condemning clericalism from the top to the lowest ranks, Francis insists on the priority of the lives and religiosity of the people, especially the poor, as the heartbeat of the Church. For many theologians and church historians, the message was clear: the arrested process of Vatican II may now advance.

If that is the case, then the process necessarily entails a pulling away from the official Church's entrenched response to modernity and toward an as yet uncharted but pastorally more promising engagement with the world. Despite its stated posture against post-Enlightenment thought, official Roman Catholicism has practiced its own modern rationalism in the form of a theology "condensed into logical theological manuals used in seminaries…far removed from the experience and feeling of ordinary people."[1] Likewise, the Church's call to resist secularity belies its having "developed highly centralized structures," starting with the formation of the Roman curia in the sixteenth century, which has devolved into "many of the predictable weaknesses of modern bureaucracies, such as resistance to change, lack of accountability to anyone but the pope, membership limited [to those likeminded with] others in the curia," all to the detriment of genuinely pastoral and creative episcopal leadership in local churches. Although the term has a wide range of connotations, *postmodern* can signal for the Church's leadership and members an awareness of the profoundly relational quality of human life, respect for the complex mix of traditions in

---

1. R. Kevin Seasoltz, *A Virtuous Church: Catholic Theology, Ethics, and Liturgy for the 21st Century* (Maryknoll, NY: Orbis Books, 2012), 24.

communities, a notion of truth as unfolding in history, and sensitivity toward the pluralism of wisdom among peoples.[2] That Pope Francis has proven committed to those very convictions through such homely imagery as calling on bishops to "smell of the sheep" and shrugging off conservative alarm over the freewheeling preparatory phase of the Synod on the Family with "I prefer a mess," makes his appeal to contemporary Christians and others readily understandable.

Pope Francis has inspired renewal for Roman Catholicism, as well as for wider Christianity and all people of good will, not by doctrinal or dogmatic change but by practicing a pastoral theology that respects people's personal and social experiences as the locus of God's salvific presence and action. Bernard Cooke, who passed away just two months after Francis's election, left a body of theological texts profoundly attuned to the thought and practice of Francis—steeped in an affective, prayerful engagement with God in the Spirit of the risen Jesus, open to lived humanity ("history") as the locus of God's revelation, reform-spirited toward Church order, and centered on the Eucharist. Cooke, whose theological career began at the same time as the preparation, historic sessions, and implementation of Vatican II, found himself immediately tasked with conveying the theology of the Council through hundreds of speaking engagements and multiple publications in the United States and abroad. Two decades later, while a professor at the College of the Holy Cross, Cooke obliged the request of the academic dean to present a series of lectures to a faculty wrestling with questions about its educational mission in an evolving societal and religious context. In his memoir, Cooke describes his years at Holy Cross as "not so much a period of discovery as they were years of integration, not only bringing together theological understandings but also relating theology to other areas of knowledge." As an exercise in such integration and application, the text of the first in that series of lectures is a veritable tour de force, concluding with five theological principles that capture the essence of his lifelong theological project. It is those principles that have guided the organization of the present book's synthesis of Cooke's experience-based (he would say "down-to-earth")

---

2. Ibid., 25, 27–28.

theology. Here follows that lecture, edited thoroughly for publication, with subtitles and minor revisions for clarity.

Interpreting and Implementing Vatican II: History and Theology

No matter how one interprets what is happening in the Catholic Church, there is no doubt that major change is occurring. In the four sessions we will be together this semester, I hope to share *an* understanding of this change. I say *an* understanding because there are a number of differing views of what is going on, and no one can claim to have *the* understanding. Having said that, I do feel that I have something to contribute to our shared understanding because the past sixty years of my experience coincide with the transition from the Catholicism of the late 1920s to that of the present moment, and because through a number of circumstances, I have enjoyed a privileged opportunity to observe and engage in this shift.

Like many of you, I grew up in a solidly Catholic home and parish, taking for granted that Church teaching and structures are unchangeable, implicitly assuming that the Church in which I lived had always been more or less that way. In a town in northern Wisconsin where we were quite clearly a discriminated-against minority, we were still confident that we had the truth, which other Christian churches did not. It did not even enter our minds to consider the claims of Judaism, much less other religions. Our assurance of being "the true Church" was strengthened by the discrimination we experienced as Catholics. One of my earliest recollections was the 1928 presidential election when Al Smith, the first Catholic to be a presidential candidate, was running against Herbert Hoover, and the Ku Klux Klan was marching in our streets and burning crosses in front of our homes. Insofar as our little northern Wisconsin city had no African Americans and scarcely any Jewish people, it was quite clear whom the Klan thought the enemy was. So we took quite seriously the prayer we recited after each Mass: "Saint Michael the Archangel, defend us in battle...."

Introduction

The religious education I received in twelve years of the parish school was solid and systematic. The religious formation I received at home was both personally genuine and intellectually alive. We discussed Sunday sermons but, more often, issues raised by *America* magazine or *Commonweal*, or by the radio talks of Fulton Sheen or Father Coughlin—until the latter began his "Jew-baiting," at which my father, in disgust, tuned him out permanently. In high school, we received rather standard upper-level *Baltimore Catechism* information, but this was more than supplemented by the course in US history taught us by the pastor, a genuine intellectual whose great heroes in the political realm were Grover Cleveland and Franklin Delano Roosevelt, and in the church, the strange combination of John Ireland, the liberal archbishop of St. Paul, and Cardinal Rafael Merry del Val, the arch-foe of modernism.

As I look back, I wonder at the excellence of the education I received, especially at the high school level, from women religious who were both well educated and open-minded. Decades before the controversy over Teilhard's injection of evolutionary ideas into Catholic thought, our biology classes were taking evolution for granted. Though ecumenism was not yet in the air, we were never imbued with what later became known as "triumphalism"—not quite, that is, for we were trained to respect honesty and sincerity and to pray for the conversion of other Christians not blessed with the truth we possessed. But the deepest level of our sense of religious privilege did not lie in the possession of truer understanding; it lay in the fact that we had *priests*, whereas Protestants only had ministers incapable of changing the elements of bread and wine into the eucharistic body and blood of Christ. They did not have Jesus in their churches as we did. This was our great treasure, and those of us who were raised with faith did truly treasure the eucharistic presence. The day of our first communion was our most important rite of passage.

I mention all this not to reminisce but to highlight what was profoundly real and important—none of which has been negated by recent change—and to express personally the deep continuity I feel with my boyhood Catholic experience. Yet even as we lived that Catholicism in basic serenity, a sea change was already well under way, more so for the moment in Europe than in the United States. The 1930s witnessed the civil war in Spain, the most Catholic of countries, where almost every city and town still has its street named after *los reyes catolicos*. That civil war's unbelievable atrocities against priests, friars, and nuns witnessed to a pent-up hostility to all things religious. Meanwhile, Nazi ideology was overtaking both German-speaking lands and much of the German soul, even as the religious establishment, both Catholic and Protestant, was conspicuous for its lack of opposition to this neopaganism. World War II, reflecting the crisis of European culture and religion, would prove to be the great watershed for Catholic thought and life.

Catholicism's Struggle with Modernity

Much earlier, however, the challenge to what was considered traditional Catholic teaching had begun. Confronted by the heritage of the Enlightenment with the rise of science and critical thought, Roman Catholic officials had managed to shield its membership, at least most of them, from these modern errors. The two decrees produced by the First Vatican Council, before the Franco-Prussian War forced its suspension, dealt head-on with the critical underlying issues: The decree on faith and revelation made it clear that the truths most relevant to human existence came "from above," with submission to authoritative teaching the path toward ultimate insight into human life. The decree on the Church—really the decree on the papacy—identified the supreme teaching authority in whose possession of truth the faithful could securely trust, thereby averting the threat of scientific methodology being applied to the faith.

Still, it was not completely averted. Historical study, literary criticism, scientific anthropology, idealist philosophy all continued to infiltrate the thinking of Catholic scholars, leading to the modernist crisis in the early twentieth century. Even as the sorting out of the issues involved continued in those early decades, many of the scholarly cutting edge of the Catholic Church were driven into silence and, in some cases, out of the Church. There seems little doubt that there

was some excessive and at times naive application of critical methodologies to the doctrinal heritage of the Church,
yet Vatican-orchestrated witch hunting stunted several
decades of Catholic intellectual advance, further alienating
Church teaching from the contemporary world. At the time,
many considered this gap a blessing. After all, Catholic theology, confined almost totally to seminaries and therefore
untouched by the dangerous intellectual currents of the university, was judged superior to other knowledge because it
drew from revelation and was certified by the divinely guided
papacy—making it capable of passing judgment on the progressive ideas within or outside the Church.

When I began formal theological studies in the early 1950s,
the major modern thinkers—Descartes, Kant, Hegel, and so
on, more generically referred to as rationalism, positivism,
and idealism—were relegated to the list of "adversaries,"
and by that very classification, considered erroneous. During
that whole period lurked the dominating fear that much of
modern critical reflection upon religion, and specifically upon
Christianity, was not so much a matter of explaining more
accurately as explaining away. This fear was by no means
without some foundation. All too often, a healthy skepticism
about the adequacy of human understanding was replaced
by cynical and snobbish rejection of religious faith as "medieval," that is, ignorant and superstitious.

Despite the surface rejection of modernity, reinforced by
the atmosphere of suspicion and fear that followed the official war against the modernists, a deep current of progressive Catholic thought was gaining strength in the years just
before and after World War II. This new wave of intellectual
development surfaced in Catholic biblical study's taking
seriously modern textual methods, in "scientific" historical
study of Catholic thought and institutions, and above all in
the creative reflection on Catholic doctrine that came to be
called *the new theology*. The progressive theologians involved
in that movement did not refer to themselves by the term;
rather, their adversaries used the designation to suggest that
this development was less than faithful to Christian tradition.

Used negatively, *the new theology* was clearly a misno-
mer. Leaders of this mid-century theological movement

7

were all eminent students of Scripture, patristics, and medieval theology. Yet, because it challenged not so much the deepest currents of Christian faith throughout history but, rather, the supposedly traditional interpretation of Thomas Aquinas espoused by some of the more politically powerful neo-Thomists, the new theology was labeled dangerous, misleading, if not absolutely heretical. It is unbelievable now that the likes of Karl Rahner, Henri de Lubac, Yves Congar, Marie-Dominique Chenu, and Jean Daniélou were silenced and in some cases removed from teaching. Not even the United States, far behind the forefront of Catholic theology, was spared. Our most prominent and probably most competent theologian John Courtney Murray was silenced through the joint efforts of reactionary professors at Catholic University and their allies at the Vatican, silenced because he proposed that the church-state relationship that exists in the United States is at least as compatible with Catholic teaching as was the established church situation that followed the sixteenth-century Reformation.

Despite repeated condemnations and repressive measures from Rome, the progressive currents of Catholic thought continued to gain momentum, even after the 1950 encyclical *Humani Generis*, which, like the earlier decrees against modernism, attacked almost every element of Catholic scholarship. But not all the official movement was backward. Hesitant though it was in its acceptance of historical critical methodologies, the encyclical *Divino Afflante Spiritu* (1943) was a breakthrough in Catholic biblical research, while *Mediator Dei* (1947) put a mild stamp of approval on liturgical studies and their pastoral applications. Still, the situation in Europe grew tenser as progressive elements in the Church, sensing pre–world war global society to be beyond recovery, pushed toward a more open, relevant Christianity. At the same time, those who considered themselves the guardians of genuine Catholicism fought to hold back this newest advance of modernism and secularism. While the explicit field of battle was a contest between two ways of thinking about Catholicism, sociology of knowledge would indicate the key role played by entrenched power and the linkage between ecclesiastical and civil politics. One telling indication was the fact that supposedly dangerous Catholic thinkers were, in the last analysis, accused not of wrong thinking but of disloyalty. Without any invitation into careful theological dialogue, they were ordered to refrain from public statements and to submit to Vatican teaching with loyal obedience under the obscure *obsequium religiosum*.

As we moved into the 1960s, the standoff continued, yet what was happening was that Catholic thinkers were more and more going their own way, doing what their scholarly honesty dictated, doing so quietly and, if necessary, in ways to circumvent Vatican control in order to survive. That this situation touched the United States as well was already clear in 1961 when, taking advantage of the invitation to give the Marquette University baccalaureate address, the new apostolic delegate, Archbishop Vagnozzi, announced his policy agenda by warning against the danger of progressive elements in the Church—biblical studies, ecumenism, contemporary sacred art, liturgical enthusiasts advocating radical ideas such as use of the vernacular in the Eucharist.

Vatican II and Its Underlying Theological Questions

Then occurred the miracle of Pope John XXIII. Thought in many circles to be an interim selection giving Church leaders time to appraise the needs of the Church, chart the course for post–Pius XII Catholicism, and then make a more important papal selection, Pope John completely belied that appraisal. A career diplomat with a keen sense of history, assigned for most of his career to the fringes of the diplomatic corps because he was not part of the Vatican in-group, pastoral in his outlook, open to the future and especially to the faith and goodness of people outside the Catholic Church, Angelo Giuseppe Roncalli in three short years changed forever the face of the Church. Most importantly, he did this through convoking the Second Vatican Council, but there was also the powerful symbolism of his own person. I remember asking a prominent Protestant theologian, an observer at the council, why Pope John had such an appeal for Protestants.

His immediate reply: "I can't speak for other Protestants, but for me the answer is simple. I can read the New Testament, then look at this man, and they fit."

Following a somewhat contentious period of preparation, with conservative forces trying to limit severely the range of conciliar discussion after their efforts to scuttle the Council had failed, the Second Vatican Council opened on October 11, 1962, with hundreds of bishops from around the world in attendance. It quickly became apparent that the Council was not going to follow the path of routinely confirming the status quo. Instead, under the leadership of great churchmen like Suenens and Koenig and Dearden, who had learned the lessons of the war years and been instrumental in rebuilding the postwar Church, the assembled bishops turned their attention to the basic issues that had long awaited official reconsideration.

There were the more obvious, easily identifiable questions that needed to be addressed, most of them dealing with Church structures and processes that derived from the Council of Trent or Vatican I. First and foremost, especially in the minds of the assembled bishops, was the need to reexamine and, at least to some extent, adjust the relationship of the pope to the worldwide episcopate. This eventuated in the Council's emphasis on "collegiality"—not a denial of papal primacy but a reassertion that this primacy was exercised within the college of bishops, not above them. In ritual matters, the Council moved toward vernacular liturgy and somewhat greater flexibility in sacramental ceremonies. Very importantly, the Council blessed and even urged further involvement of the laity in the ministries of the Church. But beneath such important practical questions lay fundamental theological issues that were at the heart of the changing understanding that led up to and followed the Council, issues that are basic to any system of religious belief, even though framed in different fashion in various religions and at different points in history.

First Cluster of Questions: Divine Revelation, Word of God, and the Human Condition

The first of these issues, one debated acrimoniously in the two decades just before Vatican II, focused on the term *supernatural*. Put quite simply, was there a level of personal existing superior to human nature that somehow became attainable through faith and divine grace? Were humans meant to be more than human, to somehow share in what it meant for God to be God? If so, did that pertain to men and women from the origins of humanity, or was it something that derived only from the salvific activity of Jesus the Christ? And if there was such a supernatural level of human life, how did it relate to the purely natural?

Now, only a few decades later, it seems strange that we were caught up in heated debate about questions that today appear so theoretical, but they were the source of such passionate discussion because what was at stake was the value of being human. Was it sufficient to be truly human, or did one have to rise above one's humanity in order to reach one's destiny? Did Christian holiness demand some denial of what it meant to be human? Translated into the social sphere, it was a question of this life, of this world and care for it versus concentration on the world beyond. Translated into Christian discipleship: Should one devote one's Christian attention to bettering this world or to preserving oneself from the world, the flesh, and the devil in order to achieve happiness in the life to come?

Connected with this notion of an "extra layer" of our existence, the supernatural, was the lingering idea of a world between humans and God, a world of angels and devils, of special powers being exerted by good or bad spirits. In a sense, it was the Christian version of Plato's myth of the cave, that is, the visible world not being the real thing, but rather the real taking place behind the curtain of our experience. It is in this hidden world that God operates, that grace works to strengthen and divinize us, where God writes straight with crooked sticks. Anyone familiar with the sixteenth-century theological controversies between Catholics and the Reformers will immediately recognize this as another version of the dispute over the nature of justification. He or she will also realize that the underlying question, which has always been the most basic religious question, is that of divine providence. Just what, if anything, is God doing in human life? This perennial question has become uniquely pressing in modern times because of the assumption not infrequently made in the various sciences that the world experienced by humans can be explained without appeal to religious belief.

Applied more directly to human knowing, the question of divine providence becomes, How, if at all, has God provided knowledge that humans could not otherwise obtain? Christianity (along with some other religions) responds, "Revelation." Christian belief has always held that in special fashion, God "spoke" to the people of Israel and then through Jesus of Nazareth, revealing to humans what it meant for humans to be human and what it meant for God to be for them. But if we accept in principle this response, the consequent theological issue becomes, What is meant by the term *revelation*? How does it occur? To whom is it given? Can any religious group such as Christians lay claim to a unique revelation not granted to others? Much of this questioning focused on the issue, What does it mean to say that the Bible is the inspired word of God?

Vatican II had the precedent of Vatican I handling revelation as a central issue, which it neither repudiated nor followed—perhaps the key indicator of the sharp contrast between the two councils. One of Vatican II's key documents, arguably its most theological, is the Dogmatic Constitution on Divine Revelation. Strongly influenced by mid-century advances in Catholic biblical scholarship, the document breaks with dictation notions of inspiration and, more generally, with a fundamentalist approach to interpretation. Going beyond identifying revelation with a formulated body of knowledge, the document situates divine-human communication within the historical experience of the faith communities of Israel and Christianity.

Second Cluster of Questions: Knowledge, Sin, and Ecclesial Power

A second cluster of underlying questions dealt with the Church's reaction to the heritage of the Enlightenment. Could one espouse the optimism regarding human progress that had flowed from modern advances in science? Could one accept the human mind as the ultimate measure of reality, accept the position that what humans could not eventually explain simply could not be or, at least, could not be important? In a sense, this naively optimistic view of human capability had already been judged by the events of the first half of the twentieth century. Two world wars, a devastating worldwide economic depression, the horror of the Nazi death camps, and "the bomb" had wiped out the illusion of unlimited human progress.

In its own ways, the Catholic Church had consistently refused to accept the ultimacy of human achievement through its classic doctrine of original sin. The teaching came into mid-nineteenth-century focus through the dogmatic definition of the immaculate conception of Mary. The dogma made explicit that Mary from the first moment of human existence was not wounded by the inheritance of sin borne by the rest of humanity. The clear implication of such a statement was that all other humans are so wounded: we are a sinful race, and because sinful, we can reach our destiny only by a gratuitous act of divine mercy; we need to be saved. Though this doctrine may have been formulated somewhat mythically, it pointed to a profoundly troubling aspect of human history, the pervasiveness of evil. Present-day postmodern reappraisal of the Enlightenment suggests that Catholicism's hesitancy to jump on the Enlightenment bandwagon was not without foundation.

These questions about the way that God acted in human history obviously touched profoundly the role of Church officials. It was they who by special divine vocation and the empowerment of their ordination, especially ordination to the episcopacy, were seen to be the mediators of salvation. Supporting their claims to such supernatural power was a hierarchical model of the world, the image of a layered universe, one in which true understanding and saving goodness flowed down from God, doing so through the intervening holy orders that stood between God and the rest of humans. In the twentieth century, challenged by other powers—political, intellectual, and even religious—Catholicism's ordained ministers as never before had to explain and justify their claims to ultimate saving power.

Third Cluster of Questions: History and Change, Church and World

A third cluster of questions had to do with the nature and value of change. It required no great insight in the early decades of this century to recognize that the world was changing. The two world wars made such recognition inescapable. Along with the rest of the world, Christianity was undergoing drastic change, although Church leaders tried to carry on with business as usual. Yet, it was difficult to contend that all was well when in France, "the eldest daughter of the Church," came the discovery that the great majority of Catholics were *non-pratiquant*. A closer look at the rest of European Catholicism made it clear that France was not at all unique.

Still it was taught that the character and above all the doctrine and ritual of the Catholic Church were unchanging and unchangeable because they were true, and truth was eternal. The idea that doctrine was developing throughout history John Henry Newman had eloquently argued decades earlier in his *Essay on the Development of Christian Doctrine*—making him suspect at the Vatican, a suspicion dispelled only when his ideas finally came into their own at Vatican II.

At the bottom of the official unease with the notion of development was, of course, the threat of relativity. If something as basic as dogmatic formulation of belief was subject to historical, linguistic, and cultural conditioning and therefore in need of both interpretation and modification, how could one ever be certain of the truth of revelation? Historical contextual examination of the Church's teaching and institutions seemed, then, to threaten the stability and eternal verity of Catholicism.

Paradoxically, this nineteenth- and twentieth-century position of the Church leadership went counter to the traditional Catholic view, for Catholicism had for centuries, and especially when faced with the Reformation's stress on *sola scriptura*, insisted on the intrinsic revelatory role of the Church's ongoing history. Yet, Catholic official theology has had a difficult time coming to grips with historical study. Only now is critical study of history being admitted, not only as a source of data for theological reflection but as an intrinsic element of doing theology.

One key aspect of this issue is the question of Christian origins: How actually did the Church get started? The belief that in some radical sense Christianity owes its origin to divine institution is as old as the Church itself. But if this is true, if the truths espoused by the Church and its central structure and rituals come from God, how can humans think of changing them? Admittedly, there are some less important elements in the doctrine and the institutions of the Church that came to be because of human decisions and the influence of historical forces; these can and often should be modified or even abolished. But at the core of the Church's existence are certain beliefs and structures, such as the doctrine of the incarnation or the ritual of the Eucharist, which go back to Jesus himself, without which Christianity would not be Christianity. Identifying and safeguarding them would seem to be of the essence.

Put simply: How much can the Church change without ceasing to be what Jesus began? From one point of view, this is the problem of continuity and discontinuity for any social body. From another point of view, it is a unique instance of this dialectic because (as Christians believe) the Church's origin and historical direction are from God. Then further: If God does guide the Church, is this in the last analysis through those in official position, or through charismatic and prophetic figures, or a combination of the two? The jury remains out after two thousand years.

The Council's Way of Addressing Such Questions

What was the response of Vatican II to these basic and burning questions? Before trying to give some brief answers, I think three or four general remarks about the character of the Council and its activity may help to understand better what the Council did or did not accomplish.

Unlike most previous councils, from Nicaea to Vatican I, Vatican II was convoked neither to condemn error nor to produce new dogmatic statements. It did not continue further the modern course of papal teaching about Mary or the

Church. It did not anathematize any heretics but, instead, opened up to the ecumenical developments of the twenti- eth century. And, as has often been remarked, it turned the Roman Catholic Church outward to recognize both the needs and the potential of the modern world and its own inevitable involvement with those needs and potential. Whereas Vati- can I was a meeting of a Church threatened by the world, Vatican II was a gathering of a Church that realized it was part of a threatened world.

In the realm of belief and theology, the Council, while reiter- ating episcopal monopoly on magisterium, that is, normative teaching, nonetheless drew heavily from the very currents of professional theology that had been so suspect right up to the eve of its assembling. Though many of the attendant bishops were still quite apprehensive about recent biblical and theological scholarship, the *periti*, the theologians who served as advisors, played a dominant role in the proceed- ings. They were the ghostwriters for almost all the bishops' speeches on the council floor, while also variably engaged in drafting the sixteen official documents ultimately produced.

Despite this theological input, the Council was not theo- logically innovative; it did not even confirm the more progres- sive views most of the *periti* espoused. What it did do was allow the more progressive currents of thought to flow above ground without being characterized as error or disloyalty. Now the leading minds of the Church could publish openly and engage in public discourse with one another without fear of reprisal—or so it seemed at that time.

For the most part, the Council did not adopt either side of disputed issues, for example, the exact extent of papal authority. Indeed, at a number of places, the conciliar docu- ments are ambiguous, bordering on contradictory. This was neither accident nor indecision. The conciliar decrees are consensus statements, representative of the diversity of views within the Catholic Church at that time, indicative of the fact that many theoretical and practical issues remained unresolved. So neither conservatives nor progressives can claim the Council completely for themselves, though in the ensuing years, some in both camps have drawn selectively from conciliar statements to validate their own views.

What did happen—and this of major importance—is that in implicit fashion, the bishops of the Council and the documents they produced absorbed underlying presuppositions and attitudes that were a radical departure from preceding centuries. Besides, they enunciated or assumed certain fundamental principles that have far-reaching implications, implications that even now are scarcely recognized. Let me give but one example: The explicit purpose of one of the ground-breaking decrees, on religious freedom, was to defend the right of all humans freely to follow their consciences in religious matters without interference from civil powers. John Courtney Murray, the decree's chief architect, reportedly remarked that it was a time bomb, for at some future time, people would realize that such freedom of conscience applied as well within the Catholic Church.

Moving Forward: Five Theological Principles, Intellectual and Practical

What, finally, were some of the deeper principles of thought and activity through which Vatican II set the Catholic Church on the new and yet ancient path it now treads? I will mention only five, trying to suggest their particular relevance for the future intellectual life of the Church and, beyond that, of the world for whose betterment the Church exists.

1. The intellectual dimension of the faith invites discovery and demands accuracy.

The first principle is that Catholics should *understand* their religious beliefs and practices. I know this sounds like plain common sense, but in many ways, it represented an important shift in the notion of religious faith. It was long assumed within the Christian churches, both Catholic and Protestant, that the ordinary person did not need to grasp the doctrines they repeated nor the rituals they performed; they simply needed to assent to the superior understanding of church leaders and attend religious services regularly. It was assumed that somehow out of such obedient fidelity Christians would fulfill God's will for them and "be saved."

As a matter of fact, more refined religious understandings were considered a subtle threat to the faith of the supposedly simple faithful; most people probably would only be confused by theological discussion. If this sounds strange, it might be good to recall a similar anti-intellectualism in US history. The profound and incisive talks Adlai Stevenson gave during his 1950s presidential campaigns won for him the damning title *egghead*. Two decades later, presidential campaign headquarters for George McGovern advised volunteers against mentioning his earned doctorate.

So, the position of Vatican II on the need to provide accurate understanding of the faith for all Catholics reflected a genuinely new approach to religion. Still, important as the Council was in this regard, it cannot lay claim to having initiated the major reversal already begun in the catechetical revival and the liturgical movement leading to Vatican II. The impact of post–World War II liturgical ferment is clearly seen in the conciliar decree on the liturgy. The perhaps most important paragraph of that document states, "The Church earnestly desires that Christ's faithful, when present at this mystery of faith (i.e., at Mass) should not be there as strangers or silent spectators. On the contrary, through proper appreciation of the rites and prayers they should participate knowingly, devoutly and actively."

The implications of the emphasis on the intellectual dimension of religious faith are far-reaching. Let me mention just two that are particularly relevant to the world of academe. Given the responsibility now of professional theologians to contribute to this desired understanding by the bulk of the faithful, the very purpose of doing theology in Catholic circles has, for the most part, shifted. For centuries, particularly since the Protestant Reformation, theology had become a polemical defense of a particular church's claims, whether Protestant, Catholic, or Orthodox, effectively making all theology post-Reformational. With and since the Council, it is increasingly accepted, except within some high official ecclesial circles, that the purpose of theological scholarship is not denominational legitimation but research and reflection that will clarify the faith understanding of all in the Church. Again, this shift had begun before the Council, for example, with the development in 1940s and '50s Europe of "kerygmatic theology," an approach to theology having as its aim the proclamation of the basic Christian message of salvation.

The deeper, long-lasting implication this shift represents is a movement toward reconciliation with the contemporary intellectual world. Modernity has been characterized by the view that the purpose of human thinking and scholarship is *discovery*. This was not, of course, entirely new, as anyone familiar with Thomas Aquinas's notion of insight (*intellectus*) and its relation to reason (*ratio*) will recognize. But with the emergence of modern science, Roman ecclesiastical leaders had attempted to maintain the primacy of their authoritative teaching by insisting that the goal of Church teaching was *indoctrination*, not *discovery*.

Clearly, this conflict represents two very different ways of reaching truth, therefore two radically different approaches to education. Having attempted, most dramatically in the case of Galileo, to subordinate even scientific knowing to their magisterial hegemony, Church officials gradually retreated to the area of religious knowing, where some still insist that theologians should function only to justify positions already decided by the episcopacy. But the dam has broken; the intellectual ferment that tried to break through several times during the past century and a half is now unstoppable. Progressive theological thinkers are still in danger of power plays directed against them personally, but the worldwide theological community, with honest respect for the intrinsic role of the official magisterium and with genuine acknowledgment of its own responsibility to serve the faith life of the Church, recognizes that the duty to search outweighs the duty to submit.

2. The Spirit of the risen Jesus is the divine power guiding the Church as a social organism, making Christ humanly present in history.

A second principle of understanding accepted by the Council, and increasingly influential since, is that the Spirit of the risen Christ, which is God's own Spirit, abides in the Church, for it is the living body of Christ. This has always been an article of belief, enshrined in both the New Testament and conciliar creeds, but for centuries, it had ceased to be the operative model for thinking about the Church. Instead, other models, particularly the political model, had controlled Christians' perception of their individual and social religious identity. They did not think of themselves as joined together in a living social reality animated by the very life principle (the Spirit) that is the source of Jesus' risen existence. Instead, they thought of themselves as belonging to a religious organization, agreed with its teaching on the authority of Church officials, and attended its religious services because that was the law of God. Granted that many went beyond this and developed a more personal approach to God, they did so as individuals, without thinking of their Church as the living mystery of Christ's continuing presence to history.

Thinking of Christ as risen, humanly present to those who accept him in faith, sharing his own life-giving Spirit with his followers, contradicts the old dominant image of Jesus up in heaven sending down the Spirit at appropriate moments, such as celebrations of sacramental ritual. It abandons the hierarchical-ladder image of God's power flowing down, through levels of mediation, replacing it with the image of God's Spirit, that is, God's life-power, dwelling within human society, even beyond the limits of the Church itself. Such an organic, life model for the Church is already challenging, in subtle but dynamic fashion, the symbolic underpinning of ecclesiastical power. But let me stress again that this is not something entirely new. At one critical historical juncture, when the Council of Constance in the fifteenth century healed the catastrophic division of the Great Western Schism, the teaching fashioned by combined efforts of theologians and canon lawyers, and incidentally ascribed to as dogma by the pope himself, held that the living Church as a whole was the seat of God's guidance and power.

Vatican II did not pick up the argument of Constance; the implications of that earlier event are still too explosive. It went a different route by drawing attention once more to the mystery dimension of Christianity, to the belief that Jesus having passed through death into risen existence abides still with humanity, making himself present to history by the continual sharing of his own life-giving Spirit, in a special way through the agency of the Church. In such a view, the model of the Church is that of a living social organism, which carries us back to Jesus' own use of metaphor in his parables, metaphor that in large part draws upon life processes such as seeds being planted, growing, and being harvested. When applied to the Church, the implications for an understanding of its institutions are radical: the living body of Christ safeguards and nurtures its life, as does any living reality, by producing the organs needed; thus, such structural elements as the episcopacy flow *from* the community and do not in the first instance produce the community. This runs counter to the preconciliar ecclesiology, most tellingly described by Cardinal Journet's massive *A Church of the Word Incarnate* (1950), which goes so far as to describe the hierarchy as maternally generating the Church.

When applied to the spirituality and ritual practice of the Church, this shift in model has equally basic impact. Instead of the long-standing notion that the risen Christ becomes present to Christians only when the eucharistic liturgy is celebrated or as long as the reserved consecrated elements are kept in a repository, Christ is now seen as constantly present to believers. Jesus' final words in Matthew's Gospel now take on renewed meaning: "Behold, I am with you always, even to the end of the age." Without in any way detracting from the intrinsic importance of liturgical celebrations, this view of Christ's continuing presence breaks with the notion that religion is a sacred realm separated from the rest of people's lives. Indeed, this emphasis is part of Vatican II's denial of the dichotomy between sacred and secular. It is not a movement toward the secular, as some fundamentalists maintain, but rather, a widening of the realm of the sacred.

3. Within this organic life model of the Church, theology is positioned to discover the symbolic dimension of Christianity and, thereby, a true sacramental theology.

This leads us then to our third principle. If God in the risen Christ continues to impart the Spirit of power, life, and truth to each succeeding generation, the lives of those humans, especially when infused with faith, constitute a continuing revelation. God's divine Word is a dynamic reality; it is the divine self-communication, the divine self-gift to created persons. Christians believe the Word is embodied in Jesus, who does not cease to be that Word in his risen life. Just the opposite: it is in full risen possession of the Spirit that Jesus the Christ is empowered to reveal God as his Abba.

Jesus as the Christ, however, is not just an isolated human individual triumphant in and over death; rather, it is the risen Jesus established as the Christ precisely in relationship to all other humans, for whom he is meant to be the source of community (*communio*). It is through these humans, related either explicitly or implicitly to him in faith, that he is able to carry on his mission of revealing the true God. To use a more technical term, humanity—and in distinctive fashion, the Christian community, the Church—is the sacrament of God's presence in the risen Christ. We have used the word *sacrament* for a long time in our teaching and theology, but in very truncated fashion as pointing only to certain ritual acts that in almost magical fashion provided grace and salvation. Now, really for the first time in the Church's history, we are beginning to examine the deeper role of the symbolic dimension of Christianity. We are on the verge of developing a true sacramental theology grounded in an organic life model of the Church.

The Council did not carry the analysis as far as we have just done, but it did consciously employ the Pauline notion "body of Christ," and at one point, it did explicitly apply the term *sacrament* to the Church. Moreover, it clearly embraced the mentality we have just described when, following Pope John's lead, it urged Catholics to discern "the signs of the times." The reason for probing the events of our world is to discover within them the working of God's Spirit.

4. The Church is an eschatological reality in human history.

In the interests of time, let me refer only very quickly to a fourth and a fifth principle. The fourth principle is that the

Church's existence is not static, for it is a community of pilgrims, itself a pilgrim reality, always "on the way." Until the consummation of history—and we know not when and how that will happen—the Church continues to live out the experience of exodus, as did Jesus himself in his life, death, and resurrection. To use the more technical term, the Church's existence is *eschatological*. It is meant to be living into the future, moving toward a fullness it has not yet achieved, ever changing as it shares more fully in Christ's Spirit; thus, *ecclesia semper reformanda*. This obviously grounds a significantly different view of the Church's relation to the ongoing process of human history.

5. Recovering the Church's mission for the salvation of the world bears implications for ministry.

But the Church does not exist for its own sake. This is the fifth principle embraced by Vatican II after centuries of insistence on an ultimacy that Christianity does not really possess. The Church is not the kingdom of God; rather, it exists to help bring about the kingdom of God, God's rule among the entire human race. While the distinctiveness of Christianity is an element of belief that we need to reexamine more thoroughly, we have finally abandoned a superficial understanding of the statement going back as far as Cyprian of Carthage: "Outside the Church there is no salvation." Not only does this broader understanding of the divine activity in history open Christians to appreciation of humanity's other great religious traditions, it demands a renewed but very ancient understanding of membership in the Church. We are once more recognizing that the primary reason for becoming a Christian is not simply to be saved but rather, as disciples of Christ, to be active in the world's salvation. The Council points unmistakably to the ministerial role of the entire people of God.

I can only apologize for my cursory discussion of complicated and critically important issues. Would that there were the opportunity here to consider with you differing interpretations within the Church of the points I have raised. To achieve only a bit of this, in our series' succeeding sessions, I hope to probe in greater detail: (1) What does it mean for the Church to claim divine input into its origin and continuing historical existence? (2) In what way can Christianity lay claim to a distinctive, even unique role in humanity's destiny? (3) How is the Church's tradition of faith to be preserved and developed? *How* is Church teaching?

Connecting Theology and Narrative: Overview of Chapters

The five principles Cooke outlined in the conclusion to the above lecture on post–Vatican II Church life and thought guide the following selection and organization of writings from his extensive corpus of books and articles. Fundamental is the question of revelation, the effort to understand more adequately (so as to promote practically) the nature and experience of "divine input" Christianity claims at its origins and through the course of history. Chapter 1, then, presents Cooke's theological method, for which the fundamental categories are revelation and history, experience and symbol. Cooke's fundamental theology interprets divine revelation in human history according to two interrelated biblical dimensions of communal and personal experience: the sacramental and the prophetic. With the person and history of Jesus of Nazareth proving the definitive revelation of "the experiential Word of God," chapter 2 considers more closely the normative character and role of Jesus for the life of the Church in its members. The Spirit is the source of divine love for human life unto death constituting the sacramental quality of Jesus' person and empowering the prophetic character of his mission. God continues such presence and action as "word" in history by sharing that same power of the Spirit of love in human lives, and in the history of the Church, as the Spirit of the risen Christ in the lives of believers. The power of the Spirit is an active sharing of love, such that the basic sacrament of divine presence and action in humanity is friendship. Chapter 3 presents Cooke's noted sacramental theology of friendship, developed through biblical traditions of covenantal bonds between God and humanity in the people of Israel and person of Jesus. The Eucharist is the outward symbolic activity revelatory of the inner, often inchoate, active presence of Christ's Spirit in the shared life of the Christian community, nourishing (ethical) lives of interpersonal and social commitments. The eucharistic practical theology of shared life—of sacrifice, love, and reconciliation—reveals the irreducibly social nature of Christianity. Chapter 4 arrives at Cooke's preference for an "organic life" model of the Church, through which the need for ministry and order prove historically essential, albeit ever evolving. The chapter closes with an exposition on the multivalent authority of tradition as practiced by, for, and among the people.

A note on content, style, and format: In the following four chapters, the content of Bernard Cooke's writings (extracts from his unpublished memoir and published books and articles) appears in regular font. The content of Bruce Morrill's commentary, organizing and integrating Cooke's thought into a narrative of his theology, appears in italic font and is indented. While the research "behind" the selection from Cooke's publications included examination of the many journal reviews of his books, reference to those and other secondary sources have been foregone due to limits of space and, more importantly, the decision to produce a book that would allow Cooke to "speak in his own voice" to a new generation of scholars and students of theology.

CHAPTER ONE

Theological Method

REVELATION IN HISTORY, EXPERIENCE, AND SYMBOL

Introduction

Cooke's theology was fundamentally practical insofar as its very motivation was the religious and theological formation of the laity and, as that work evolved early in his professorial career, the reform and renewal of the Church's rites and ministerial structures. Thus, his methodology as a professor and religious educator coincided with that of his theological writings. For both, the categories of history, experience, symbol, and revelation proved fundamental to the ongoing quest for truth as practically discerned in Christian lives, individual and communal. Such a method makes prayer, faith, and perceptive, ethical living the "primary theology" (to draw on a dominant liturgical-theological term) of the Church. Liturgical theologians, by the 1970s, had located primary theology in the actual practice of the Church's rites (the lex orandi*), arguing that theological formulations (the* lex credendi*) arise from and must answer to how the liturgically assembled Church prays. Only over the next decade did liturgical theology begin to articulate the necessity of including the practical living of the gospel message (the* lex vivendi *or* lex agendi*) in relation to liturgy and doctrinal theology. Cooke, on the other hand, from the start, identified personal, interpersonal, and communally shared experience—for which the interpretive, biblical keys* *prove to be Jesus and the Eucharist—as the locus of Christian faith and, thereby, theology. For Cooke, the work of academic theology, in print and classroom, is to reflect critically on the history of such experiences and to propose constructive ways forward for the Church (as the people of God) in an ever-changing world. Invited by the* Journal of Ecumenical Studies *in 1980 to respond to a proposal by Hans Küng, Cooke argued (JES 71),*

One of the critical methodological challenges facing us today is utilization of history in our theological reflection, not just historical "data" distilled from the multitude of detailed historical researches but the very modality of consciousness that has come in recent centuries from increasing awareness of the historical nature of our human existence. Beyond the questions of how far we can reconstruct events of the past "as they really happened" lies the deeper heuristic issue of how vicarious experience functions to give us insight. Ultimately, the reason for studying history (or any of its cultural expressions, such as literature) is to transcend the narrow limits of our own direct experience and enrich our consciousness by sharing in the experiences of others. This, of course, is especially relevant in the matter of religious awareness where present-day believers claim a community in faith and belief with previous generations. Given the importance of this matter, I think that any attempt to work toward a consensus in method must investigate the role being assigned to historical understanding.

The selections here in this chapter explore the principle axes of Cooke's theological method. Fundamental to his method for both written argument and educational engagement was his situating of personal and communal Christian development within the broader, reflective experience of being human in time and space—that is to say, historically.

Doing Theology Historically

With history, as communal experience interpreted over time, having emerged as a fundamental category for his theology, Cooke's memoir includes attention from childhood onward

*to clues for not only why history was so important but also
what the very notion of history itself means for Christianity.
The pivotal moment appears to have been the intense several
years of his getting the nascent graduate program in theology at Marquette, with its limited faculty and administrative
resources, up and running in the early 1960s.*

On the surface, all the time and effort, much of it administrative, would seem to have precluded any development of my own
theological advance. Certainly, many of my own research interests
could not be pursued, but the need to think through the structures of the emerging graduate formation demanded an integration of theological issues that probably would not have otherwise
occurred in my understanding. More than that, the interaction
with a very talented group of graduate students meant a constant
input to my theological insights. Any alert teacher knows that
student questions are a precious challenge to one's already existent understandings. Then, too, the need for me to teach a wide
range of courses when we were still short on professors meant
that I was forced to do a great deal of reading, research, and study
over quite a range of religious thought, leading to much clearer
realization of the interlocking of theological issues. Perhaps most
importantly, as we worked through the sequence of doctoral-level
courses, we were actually developing a methodology for doing
theology historically. We realized that the historical development
of Christian thought was itself the central "logos" that interpreted
and unified the whole of theology. All this led to a fundamental
shift in the overall context of my doing theology, a shift that would
affect not just my thinking but also my personal life.

*The narrative character of both biblically based religious tra-
dition and, more fundamentally, all viable human social bodies compels recognition of history itself as a governing symbol
("the central 'logos'") for Christian theology—notwithstanding
whatever challenges postmodern theories might pose. Such a
modern theological approach, Cooke realized on further reflection, was already emerging during his doctoral study years in
1950s Paris, where not only the breakout of Catholic biblical scholarship but also forays into modern philosophy would
have a lasting impact. In the "Paris" chapter of his memoir,
he describes how participation in a small discussion group*

29

during the second year of those studies led to a summer of intensive reading in Hegel. While it might seem a digression for purposes of this present volume, his brief explanation of the unusual Jesuit house where he studied that summer provides an example of what to his mind, as a Christian theologian, mattered historically (indeed, attention to Judaism would become essential to his work in Christology, sacraments, and history as theology).

Seven of us had been gathering every Thursday morning, led by Gaston Fessard, one of France's leading Hegelians. We spent the entire morning during a full academic year discussing texts of Hegel and Marx. It was loads of fun because I could play devil's advocate, not being a dedicated Hegelian like the others. With my philosophical background of three years probing the thought of Aquinas at St. Louis University, I pitted Thomistic insights against the philosophy of Hegel, sometimes seriously and sometimes facetiously. The upshot was that Jean-Claude Guy, my closest friend during those Paris years, dared me to spend that summer's afternoons seriously reading Hegel with him.

We did this at the Jesuit house of study (the "scholasticate") in Chantilly, outside Paris. The setting was ideal. It had a great library with almost everything I needed for work on my doctoral thesis, which occupied my mornings. The residence was unusually pleasant for a Jesuit house of study. Originally, the buildings were the home of the Rothschild family, but during the Nazi occupation of Paris, the Germans confiscated them for their headquarters. Because of all its connections with the Nazi regime, the Shoah, etc., the Rothschilds had no desire to live there again. They gave the entire estate to the Jesuits in gratitude for all they had done to aid French Jews and resist the Nazis. A property that the Society of Jesus could never have afforded to buy, Chantilly provided housing the Order needed for its students in the postwar years. It was in this beautiful setting that Jean-Claude and I spent our afternoons reading Hegel's *Phenomenology*, guided by Père Gauvin, another of the country's leading Hegelians. I was not converted to Hegel, but it did a great deal to challenge my own philosophical understandings and to give me greater insight into modern philosophy. Above all, it led me to reflect even deeper on the nature of time and history, feeding directly into my doing theology historically.

Some thirty years later, in the second of two articles published in the 1987 volume of the journal Philosophy and Theology, *Cooke argued for history as a key symbol for Christian faith and, thus, for theology, to the effect that one might wonder whether Hegel's thought, while not completely convincing as a system, did not have more of an impact over the years than he seemed to realize. In any case, "History as Revelation" (PT4), presented here in full, occasioned Cooke's articulating in condensed fashion the methodological principles operative in his magnum opus,* Ministry to Word and Sacraments (1976), *which had actually begun to take shape in his earlier books and, then, continued to govern his later work, both scholarly and popular.*

History as Revelation

1. Introduction

One of the most important influences on theology in the twentieth century has been the historical consciousness that one associates with Western modernity. While we are beginning to appreciate the enrichment that a historical perspective brings to our understanding of Christianity, the struggle to use history as the context for understanding faith has been long and bitter— and the resurgence of fundamentalism in the Church makes it clear that the fight is not yet over.

My purpose is not to detail this conflict, nor even to analyze the underlying philosophical shift from the absoluteness and immutability characteristic of the Platonic heritage to the relativity and impermanence of insight that accompany more empirical thinking. Rather, I wish to look at the manner in which history— and I am using the word *history* to refer to the sequence of past and present human happenings as understood by a group of people —functions as the symbol in which revelation occurs.

Without pretending that they follow in logical sequence or that I will establish their relationship to one another, I will treat four questions: (1) What is the validity for arguing, as the biblical traditions do, that "the acts of God in history" constitute a special revelation? (2) Is there one history of divine revelation which involves the entire human race? (3) How are we to appraise the history of Christianity as "revelation"? (4) How does history function as a symbol in the process of "revelation"?

2. The God Who Acts

Anyone who experienced the evolution of biblical studies during the past half century remembers the emphasis that was placed at one point on the notion of "salvation history." As scholars became increasingly unhappy with explanations of revelation and inspiration that implied some sort of verbal communication, became more critically aware of the contextual influences on the humans who produced the biblical texts, they looked for some more open and uncategorized medium for divine revelation. The events themselves of the life of the biblical people seemed to provide the clue. It was the events themselves that from Moses onward, perhaps even from the patriarchs onward, carried the divine message of salvation. And obviously for Christians, the great event was Jesus' Passover, in which revelation found its fulfillment.

However, before very long, it was apparent that this was at least one step away from the answer. For one thing, textual research early on established that there was not a theology of the Bible, despite efforts by first-rate scholars to reconstruct such a "theology of the Old Testament" or "theology of the New Testament." One of the very best books bearing such a title, Gerhard von Rad's, provided clear evidence that one was faced with a multiplicity of theologies; the historical happenings obviously did not speak unambiguously about the divine. This was not to deny that God did perhaps intervene specially in the happenings of human life, nor to deny that these happenings could in some way speak about the God who so intervened.

The issue was and still is what leads people to interpret their experiences as influenced by God and therefore as speaking for God? Are we dealing only with the universal phenomenon of humans trying to make sense of their lives, trying to understand the mixture of order and chaos, the mixture of life force and death force, that they encounter—a phenomenon that finds expression in more or less sophisticated myth making? If that is the case, we are simply employing metaphor, using aspects of our experience of ourselves and proceeding anthropomorphically to imagine what the divine must be like. Or in the case of the biblical traditions, are we dealing with something beyond this? Are we claiming that the happenings of history as we experience them, or at least some more kairotic happenings, are saying something more directly from God, that they are special "word of God"?

I believe that we do espouse the latter, more direct, understanding of "word of God"; as a matter of fact, I believe that the revelation about God that the faith communities discover in history stands in stark challenge to some of the mythic anthropomorphisms of our culture. More of that in a moment.

If we do opt for some direct manifestation of God in the happenings of life, what are the grounds for doing so and where do we find guidelines for reading "the signs of the times"? It is here that the prophetic ministry provides a clue. It is the role of the great prophetic oracles of Israel to instruct the people in the true interpretation of their historical experience. Always the prophetic voice comes to challenge the prevailing wisdom, the "official line," the temptation to create myth on the presumption that God acts as we do—the prophetic text reads, "My ways are not your ways, says the Lord." What ultimately tells a faithful people what their history is, i.e., what the happenings of their experience really mean, is the intruding presence of God-self-giving in the prophetic experience we tried to examine in "Prophetic Experience as Revelation." *[Editor's note: That essay appears further below.]*

On the basis of such prophetic interpretation, the community of faith can see human history as structured most profoundly by the sequence of *magnalia Dei*, the great acts of God. For Israel, the pattern of divine activity was already apparent in the exodus from Egypt: an enslaved group without social cohesion or identity, they were singled out by Yahweh, freed from domination, guided through a period of trial and utter dependence on divine help to a promised land of their own where they could gradually work out their destiny as witnesses to the true God. Correlative to this divine activity, the people were required to respond by adherence to the path that God had laid out for them in the Law and to relate to no other divinity than God as revealed to Moses.

With the advent of the Davidic kingdom there comes an increasing maturity and autonomy in working out their history;

the people enter upon a new phase in their corporate life—but this shift is itself interpreted according to the exodus/covenant model; the stability of the Davidic dynasty is seen to be rooted in a special covenant with David and his successors, a covenant that is situated within the Mosaic covenant so that this latter can be better implemented.

So, too, the ninth-century-BC career of Elijah and the origins of charismatic prophecy in Israel are interpreted in the light of the Mosaic-Davidic covenant. Like Israel in its infancy, Elijah flees a wicked ruler to spend forty days in the desert on his way to the sacred mountain, and there on the mountain, the revelation of Yahweh comes to him, not in thunder and earthquake but in a gentle breeze.

And finally, when the remnant of Judah returns in mid-sixth century to rebuild Jerusalem and its temple, the prophecy of Deutero-Isaiah that invites them to this return images that return as a new exodus, led this time by Yahweh himself.

For Christians, the culmination of such deeds occurs in the life and death and resurrection of Jesus. Faced with the need to give some meaning to the apparently contradictory event of Jesus' death, the earliest Christians drew from their Jewish background and formed a Christology shaped by the model of the exodus—very logically, since they believed that it was the God of Moses who had raised Jesus from the dead. Jesus is a new Moses, leading the new chosen people into the final promised land of eternal life; Jesus is a new David, the fulfillment of the Messianic covenant promise, but fulfillment by way of prophetic rather than political mission. Behind this theology of history that characterizes the outlook of both Hebrew and Christian Scriptures lies the faith conviction that the one transcendent God reveals self in the guidance of human history.

As the Acts of the Apostles describes it, this revealed interpretation of human happenings, and specifically of their experience of Jesus' life and death, comes only with the community's reception of the Spirit of prophecy. And because this Spirit abides with the Church from the first Pentecost onward, the developing memory of the community that we call "tradition" is not simply a handing on of previous understandings; it is a continuing absorption of earlier chapters in the story into the revelation provided by later events.

3. Universal History as Revelation

Up to this point, we have been talking about human history in the rather narrow context of Christianity and its historic antecedents in Israelitic religion. Twentieth-century discussion of religion, particularly since the probing reflections of Ernst Troeltsch, has moved into a worldwide context and demands that our questions address the issue of revelation as it touches the other great world religions and culture to which they relate.

Obviously, when dealing with the many peoples who have come and gone during past millennia, we are faced with a multiplicity of histories, both in the sense of many sequences of events and in the sense of multiple interpretations of those events. And the existence of many religions testifies to the existence of many stories about divinely guided histories. Now the bottom-line question: Are we to deal with these various "salvation histories" as discrete human traditions that ultimately relate to one another only in overlap of some mythic elements, or can and perhaps should we move toward discovery of some fundamental history of salvation in which all of them share?

Several thoughtful theologians and historians of religion—and I would not wish to draw that distinction too sharply—have argued for the existence of an overarching religious history. Perhaps no one has argued the case more persuasively than Wilfred Cantwell Smith in his *Towards a World Theology.*

Let me cite Smith himself:

What is beginning to happen around the earth today is the incredibly exciting development that will eventually mean that each person, certainly each group, participates in the religious history of humankind—as self-consciously the context for faith. I do not mean that Christians will cease to be Christian, or Muslims Muslims. What I mean is that Christians will participate, as Christians, in the religious history of humankind: Muslims will participate in it as Muslims, Jews as Jews, Hindus as Hindus, Buddhists as Buddhists. I am a Presbyterian, yet the community in which I participate is not the Presbyterian, but, at this level, the Christian. I participate as a deliberate though modified Calvinist

in the Christian community, and the Christian process. In much the same way, I choose to participate as a
Christian in the world process of religious convergence.
For, ultimately, the only community there is, the one
to which I know that I truly belong, is the community
worldwide and history-long, of humankind. (p. 44)

There is a simplistic and long-standing response to the questions raised about the relation of Christianity to the other great
world religions: of course there is a universal history of salvation;
it is Christian history and all humans are saved by somehow relating to it, which implies that all other religions are at best inadequate and preliminary. There is the other extreme which handles
the multiplicity of religious traditions, including Christianity, like
a supermarket; they all have something to say and there is little
ultimately to choose among them. They represent a recurrent cultural phenomenon; but none of them can really lay claim to special divine origin. However, if one wishes to retain the belief that
the God who is revealed in Jesus is the transcendent reality whose
compassionate providence guides the existence of all humans
and to retain the belief that this God saves humans precisely by
self-revelation, one cannot resolve the issue simply.

Unless one is willing to say that in all other cultures and in all
other communities of sincerely faithful people, such as Muslims or
Buddhists, the providential power of God's Word and God's Spirit
has been either absent or overshadowed by the power of evil, one
must admit, I believe, that these other histories have functioned
in some way as "word of God." If this is true, these other religious
traditions give expression to elements of divine revelation which
we as Christian theologians can no longer ignore.

Let me illustrate this by reflecting on two instances, the historical career and insights of Muhammad and the present-day conversations between Christians and Buddhists. When one brackets
as far as possible both the legendary idealizing of Muhammad
within Islam and the centuries-old defamation of him within
Christianity, it seems difficult not to admit some out-of-the-
ordinary intervention of divine presence in his religious experience. Discovering the profound cultural betterment and more
importantly (for our discussion) the revolutionary refinement
in the understanding of God that resulted from his preaching,

and then applying the gospel principle "By their fruit shall you know them," I would argue that Muhammad can lay claim to identity as an authentic charismatic prophet through whom the same God worked as worked through the prophets of Israel. I realize that this is an extremely sketchy proposal that demands much greater justification; but I believe the justification can be given.

The second instance is one with which many of you are familiar, the rather widespread religious interchange now going on between Christians and Buddhists, particularly in countries like Japan. I am not referring to the somewhat faddish popular interest of US and European Christians in the religions of the Far East, but to the serious exchange of religious insight and experience between scholars of the two spheres. Theoretically, there would seem to be little room for this kind of thing, since Christianity speaks of God in a theistic context and through the metaphor of personhood whereas Buddhists think of the transcendent in terms that classify as "impersonal." But fruitful interchange is occurring; each group has learned from the other—which seems to me to argue that their religious pasts and presents are not completely discrete.

4. The Revelation of Christian History

But to return to our own faith tradition, how are we to discover how divine revelation has been occurring during the past twenty centuries of Christian faith experience? That we should be searching for such evidences of divine self-giving seems clearly indicated by Vatican II's decree on divine revelation, which abandoned the notion that Christian revelation ended with the apostolic period. Without being excessively negative, I think one could safely say that not everything in the Church these past centuries has been from God. But having said that, how are we to determine what in the actual experience of people being Christian has been "word of God" for them? Or to put it another way: What is the real history of Christianity? Is it the sequence of public activities and official statements that institutionalized leadership had passed on as the "important" events? Does it include the countercultural elements that often found their way into the standard histories as "heresies" or "schisms"? How much of what is still considered history of the Church is part of an ideological explanation of Christianity?

These are more than historiographical questions; unless we can find some response to them, we do not know where to look for the divine input; we do not have the starting point for our ecclesiology.

I believe we have tended to think of the activity of God in Christianity—and, for that matter, in life as a whole—as a mysterious inner process of grace and revelation that is cloaked and to that extent hidden by human cultures. Popular adages such as "God writes straight with crooked sticks" reflect the view that God works behind the scenes, often contrary to what seems to be the course of affairs, and that we must learn to look beyond the sensible world of experience in order to discern the divine saving action. Yet, even the currents of Christian thought deeply influenced by the Platonic dichotomy of spirit and body spoke of traces of divinity, the *vestigia Dei*, sensible things. At times, for example in the twelfth century, this appreciation of the created world intensified and triggered a cultural and religious awakening; but each time, it was gradually suppressed as being too "secular."

To some extent at least, however, what was at stake was the sacramentality of the created world; in the medieval West, it focused on the disputes over the symbolic dimension of the Eucharist; somewhat earlier in the East, it had been to the heart of the iconoclast controversies. In both portions of Christianity, there were close ties to the developing theories of Christian spirituality, especially the relation between contemplation and action. Unfortunately, as systematized reflection about sacramental liturgies crystalized toward the end of the twelfth century, the intrinsic questions about symbolism were overshadowed by canonical considerations and by a scholastic metaphysics of causality. The result was the relatively nonsacramental view of sacraments that passed into the Council of Trent and into the past four centuries.

There has been, though, a consistent undercurrent of appreciation for the revealing power of "ordinary" created things. To cite just one important influence: the emphasis on *in actiones contemplativus* that characterizes Ignatian spirituality implies a discovery of divine presence *in* the experienced world.

Today, we seem to be into a period of new theological insight into creation's sacramentality, insight made possible by modern advances in study of symbolism. Now we are realizing that human cultures are not a shell covering over the divine actions we associate with the terms *grace* and *revelation*; rather, the divine saving presence is communicated through those cultures. This lays on us the difficult task of discerning within a culture the elements that authentically communicate revelation and the elements that distort or negate it. "Grace" and "sacrament" both have important social dimensions that we have tended to overlook; God's saving and revealing power works, not just to redeem our individual human sinfulness, but also to transform human history into the eschatological realization of the kingdom of God.

Let me mention just one more aspect of the task facing us when we try to find in our Christian history the traces of divine revelation. What we are really looking for, if I do not mistake the quest, is the manifestation of God's Word and God's Spirit working in the Church's language and institutions and activities. But an essential element of the hermeneutic which would equip us for this task is an adequate Christology—which would coincide with pneumatology. For the moment, we do not have such a Christology which would probe the risen existence and continuing historical role of Jesus as the Christ, a Christology which would be indistinguishable from both pneumatology and ecclesiology. What we have now is a Jesusology that is struggling to reevaluate the historical reality of Jesus of Nazareth and bring it to bear on traditional explanations of the incarnation of the Word of God.

Exciting developments along this line are occurring in theological circles today. Symptomatically, Yves Congar, the acknowledged dean of Catholic ecclesiologists, has increasingly turned his research to pneumatology; and the breakthroughs in understanding what is meant by "the resurrection of Jesus" have continued since Durwell's pioneering book in the mid-1950s. When we are further along the road in such theological reflection, we will have resources as never before to discover the true history of Christianity, for it is the working of the risen Christ and his Spirit that is the heart of the history of the Church. And then the model of "a community of disciples" that Dulles singles out as one of the more promising new models for the Church will receive deeper resonance as it points to the sacramentality of the Christian people.

We can never completely resolve the issues we have mentioned, but we must at least recognize their existence and allow them to set our theological agenda.

5. History as Basic Symbol of God

The fourth and final topic that I wish to open for discussion is the role of history as the basic symbol in and through which we gain insight into the reality of the divine and of Christianity. The immensity of this topic makes the brain reel, so we will do no more than point to it as part of our intellectual future, perhaps the principal item of theological research for some decades.

Today, there is much talk about myths, models, and metaphors —some of it truly innovative and groundbreaking, some of it repetition in obscure technical language of ideas that have been around for decades if not centuries. Unquestionably, we are at a point in our intellectual history where we deal with the metaphorical dimension of thought and language in a more self-conscious and analytic way. This gives us an increased capacity to recognize critically the interpretive elements in our knowledge and, consequently, to gain more accurate insight into the reality we are attempting to understand.

Along with this, there is the widely recognized shift in the models being employed in Christian theology and official doctrine—the instance most often mentioned being that of the partial shift at Vatican II away from the institutional model for the Church. One can notice easily today theologians' use of various models; we have already entered a period of ecclesiological reflection quite different from the post-Tridentine and post–Vatican I era. But the long-range and more radical model shift will take some time to become evident, for it is operating at the grassroots level of Christians' individual and community self-identification. It will probably take a generation or two for most people to interiorize the notion that they are the Church, that they are agents as well as recipients of salvation, that they are prophetic and priestly family of God.

As this movement from organizational to familial self-imaging occurs, there will obviously be a major change in the metaphorical extrapolation from experience that Christians will employ to understand Christianity.

But if our accustomed ways of modeling the Church are being questioned and modified, the challenge to our metaphorical understandings of God is yet more radical. Challenge from linguistic analysis of "god-talk," challenge from feminist thinkers objecting to masculine monopoly on language about God, challenge from sociological clarification of the human tendency to project a God who can legitimate their institutions and structures—these and many more had forced us to think through more carefully things that we had known at one level for a very long time.

We had always known that "person" could be applied to the divine only in very analogous fashion, yet we almost inevitably drifted into thinking of God as supremely personal, i.e., supremely like what we are. Again, we had unreflectively called God *Father* without adverting to the revolutionary implications of the term *Abba* as employed by Jesus and the first Christians. And we had not differentiated that application of *Abba Father* to God from the biblical application of both paternal and maternal imagery to the divine. Then, too, over the centuries, we had frequently referred to God as *king* in ways that placed the divine within whatever happened to be the prevailing context of political experience.

But if all such images and metaphors are inadequate, where can we turn for something less idolatrous? At least part of the answer comes in realizing that what we need is not some metaphor for the transcendent. In a way, that is a contradiction in terms: what we need is a model for the *process* of divine revelation in which God is discovered. That process is, as we have been saying, human history as guided by divine providence through prophetic intervention. And how are we to model that process? As little as possible.

It seems to me that a very different kind of modeling can and should be employed, one in which a critically refined community memory of experiencing the divine—i.e., tradition made more accurate by painstaking historical research—is the symbol employed to gain insight into the transcendent. In addition to hearing God in the word of our own experience, we must hear God's word by vicariously experiencing the faith of past generations. To the extent that we can gain some entry into the actual developing faith experience of Christians over the centuries, we will have understood the revealing action of God's Word and Spirit. This will involve much more than accumulation and synthesis of historical data; basically it will be, as we have just said, vicarious experience used by the present generation of Christians to flesh out and interpret its own experience of the God revealed in Jesus as the Christ.

Inevitably, any experience of human life, be it direct or vicarious, is interpreted through use of ideas and images; and so we cannot avoid using ahistorical models like *parent* or *person* along with history itself as a model. Nor can we avoid distilling our shared faith in more abstract doctrinal formulations; these help keep our interpretation of history more accurate. However, we must strive to discover the way in which particular historical contexts relativized the understandings that believing Christians, including ourselves, gained through these models and formulations. We hope by so doing to reconstruct in a not-too-inadequate way the historical experiences of faith that sacramentalize the saving self-revelation of God.

Ideally, present-day Christian experience of a revealing God and vicarious sharing in the faith experience of previous Christian generations should intersect most focally in celebration of Eucharist, for it is *anamnesis* and sacrament. So, I end my theological remarks by a pastoral plea: we need encouragement, support, and freedom as Christians to create appropriate eucharistic liturgy. Without the kind of Eucharist our Christian faith needs, none of the promising theological and ecclesial developments to which I have referred can come to fruition. Without it, God's revealing presence through Word and Spirit cannot find appropriate expression, and we cannot become fully "hearers of the word."

Personal and Communal Experience: Symbol and Interpretation

The "turn to experience" was long underway in modern philosophy and Protestant theology by the time Cooke, among other European and American Catholic thinkers, went about his own work. While the concept has undergone no small amount of scrutiny by such emerging postmodern disciplines as critical theory, talk of experience in popular usage remains prone to limiting the notion to whatever one senses or does directly, as opposed to hearing about it from someone else (and on that rides the entire valuing, or not, of history). This, Cooke realized, is a category mistake ignoring how greatly our individual and communal worldviews are influenced by

*the experiences of others, as conveyed through symbols
and, in a heightened way, through language and, even more
powerfully, writing. This was a lesson, Cooke realized upon
reflection, that he learned in the undergraduate stage of his
Jesuit formation at the "juniorate" secluded outside St. Louis
in 1940s Florissant, Missouri:*

One thing did occur in the second year of juniorate, something that over the years continued to influence my theological
interest in symbols. I became fascinated with the way in which
language functioned. I didn't then know how to identify it, but
when I spoke to the dean about it and asked him for suggested
reading, he told me that my interest was in linguistics. He took
me into the inner sanctum, the faculty library, and together we
browsed through books on the topic. Much later, this would flow
into a broader fascination with symbolism and my reflection on
sacramentality and sacramental rituals.

What I gleaned from these two years that would figure importantly in my later theologizing was a feel for literature—quite simply, how to read. Was there more than that, some elements that
were constitutively theological? I think that experiences as we
pass through the years comprise a springboard for our "discovering" God. Literature expands that experience, giving us vicarious awareness of the human condition and thereby an expanded
starting point for theologizing. Certainly, the great Greek trag-
edies highlight the psychological dynamics that play a part in our
deepest human experiences. They point to the perennial questions about the ultimate forces that work in human consciousness
and freedom and that help shape our destiny. Reading genuine
literature probably should be considered an intrinsic part of theological method and great literature, part of the "biblical" canon
from which we draw. For one thing, I have found myself in teaching theology often drawing from Greek authors, particularly
Sophocles.

One author I discovered during those years was Chesterton,
not his *Orthodoxy* (which I had read in high school and did appreciate) but his autobiography. Somewhere during my second year
of juniorate, I "dried up." Much of our study dealt with the forms
of literature with relatively little concentration on the content,
and I suddenly felt glutted and didn't wish to read anything. For

some reason, I stumbled on Chesterton's autobiography, and his poetic awareness of the world around him saved me.

Doctoral studies at the Institut Catholique de Paris only heightened Cooke's convictions about the fundamental nature of experience, including what he would eventually call "vicarious experience," as the symbolic medium for every person's knowledge of God. Cooke comes to argue that experience—either one's individual experience or the sequential experience (aka history) of a society or community—itself is a symbol. How strange it might appear to speak of experience as a symbol! In places, he seems to identify it with self-awareness, but how does such a seemingly unbounded or ephemeral notion comprise a symbol? That a person might function as a symbol to others is not hard to grasp if one considers such examples as president of the United States or pope of the Catholic Church. In those cases, the symbolism resides primarily in the societally sanctioned office. But can one's entire life, encompassing all its experiences, itself be called a symbol?

Perhaps Cooke's thesis is best grasped by recognizing that people experience their lives as a story, doing so with such immediate conviction that they would assert that they are their story. For example, in a negative context of feeling stereotyped or having one's character or motives impugned, a person might exclaim to the other(s), "You don't know me!" That me, in such a single small word, entails the offended person's entire life, entire sequence of experiences continuously interpreted, yet, in that moment of confrontation, comprising a singular awareness of oneself. A positive example recently appeared in a younger theologian's book-length effort to argue for evangelization as participation in self-giving love. At the outset, Timothy O'Malley adverts to the experience of falling in love as "a moment in our lives in which our history is rewritten by the good news that we are indeed loved." He continues,

> As we grow into this love in the context of marriage, the name of our husband or wife takes on the contours of our common narrative, of the maturing love that we have embodied in specific times and places.

> *For me, to say the name "Kara" is not simply to utter
> four letters, consisting of two syllables, a word whose
> root is the Latin caritas; instead, this name recalls
> the person of my wife, the sorrows and joys that we
> shared as our mutual love has slowly formed us over
> the last decade.*[1]

One might argue that the symbol in this case is the word
husband or wife, but I would counter that O'Malley is insisting
on something utterly resonant with what we shall find Cooke
arguing in the passage below, namely, that the comprehensive,
shared life itself is experienced as a symbol; name and story
and history and self-awareness altogether comprise an image
bearing a reality beyond any word(s). The further movement is
between the individual (or in this example, the couple) and the
communal, the self and others, in space but also time. Cooke
is wrestling at a primary human level largely avoided theologically, it seems to me. He's pointing to something, namely our
experience, which is such a powerful symbol in our discourse
(think of how conventionally marketers invoke "the shopping
experience" or ask one to evaluate one's "dining experience")
yet so hard to explain (hence the philosophical efforts of phe-
nomenologists, existentialists, and so forth).

The following passage comprises the first move of Cooke's
conclusion to The Distancing of God *(DG 349–55). The final
chapter's argument for experience as "basic symbol" for individuals and peoples—and them in relation to God—follows
upon previous chapter-length discussions of theories of symbol and ritual in cultural anthropology, modern psychology,
and linguistics and literary criticism (and is followed by his
discussion of "History as Key Symbol" and "Christian Experience," moves that rehearse his arguments in the 1987 article,
above).*

Experience as Basic Symbol

In one sense, it is immediately obvious that each person's
own personal experience is the basic symbol through and in

---

1. Timothy P. O'Malley, *Liturgy and the New Evangelization: Practicing the Art of Self-Giving Love* (Collegeville, MN: Liturgical Press, 2014), 10.

which that individual comes to know both self and world; and recent research in the fields that we have examined details the manner in which this experiential symbol functions. Still, recognition of daily experience as a key symbol has come slowly, perhaps because of the tendency of researchers to focus on more intense situations of human consciousness—psychological pathology, poetic creation, ethnic rituals—where the dynamics of symbolic causation are more evident.

Experience is not, as some earlier theories of knowledge contended, a matter of consciousness mirroring a prestructured outside world. We have become increasingly aware of the extent to which each human, most basically in early childhood years, needs to sort out the complex manifold of sensible stimuli and fashion it into an intelligible world. Any number of influences contribute to this process of interpretation, construction, and integration, but ultimately the individual's unique state of awareness is that in which and through which all else is known.

All this rests on humans' power of symbolizing through language and ritual and of communicating with one another through these symbols. The process of intertwined symbolization and communication involves a constantly evolving dialectic between the conscious self and "the other"; people identify themselves as they construct their world. Through this creative self/world experience, people establish the "space" within which they can act with benefit to themselves and others.[2]

Accurate or inaccurate, one's experience of surrounding reality and particularly of significant other persons is, for that person, what reality is all about. The experience can be educated, deepened, altered, criticized, and corrected, but there is nothing that can replace it as the foundation of all one's knowing. Even if one has psychologically retreated to a world of illusion, the illusory awareness is for that person what reality is all about.

If the sequence of experiences, with its intentionality constantly polarized by "others," is the fundamental symbol that breaks human isolation and provides an unfolding bridge of knowledge to the outside world, it is also the symbol within which a person comes to discover and identify himself or herself. There

---

2. See Leland Elhard in *Dialogue between Theology and Psychology*, ed. Peter Homans (Chicago: University of Chicago Press, 1968), 140–41 (hereafter cited as *Dialogue*).

are degrees of insight into one's experiences, there are more or less educated interpretations of those experiences, there are varying capacities to confront with open self-confidence the implications of experience, but there is nothing that speaks more fundamentally to each person about their distinctive identity.

Experience as Symbol of God

It would seem to follow unavoidably that their intertwined experience of self and world is the basic and enduring symbol through which humans can come to whatever knowledge of the transcendent, that is, God, is possible. Other "words of God" there may be, such as Scriptures or ritual, but these can find their meaning only in interpreting and being interpreted by people's experience. Various religious traditions have expressed this in distinctive but overlapping fashion—"finding God in all things," "being contemplative in action," discovering "that thou art."

There are, however, two paths that can lead from personal experience to some awareness of the divine. The one proceeds—though not all philosophical traditions agree that it can so proceed—by ways of reasoning from such things as the perceived contingency of one's self and one's world to the existence of a noncontingent. The other proceeds from religious experience, that is, one's own immediate consciousness of God or a mediated consciousness that comes in trusting acceptance of someone else's experience of the divine. It is in this second instance that one can speak about "the presence of God," a being-for-another on the part of God that is grounded, as is all personal presence, in a self-communication. All presence is conditioned by the free "listening" of the recipient of the communication; what is distinctive about presence in this religious instance is that the "listening" consists in the faith of the religious believer. Divine presence in religious experience is dependent upon humans being "hearers of the Word."

Current studies in hermeneutics have helped us to appreciate the extent to which and the manner in which one's presence to oneself as well as the presence of others is dependent upon the subjective interpretation that is intrinsic to all experience. Thus, religious experience of divine presence, no matter how genuine,

47

is always conditioned by one's culture, by the doctrinal instruction provided within one's religious community, by the experience of liturgy—and so constantly in need of ongoing criticism and purification. At the same time, there is an underlying core awareness of divine presence that provides essential continuity in the midst of developing consciousness, much the same as does one's self-awareness.

In recent decades, both theologians and religious educators have become aware of the foundational role played by personal experience. A half-century ago, almost all mainline Christian theologians were still following the time-honored method of starting with a classic formulation of faith, for example, the christological creed of Chalcedon or a passage from the New Testament, and attempting to probe its meaning in the light of some other knowledge. Now theologians are increasingly aware that their starting point must be the shared faith experience of a believing community—though the large fundamentalist wing of theology in the United States still insists on the biblical text itself (read "literally") as that from which Christian reflection must begin.[3]

Much the same shift to stress on religious experience has marked the past few decades of religious educational theory— and to some extent religious educational practice. Benefitting from research in the psychology of religion as well as from the more experiential approach of theology, catechetical training and catechetical materials have stressed the role both of the student's general human experience and of his or her experience of sharing faith within a believing community.[4]

However, in both theological reflection and religious education, there has been a laudable emphasis on awareness of self-as-related to the transcendent and on awareness of the community in which one finds oneself situated, but comparatively little stress

---

3. On European "discovery" of experience as a starting point, see the dialogue of Hans Küng and Edward Schillebeeckx with US theologians in *Consensus in Theology?* ed. L. Swidler (Philadelphia: Westminster Press, 1980). However, the shift in Catholic theology was already observable as early as Congar's 1946 article "Theologie," in *Dic. Theol. Cath.* 15, cols. 342–502.

4. See especially the work of Thomas Groome, *Christian Religious Education* (San Francisco: Harper & Row, 1980). Also W. Meissner's two books, *Life and Faith* (Washington, DC: Georgetown University Press, 1987) and *Psychoanalysis and Religious Experience* (New Haven, CT: Yale University Press, 1984).

on awareness of God-who-is-present. Symptomatic of this, and perhaps its basic cause, is the relatively minimal awareness of divine presence in the celebration of Christian liturgy. Ritual is, as we saw in earlier chapters, meant to be a privileged context for a community and individuals within community experiencing ultimate meaning through becoming aware in symbolic activity of ultimate reality. If ritual is not this for people, they lack the indispensable starting point for growth in understanding of their faith.

Vicarious Experience

In all human psychological existence, vicarious experience plays a major role. For each of us, present and remembered experience is a very limited affair—linguistically, geographically, culturally, and socially, we have but one context of immediate happening, even with all the advantages of modern travel and communications. Yet, this severe limitation is overcome by the ability we have as persons to share in the experienced selfhood and worlds of others. This ability is so basic and so constantly relied on that people scarcely advert to it—which is another way of saying that we take for granted that we can share human life in communities of various kinds.

Daily conversation is the most common source of complementing one's individual and immediate experience by sharing in other people's. Taking for granted a fundamental human commonality in conscious awareness of the happenings of life, people are constantly communicating to one another the events, major or minor, that constitute their ongoing life history. In this way, people share in the intertwined happenings that make up the history of a neighborhood or town or nation, and consequently, interpret themselves and their individual experience in the light of this broader reality.

The recent explosion in communications technology has widened the exposure of people to others' experience, not just in their immediate vicinity but throughout the world. For the moment, this enrichment of consciousness is limited because of most people's relative inability to resonate with cultures other than their own; but media such as television appear capable, if used judiciously, of broadening people's horizons and opening them to appreciate the happenings in human lives worldwide.

If the phenomenon of vicarious experience can be extended spatially, it can also reach back in time through the shared memory of human communities. This can be informally realized through folklore and sagas and storytelling; it can be structured into the traditions that a group consciously transmits from one generation to another through education or ritual or law; it can be even more formally organized into the unified narrative we refer to as "history." Despite all the differing theories as to what truly constitutes history, there is an underlying agreement that historical study is meant to acquaint today's humans with what it meant for people of an earlier age to experience being human. And we often voice the hope that today's women and men can learn from this earlier human experience, that is, that vicarious experience can provide a broader source of insights to guide our present-day decisions.

Even though von Ranke proposed as the ideal of historical study the reconstruction of past happenings "as they truly were," scholarly historical research does not pretend to recapture the psychological states of those who lived in past epochs. Such is left to the arts, particularly to literature, where imagination enters in to re-create for both the artist and the observer a vicarious experience which, because it is highlighted, can both deepen and challenge the meaning of ordinary daily experience.

Today, film and television provide an unprecedented expansion of such vicarious experience, to such an extent that the basic sequence of exposure to human life is changed for young people as they grow up. Besides, there is an almost limitless range of vicarious experiences to which people can choose to expose themselves, from documentaries to first-rate dramatic presentations to professional athletics to soap operas to television evangelists. And then there are the experiences of fulfillment carefully suggested by television commercials. All this creates a complex symbol of human life today in the light of which people situate and appraise the happenings of their own individual lives.

Interpreted Experience

As never before, then, experiences of all kinds act to symbolize and interpret for people what it means to be human. But the other side of the coin is that all these experiences, whether individually immediate or vicarious, are themselves already interpreted experiences. We have seen in previous chapters the insight into such interpretation that has been provided by the social and behavioral sciences as well as by literary criticism; and we can, then, summarily list the principal interpreting agencies and note the central role played by symbols.

People's lifestyle and housing and dietary patterns, their family and civic and religious celebrations, their occupational and recreational use of time, their technology and art, their processes of education—in short, all the things we lump under the notion of a people's *culture*—constantly speak symbolically about the meaning people attach to human life and incarnate the values that govern the conduct of life. Which is to say that the basic day-by-day experience of people, as they interpret it in their particular historical time frame and with the ever-present mindset of their mother tongue, is an all-embracing symbol that synthesizes the manifold interpretive elements of their culture.

Another major source of interpretation is the particular happenings to which the person has been exposed in his or her past, either individually or as part of a group. While, as we indicated, this can be expanded by vicarious experience, such extension has meaning and can enter into one's hermeneutic only in so far as it can be related to some personally experienced reality. A teacher knows that there are many topics about which students can gain understanding (as opposed to mere informational knowledge) only if they are given the opportunity to experience directly what is being discussed in the classroom. Enrichment of one's experience by exposure to a broad spectrum of happenings—for example, by living in another culture for a time—provides, then, a greater capacity to discover meanings in life.

Simply being involved in happenings is not enough, however, to guarantee a person's ability to interpret experiences accurately. If there is anything that constitutes a gain in modern thought, it is the insistence that our observations of the world around us, or for that matter of ourselves, must be questioned regarding their accuracy, that our opinions and even our convictions must be tested to see if they are solidly grounded, that our knowledge must be seen as always incomplete and in need of amplification.

One is not born with such a developed ability to experience accurately and in depth. Modern development of the social and behavioral sciences has made us realize the need to discern the underlying dynamics of our actions as individuals and as groups if we are to grasp what is really happening, and made us aware at the same time of the need to employ the methodologies of these sciences if we are to have more than a superficial grasp of our experience. At the same time, such technical knowledge needs to be combined with a developing sensitivity to our surroundings so that it becomes realistic instead of purely academic. And any particular happening needs to be viewed within the broader context of present and past happenings, so that its meaning can be appraised with balance and perspective.

As we have tried to indicate, the symbols that people use in this process of interpreting their experience are of central importance, for they are intrinsic to the actual experience of people— as things happen, people shape their personal awareness of those happenings according to certain models, though for the most part they are not aware of the interpreting role of the most basic of these models precisely because they are so basic.[5] Much of the task of education in today's world consists in helping people to discover the models (that is, symbols) they are actually using, to evaluate the appropriateness of these models, and to help them develop the capacity to find and use symbols that will most accurately and beneficially shape and communicate their human consciousness.

In a word, we must pass from naive awareness of reality to critical awareness.[6] This requires a process of consciousness raising which, if one is thinking of accomplishing this for the bulk of people, is an immense undertaking. Yet, there can be no more fundamental educational task, for the consciousness people have is the measure of their own capacity to exist humanly and to enter into the creation of their personhood.

The very fact that such conscientization cannot be accomplished by a person without outside help makes clear the key role of a community's transmission of tradition. Each individual

---

5. On one's name as the central symbol of a person's existence, see Elhard in Homans, *Dialogue*, 140.

6. This progression toward critical awareness has been the onus of several of today's leading thinkers: for example, Paul Ricoeur, *The Conflict of Interpretations* (Evanston, IL: Northwestern University Press, 1974); Bernard Lonergan, *Insight* (New York: Harper & Row, 1957); Karl Rahner, *Spirit in the World* (New York: Herder and Herder, 1968); and Paulo Freire, *Pedagogy of the Oppressed* (New York: Continuum, 1970).

human is born into a particular way of life that is grounded in an understanding of what being human is all about and inherits a particular understanding of what the good life could and should be. That distillation of previous generations of experience constitutes a group's wisdom, a synthesis of the values by which it tries to survive and prosper, and the hopes by which it guides its management of social existence. Naturally, explicit verbal instruction plays the most obvious role in the process of handing on this community wisdom generation by generation, but it must be accompanied by congruent ritual and lifestyle if it is to be heard and translated into people's lives. But if all these traditional societal influences mold the individual's awareness of what seems to be immediately objective experience, the experience itself gives a unique translation of the tradition that the community has been sharing with the person. Thus, neither experience nor interpretation can exist independently of the other.

Prophetic Experience: Interpretive Key to History as Revelation

The tradition of a society or community bears a history, Cooke is arguing, even as the interpretation of experiences as history is shaped—indeed, performed—through a society or community's traditions of symbol, narrative, and ritual. Thus can he speak of history as a key symbol in the lives of both societies or communities and individuals. The symbolic power of history, as we saw in the second section ("Doing Theology Historically") above, is essentially, crucially true of Christianity as a biblically based, communally shared tradition of people's experiences of God. But what enables people of biblical faith to interpret history, with its myriad experiences both individual and collective, as revelation? Cooke summarily pointed to his answer toward the end of "History as Revelation": "Human history as guided by divine providence through prophetic intervention" (see p. 41). In prophetic experience, the individual and communal—people's immediate and mediated experiences of God—converge in sacramental transparency. For Christianity, the classical Hebrew prophets model this, with

53

Jesus the eschatological prophet becoming the definitive reve-
lation or Word of God in history and, thus, for the Church (PT3).

Prophetic Experience as Revelation

1. Introduction

In his valuable study on *Models of Revelation*,[7] Avery Dulles suggests five definitions that can serve rather adequately to group the principal explanations of revelation that one finds in theological circles today.

Let me quickly mention these and as I do so indicate why, in my opinion, each of them touches on one or other key aspect of revelation but still fails to answer the key question: "How does the divine input occur? How does God communicate to humans something previously not known about the reality of the divine?" Doing this will, I hope, set the stage for examining the experience of the great charismatic prophets as possibly providing some response to these questions.

The first definition: "Revelation is divinely authoritative doctrine inerrantly proposed as God's word by the Bible or by official church teaching." For those who accept the Bible and/ or Church teaching as "word of God" the formulations of belief that they provide are invaluable aids to knowledge about God; but the fundamental query must be, how does the understanding of God to which both Scripture and Tradition bear witness come to be communicated to humans? Any formulation is second-stage; it depends upon a prior event of revelation.

The second definition comes closer to that prior event: "Revelation is the manifestation of God's saving power by his great deeds in history." We [studied] this approach more thoroughly in the [essay "History as Revelation"] when I talk about history as revealing symbol; for the moment, let me point to the question it triggers: "What justifies any group in saying that they can argue so directly from their historical experience, that they are doing something distinctly different from the common process of humans giving a mythic interpretation of their life?"

Perhaps the third definition leads us still closer to the reality we

---

7. Avery Dulles, *Models of Revelation* (New York: Doubleday, 1983). *(Ed. note.)*

wish to grasp, for in saying that "revelation is the self-manifestation of God by his intimate presence in the depths of the human spirit," one is dealing with a seemingly unmediated communication that is prior to formulation or to resultant interpretation of history. The problem with this definition is that it seems to provide no basis for a normative revelation that could ground the existence of a faith community, no criterion for judging the truth or falsity of anyone's claim to receiving such revelation, no structuring of consciousness that would allow the divine self-manifestation to be shared with others.

The fourth definition is closely associated with the influential views of Barth and Bultmann, different as these two are from one another. It reads, "Revelation is God's address to those whom he encounters with his word in scripture and Christian proclamation." Anyone familiar with either Barth or Bultmann or with the major currents of contemporary Christian thought they initiated knows the richness of this approach to revelation. It brings together the normative structuring of the inspired word with the faith event of God's experienced presence; but it does not explain the genesis of scriptural proclamation as privileged source of understanding the God experienced in faith.

Finally, revelation can be defined as "a breakthrough to a higher level of consciousness as humanity is drawn to a fuller participation in the divine creativity." This understanding of revelation recommends itself because of its acceptance of the human as the medium for insight into the divine, because it seems to fit neatly with liberation theology's use of Christian *praxis* as starting point for theology, and because it integrates the realities of revelation and grace. But there seems to be a lurking danger that one is dealing only with a better insight into "the human" rather than a knowledge of God.

2. Prophetic Experience in Jeremiah

In moving on to an examination of prophetic experience, I do not propose a sixth definition. Instead, I would hope that in looking at a concrete instance of revelation, namely the breakthrough experience of a great charismatic prophet, we may together appreciate better both the pluses and minuses of the five definitions we just discussed.

Jeremiah has always held a great fascination for me, so I propose to concentrate on him as our first "case study." Besides my personal attraction, other factors make him an appropriate object for study: no other Israelitic prophet is so personally knowable through the biblical texts, no other prophet's exposure to and reaction to the divine is more clearly expressed, no other person had to struggle more painfully to make the God of his prophetic awareness fit together with cherished religious traditions and with the experiences of life.

Jesus of Nazareth provides, of course, an even more important object of study; he is described for us in the New Testament texts as "the eschatological prophet" and seems to have thought of himself as such. The complexity of his person and of his salvific role are so great that I hesitate to use his experience of God as a means of clarifying what we mean by "revelation." However, to discuss what Christians mean by "revelation" and omit reference to what happens in Jesus would be too severe a limitation of our theological reflection. So, after discussing Jeremiah, we can make a quick comparison with Jesus, acknowledging that the treatment will be all too brief and merely suggestive of our future christological agenda.

What then can we learn from Jeremiah? First of all, if we give any credence at all to his prophetic witness, we must admit that he was aware of God in a special and immediate way. Prior to the vocation experience that lies behind the opening verses of the book, he had already shared in the communal faith of Israel, been aware of a guiding providential presence of Yahweh in the life of people, felt himself related to this God through prayer and the liturgies of the temple. Yet, this new experience was just that, radically new—overpowering, unavoidable, demanding, shattering. And there are recurrent indications in the book that this initial experience was not isolated; rather, it set the pattern for a continuing intimacy and communication between the prophet and the God of Israel.

Strangely, as one probes the passages that reflect Jeremiah's ongoing awareness of God and his attempt to bring this awareness to his contemporaries, one struggles to identify the elements of newness. Even the great prophetic oracle of "the new covenant" in chapter 31 invokes the traditional language of the Mosaic covenant promise: "I will be their God and they will be my people." True, one can talk about a more spiritual approach as reflected in the language of "a law written on the heart"; one can point out that the new dispensation will not be like the covenant of old. And Jeremiah clearly is talking about something that is not yet, something that will come to be, something that will not be like what is—even though it will exist in profound continuity with what has been and is.

There are no new categories of explanation that structure Jeremiah's consciousness; the images that he uses in his oracles or in his prayers are the classic images of Israelitic prayer and prophetic exhortation. What, then, is new in his religious experience, something new that we might point to as a divine communication deserving of the term *revelation*, something that added to the religious insight already possessed by the true faithful of Israel?

Though it sounds trite, the more one reflects on Jeremiah's experience of God, the more one becomes convinced that the "new" reality is God. The God is not another divinity than the object of Mosaic faith, but the reality of the divine as it "swamps" the consciousness of Jeremiah is so beyond what he had understood in his previous religious knowledge that it is radically new. Now Jeremiah knows that, in a very true sense, he had never known God before, that his understanding of the transcendent had been in large part so inadequate as to be idolatrous. What has taken over the human awareness of the young prophet is not some provocative idea of what God must be like, not some sharpened realization of what he had been taught about the divine, but God become present to him.

In the new awareness of divine reality, everything in Jeremiah's human knowledge is challenged, his formulated knowledge of God, his understanding about the truth and role of Israelitic religion and social institutions, his self-identity as a believing Israelite, his interpretation of the world around him and of the history in which he played a part. None of the categories he had employed to think about God fits, none of the images applied metaphorically to the divine was appropriate, none of the behavioral dictates he had been taught did justice to the implications of the experience he now had. Yet, being human, he had no recourse but to employ inadequate, even distorting, images and ideas as he tried to grasp and communicate the "new God."

Out of this came the fearful isolation that is the fate of the authentic prophet—he did not fit. Future generations would reflect on what he had said and would draw, particularly during the anguish of Babylonian exile, both insight and hope from his experience. Gradually they would come to appreciate the truth of his oracles. But all that would come later; during his own life, the prophet would be out of step because he belonged intellectually to a future generation; he was living literally in another historical period. The prophet, however, was not only already a part of the future; he was a creator of that future; he was the bearer of the newness that would shape that future.

At this point, it seems to me that three realities come to focus and coincide: divine revelation, divine presence, and divine providence: God's presence in the divine self-giving is the revelation which in shaping human consciousness, motivations, and freedom, provides immanent direction for history. However, there are two other aspects of Jeremiah's religious experience that need probing—the sacramentality of his own human involvement with his people and the compelling drive to speak.

More than once in reading the Book of Jeremiah one is hard put to distinguish whether the anguish over Jerusalem's infidelity about which the text speaks is Jeremiah's or Yahweh's. Jeremiah loves his people even in their folly and stubborn sinfulness; he wants them, particularly the priests and prophets and sycophantic courtiers, punished for their rejection of divine truth and love as he conveys it to them—but one cannot separate this from his prayer that they be punished for their rejection of him; at the same time, he pleads with Yahweh not to destroy the people.

Perhaps I am drawing too much from the texts, but it seems to me that it is futile to draw a line between the human word of the prophet and the word of God in his oracles, for there is no such line. It is in his own anger and compassion and despairing hope of turning the people from their self-destructive course that the prophet discovers "the mind of God." In venting his own frustration and judgment upon the apostasy of Judah, Jeremiah is conscious of the congruence of this with the God he experiences and so knows that his own words speak for Yahweh; he is truly oracle, or (to put it in later theological terms) he is sacrament of the divine communication.

It is significant that Jeremiah's awareness of Yahweh's relation to the people comes in the prophet's oracular statements, for the prophetic experience involves not only awareness of the divine, it involves the compulsion to communicate. As Lindblom pointed out years ago in his study of prophetism, what distinguishes the prophet from the mystic is precisely the irresistible urge to share the experience of God. The prophet is possessed by God's Spirit as an oracle, an instrument of revelation; the divine self-giving to a community—as Paul will say much later in a letter to the Corinthian Christians, prophecy is given for building up the body of Christ. The prophetic experience is both awareness and mission. Because it is this essentially social reality, the prophetic experience is normative revelation; it is word/law of God.

All five definitions we drew from Dulles find some verification in our reflection on Jeremiah: the doctrinal formulations that later find their way into the biblical text are grounded in but never exhaust his prophetic awareness; God-present-to-the-prophet acts as the source of Jeremiah's interpretation of historical happenings as "acts of God"; God's revelation does occur in the intimate depths of Jeremiah's consciousness but precisely as knowledge to be communicated; because it gives expression to God's Spirit, the oracular language of Jeremiah that passes into the Bible can continue to be "word of God," word of revelation, for later generations; and the prophetic experience, precisely because it is awareness of God, clearly represents a heightening of consciousness and greater participation in the divine creation of history.

Put simply, reflection on prophetism as illustrated by Jeremiah suggests that revelation is the divine self-communication. It is God giving self in love. What impinges on the understanding of the prophet is nothing more or less than God, and while this immediately triggers ideas and images already present in the prophet's psyche, there is no infusion of new ideas or images. Instead in the context of immediate exposure to the divine the already-existent structures of religious perception and insight are transformed by the prophet's new knowledge of their divine referent.

3. Prophetic Experience in Jesus

The element of immediacy takes on more profound meaning when we turn to the case of Jesus, the eschatological prophet. Given the detailed care given the matter by the past twenty years of New Testament scholarship, I think we are quite secure in

59

saying that both earliest Christianity and Jesus himself looked on him as the eschatological prophet. The theology of the Lukan Gospel is particularly suggestive in the way in which it describes the prophetic Spirit working in and through Jesus from the very moment of his conception.

We have no shred of evidence about Jesus' distinctive religious awareness until the Gospel scene of his baptism at the Jordan, and the description of that happening is heavily theologized. Still, it seems that the intent of the evangelists is to describe the baptism as Jesus' call to prophetic mission, parallel to that of Israel's great prophets. And quite clearly, the experience of Jesus is one of a divine self-revelation so intimate that it touches creatively at the very heart of his own personal identity.

Obviously, we are here dealing with Jesus' "Abba experience." No end of New Testament scholars will insist that it is impossible to probe behind the faith-controlled reflection of the biblical texts and contact the human consciousness of Jesus. Granted the minimalism that we must accept if we are to proceed with scholarly care, I find it hard to deny the statement about Jesus' "Abba experience" that Schillebeeckx makes in his *Jesus* after lengthy and painstaking appraisal of contemporary Gospel study: "...trying to delete the special relation to God from the life of Jesus at once destroys his message and the whole point of his way of living; it amounts to denying the historical reality 'Jesus of Nazareth' and turns him into an 'unhistorical,' mythical or symbolic being, a 'non-Jesus.'"

What one arrives at by theological reflection on the New Testament depiction of Jesus is that his consciousness was totally and uninterruptedly permeated by the presence of his "Abba"; the constancy and fundamental character of this awareness can be deduced from the fact that it is inseparable from his own self-awareness as the *pais agapetos*. Just as our self-awareness permeates each and every experience we have had makes it *our experience*, so Jesus' self-awareness and the accompanying awareness of his Abba's loving presence to him transformed the entire course of his human experience.

Just as Jeremiah spoke and to some extent existed as oracle, so too in more profound fashion did Jesus of Nazareth. A multiplicity of New Testament texts give us solid grounding for the conclusion that Jesus lived with the conviction that his Abba's Spirit worked in and through him, that what he did was God's doing as well as his own, which was why what he did was God's glory. While it may have taken a generation or so for early Christianity to formulate its understanding of Jesus in terms of his being "the word made flesh," Jesus' own experience seems to have been that of embodying what his Father wished to convey to people.

One can say that Jesus is God's parable, or that he is the sacrament of our human encounter with God, or that he is the Word incarnate—they all express the same mystery of unique divine presence to a historical individual and through him to other humans in history. This finds full realization in Jesus' Passover through death into risen life: whereas a prophet like Jeremiah has the undeniable impulse to communicate his awareness of God, the very finality of Jesus' risen existence consists—if I can use a rather barbarous expression—in an ontological urge to share the life-creating Spirit of God. Thus, it is the conjoined communication provided by Jesus as embodied divine Word and by the divine Spirit he shares with us that constitutes the continuous self-giving we call "revelation."

4. Social Orientation

Once we have reached this point in our explanation where we talk about Jeremiah or Jesus sharing with others their own distinctive awareness of God, we have moved to the second stage of revelation. Because the prophetic charism is granted an individual in order that he or she can speak for God, the revealing act of God has an essentially social orientation. The Word and the Spirit of God work in history to form a people by shaping its consciousness and motivational structure, and to do this most profoundly by divine presence to people.

While this divine presence to a believing community does not have the overpowering immediacy nor the irresistible urge to speak that characterize the special prophetic experience, it does share in both. In its beginnings, the faith experience of the people draws from and rests upon the authenticity of the charismatic prophet, but it is meant to proceed from this to the people's own shared experience of God in faith and prayer. Awareness of God immanently active in human affairs through the mystery of personal divine presence constitutes a continuing revelation.

This subjective awareness depends for its accuracy upon the normative prophetic experiences of the great charismatic figures whose consciousness of divine reality is distilled in the biblical texts, depends most importantly on the experienced presence of God in Jesus, depends upon that cumulative experience of God we call "tradition," depends upon those voices within the community today that in various ways testify to God's Word and Spirit in our midst. But though the awareness of God with us must be tested in these ways so that we can discern the elements that are truly "word of God," the basic experience itself is the irreplaceable core of faith. We are meant to know God—the prophetic judgment upon ancient Judah that opens the Book of Isaiah says it much better: "The ox knows its owner and the ass its master's stall; but Israel, my own people, have not known me."

Revelation, then, in the special meaning we give it in reference to the Jewish and Christian traditions of a God-guided religious history, consists in a two-stage self-communication of God, the swamping and outreaching infiltration of the prophet's consciousness and the transformation of a group's consciousness as it becomes a community of faith. Christianity sees this as culminating in a continuing event of Pentecost whereby a sacramental community of discipleship embodies God's Word and Spirit. So far in our Christian history, we have viewed this almost exclusively in terms of the structured Church; we are only beginning to go further and to study the reality of God speaking in other human contexts, to ponder the possible implications of Acts 2 when it tells us that the crowd gathered on the first Pentecost wondered that "we hear them telling in our own tongues the great things God has done."

5. Conclusion

Before ending what I concede is a bit of theological ruminating, I would like to indicate briefly why I think our reflection is grounded in the evidences of faith provided by Christian tradition.

First, any understanding of "revelation" must honor the genuine transcendence of God. While we cannot avoid anthropological language about God's speaking, about God being personally involved with humans, and probably cannot avoid overtones of spatial and temporal imagery when we think about divine presence to humans in history, we must remain aware of the need to take account of these anthropomorphisms. I believe that the discussion we have had together did try to do this by speaking of the divine reality itself in all its undifferentiated simplicity as that to which the consciousness of the prophet is exposed. Any structuring of this experience in terms of imagery or categories of thought comes out of the prophet's own psychic depository.

Secondly, traditional Christian teaching has always maintained that revelation involves some real communication of knowledge from God to humans, knowledge about human life and knowledge about the divine. As we have described the prophetic experience and its overflow into the faith of the community, there is both knowledge *about* God and knowledge *of* God. And while this knowledge is always framed in ideas and images and words, none of these is in the first instance intrinsic to the communication.

Thirdly, both biblical and ecclesial traditions place the divine revelation in a social context; the word of God is spoken to bring a people into existence and through them to establish the kingdom of God. Our discussion has taken account of this element of tradition. We have seen that the revelatory experience of the prophet of its very nature is directed to formation of a community of faith. The words and even the person of the prophet—and a fortiori of Jesus—are creative and normative of the faith in God that is the principle of unification in a community of discipleship.

Fourthly, the sources of Christian faith have always viewed God's revelation as the ultimate story, the only completely adequate explanation of that sequence of human experiences we call "history." This also seems to be taken into account by the explanation we have given, for it views revelation as a continuing divine presence and self-giving that transforms humans' experience of being in time and space....

Finally, Christian understanding of divine revelation has implied the communication of *new* understanding. God told humans something they had not previously known. The question has always been, where does this newness come from if, in the context of admitting the transcendence of God and the genuinely personal experience of the prophet, one would not think of God employing words as such nor of immediately placing ideas in people's minds? I think that the line of reflection we have followed offers at least the possibility of explaining the "new" element we attach to revelation.

Does such a line of theological reflection explain "revelation"? No more than it explains God, for revelation is God, God-for-us.

Theology's Service to the Experiential Word of God

Cooke recognized that the catalyst for his theology of revelation as the "word of God" that people experience in their personal and communal histories to have been was "tertianship," the final year of his Jesuit formation. To be more precise, his great inspiration was the tertian director, Fr. Karl Wehner, a wise and courageous German Jesuit who served no less than three terms as a provincial superior. During his third term as tertian director, he was transferred and put in charge of the Jesuits behind the Iron Curtain in East Germany. That Cooke would extol Wehner, and not some prominent author or professor or academic program, as the single most important influence on his theology is indicative of how he understood the practical and "personal" nature of the discipline, locating its primary content in persons' unique and communally shared lives of practiced faith.

Whereas his superiors had determined while he was still a seminarian that Cooke would pursue doctoral studies in Europe after his priestly ordination, one further step in Jesuit formation needed completion. Tertianship, so named for its function as a third year (in anno tertio) appended to the noviceship completed years before, featured once again making the full thirty-day Spiritual Exercises of St. Ignatius, study of the Jesuit Constitutions, and some short-term pastoral assignments. Rather than undergo the process in his own province, Cooke persuaded his superiors to assign him to the tertianship in postwar Münster, not only so that he could acquire the German language essential to a scholarly theological career (the explicit reason) but also to be spared the rigid, lectured approach to the Ignatian Exercises that still dominated his

home province (the tacit motive): "I knew that there was a dif-
ferent reading of the Spiritual Exercises in some quarters in
Europe, a reading flowing from research into Loyola's personal
history and writings. This hunch proved highly justified." After
a journey traversing the Atlantic by boat, then France and Ger-
many by train, Cooke spent the summer in Bavaria, becoming
basically conversant in German.

In Pullach, I stayed at the house where young Jesuits studied
philosophy. It had been the place of Nazi internment of prominent Jesuits before and during the war. As I entered the front door
and stood in the lobby waiting for someone to answer the door-
bell, I noticed a banner on one wall with three lists I will never
forget: "Lost on the Eastern Front," fifty or so names; "Lost on the
Western Front," about thirty names; and "Witnesses to the Faith,"
i.e., killed by the Gestapo, eighteen names. For the first time, the
reality of Nazism and World War II hit home to me, as did the
Society of Jesus' heroic resistance to Adolph Hitler. To this day, I
retain immense respect for them, especially for Karl Wehner....

After three months, I bid Pullach farewell and headed north
for tertianship in Münster, Westphalia. I purposely arrived a day
early so I could make the tertian master aware of my linguistic
disability and apologize for it. When I had my room assigned and
baggage settled, I knocked on the tertian master's door, expect-
ing not the worst but certainly not the best. The response to my
knock was a "*Herein*" that sounded friendly enough, and entering
his office, I received a warm welcome and a bit of a surprise. Karl
Wehner did not look at all as I had expected. I had imagined him
to be rather austere, strictly German (whatever that was), and
rather demanding. Just the opposite: here was this somewhat roly-
poly man with a wide smile and completely nondominating manner. When I apologized for my still halting German, he responded
with a reassuring laugh, "You should see some of the other non-
Germans who arrive here."

This was my first encounter with the man who more than anyone influenced my life and theology. Though I always respected
the official distance that separated us, and though none of us thirty
other men in tertianship received special treatment, he and I did
by a series of accidents become friends. Shortly before the "long
retreat" (the thirty-day Spiritual Exercises of St. Ignatius Loyola),

we made a pilgrimage, fifteen miles each way on foot, to a well-known shrine of the Blessed Virgin at a place called Telgte. The place was highly familiar to Wehner because in the town's marshaling yards were assembled scores of box cars where thousands of war refugees from eastern Europe were housed, refugees to whom he ministered each weekend. My good fortune was to be his hiking companion on the pilgrimage, and I took advantage of the situation by plying him with questions about himself. I already knew a few facts: that he had twice been a provincial superior, in Bavaria and in Berlin, the latter during the high point of Hitler's power; that Jesuits were always in trouble because of opposition to the Führer; and that they paid for their opposition by being executed or imprisoned in Dachau.

Naturally, I asked if he had ever personally encountered Hitler. "Three times," he responded, in a matter of fact way that seemed to say, "What did you expect?" Of course I had to pursue the point further: What was he like? "Well, when one was summoned to see him, presumably as prelude to some punishment, you would be kept in a waiting room outside his office. In this waiting area there were two huge SS guards and two huge attack dogs, obviously to intimidate you. I happen to like dogs," he added with a smile. "Finally you would be admitted to his office, which was a very large room almost completely empty of furniture where himself stood on a raised platform at the end. Immediately, he would begin to berate you, but if you stood up to him, he crumpled. Quite simply, the man was a coward who covered it up by being a bully." What amazed me as I listened to him was how he managed to escape with his life. My guess is that his calm fearlessness baffled Hitler. As he talked more about the years of the Nazis and the war, it was without the slightest suggestion that he had done anything unusual or courageous, but I could fill in the story with things about those years that I learned from others who suffered under them. It wasn't that he did not appreciate what had happened in Germany in the 1930s and '40s. When a film entitled *Five Minutes after Twelve*, a documentary on the rise and fall of the Third Reich, appeared in theaters that year, Wehner strongly urged the non-Germans among us to see it, so as to get some idea of the catastrophe that had occurred.

Another of Wehner's qualities was the immense respect he had for the views of one like myself. Before we went into the long retreat, where he was to serve as the guide to our forming a spiritual outlook that would probably shape us for the rest of our lives, he had an individual session with each of us. In it he asked one to describe the spiritual formation he had received up to that point. I hadn't got more than three sentences out of my mouth when he grinned and said, "Meschler." Meschler was the name of the German Jesuit of the "old school" whose writings had been central to my novitiate at Florissant. Meschler epitomized the approach to Ignatian spirituality with which I had long felt uneasy and from which I had managed to escape by getting to Münster. When I went on to describe further my exposure to this interpretation of Loyola, Wehner's response surprised me: "I disagree with that, as you can see. However, if you feel at ease with this previous formation and it has helped you, stay with it and ignore what I will be saying." I assured him I had no inclination to cling to Meschler. I later learned that Wehner was heir to the revolution in Ignatian spirituality that had taken place among prominent European Jesuit historians and theologians. Wehner's own tertian master was actually sent from Germany into exile in Buffalo for his role in that movement.

Another question he posed was very different. Did I have any special project, any particular agenda for the tertianship year? I mentioned that one hope was to bring together for myself Aquinas's notion of wisdom and Ignatius's *Contemplation to Attain Divine Love.* "Great," he replied, "and if you are in the midst of research on that and it is time for one of my conferences, just skip my conference." I wouldn't have missed one of his conferences for the world. They were opening up a vision of Christianity and ministry to the gospel that was immensely exciting and yet very simple and down to earth. What was beginning to happen, and would deepen over the year in Münster, was the integration of my academic theology with my experience of faith. Theology was becoming my ministry, ministering was becoming my theologizing and my prayer.

That brings me to the thirty-day Spiritual Exercises, the long retreat. Wehner did not preach the retreat; instead he followed the guidelines comprising the original text. He did provide brief introductions to the meditations sketched out in the Exercises, but principally he helped each retreatant understand what was happening to and within him as he followed the prescribed meditations and contemplations. He helped the individual discern the decisions he faced. One innovation reflects his approach. The long retreat is divided into four "weeks" with three break days in between. We did, of course, have the break days, the opportunity to blow off steam and rest up a bit from the intense mental effort. But at Münster, we also had an extra day at the end of each "week," when we did not follow any prescribed exercises but just relaxed mentally and browsed thoughtfully through what had happened in the preceding days. It was amazing the effect that had on the spiritual discernment so central to the Exercises. It was another instance of the regard Wehner had for each of us as distinctive individuals. Incidentally, the experience of those "extra" days initiated a quest for understanding the Spirit of God that continued the rest of my life and eventually found expression in my last book, *Power and the Spirit of God.*

At the heart of my theological reflection that year was the notion with which the Exercises end: contemplation in action. It brought together all the ramifications of divine presence that had been such a "bombshell" for me in the earliest days of novitiate and continued to resonate throughout my years of studying philosophy and theology. Not only did it interpret my own life experience, it proved to be the key to the theology for the laity that I was commissioned to develop. Not only did Wehner encourage me in the research I did, but on more than one occasion invited me to share with him my insights, doing so with genuine interest in learning. I must confess that it felt like carrying coals to Newcastle.

Two other more technical contributions to my doing theology should be mentioned. The first flowed from the character of my fellow tertians, not only their companionship but also the variety of their previous experiences. About half of them were slightly older Germans who had survived the Nazi years and military service, who had endured the temptation of rampant nationalism and military power gone awry and come through as metal tested in fire. Others were Dutch, Belgian, or French who had shared with their people the sufferings inflicted by the early years of World War II and who had resisted "underground" the extermination of the Jews. How different from the memories we few Americans in the group had of what it meant to be Jesuits and Catholics. For me, it fostered an appreciation for the diversity that needed to be honored as we thought about and worked to nurture Christian and human community, as well as an understanding that fidelity to the gospel involved honest and responsible confrontation with the happenings of life much more than it did conformity to institutional demands.

Although such autobiographical testimony might prove a sufficient concluding demonstration of Cooke's objective in shaping his fundamental theology through the categories of immediate and vicarious experience, history, and revelation as "word of God," a final short excerpt from his academic writing can serve as a summary and set the stage for chapter 2. The following passage returns us to the 1980 article in the Journal of Ecumenical Studies *with which this present chapter began. Having analyzed and respectfully taken issue with Hans Küng's proposal for a new "consensus" on correlational theology, Cooke proposed (JES 73–74):*

Let me, then, sketch very quickly an alternative model for the theological enterprise—using "alternative" rather loosely, because it will quickly become apparent that it is basically open to the kind of thrust that Küng describes in his own method. Instead of viewing the theological task as one of bringing two poles, "the gospel" and human experience, into creative contact with one another, I see a person's experience (and by extension, a community's experience) as the basic and, to some extent, all-encompassing "word of God." For each of us, it is the sequence of experienced happenings that tells us ultimately who and what we are, what the world around us is all about, what transcendent influence works with and upon us, and what response we are called to give as we help shape the future.

Obviously, the happenings that make up a given person's experience are being constantly interpreted—necessarily so, because in many instances, the meaning of the happenings is obscure or ambiguous. And the very factors that enter into the interpretation—explanations given by family or friends, education and reading and discussion, "hearing the gospel," religious doctrines and catechesis, exposure to the arts and literature, and other expressions of human culture—are all integral elements in the experience itself. Perhaps most basically, any given experience is interpreted in the light of other experiences, either one's own recalled past experiences or the experiences of others in which one has shared vicariously. These experiences of others, which for them were an immediate "word of God," function also for me as "revelation" in proportion as together we form one truly sharing community of belief. Each person is, then, sacramental in some very fundamental sense; each true believer is a "theological source" more ultimate than any doctrinal or theological formulation—though, clearly, the generalizations that take place in doctrine and theology have an indispensable role in creating a unity of understanding and making interchange of personal belief possible.

In order that the experiential "word of God" might be genuinely fruitful for each of us, it must be read with accuracy. This is where theological input occurs, hopefully. No brief summation of theology's task is satisfactory, partly because the very boundaries of theological reflection are expanding as new modern disciplines of knowledge become part of theological method. Let me suggest just three or four contributions theology can and should make.

1. Theology should help one discover and identify the religious components in the implicit and explicit structures of interpretation that influence any given experience. That there are such presuppositional structures is certain, that they both limit and enrich our perception of "reality" is well-known; and the recognition of religious presuppositions in this "hermeneutic of experience" is required if we wish to ascertain what in our experience is revealing word of God. Not only should theology provide the categorical clarifications enabling us to identify these religious presuppositions, it should also, by situating such understandings relative to established credal and theological traditions, indicate the extent of historical relativity in our presuppositional structure.

2. Theology should describe as accurately and critically as possible (as a basis for comparative evaluation) those principles for interpreting one's own experience that are provided by previous expressions of faith—including the Scriptures. A distinctive element in this task is the critical examination, in historical

perspective, of the various *logoi* or structuring categories that people used to give rational theological structure to their religious understandings.

3. Theology should help suggest the (providentially directed) pattern of ongoing religio-human development into which our own experience fits. This would include a practical extrapolation of our present historical dynamics, a hypothetical projection of what the future could (and, according to the gospel imperative, should) become, so that this could influence practical moral decisions.

4. Christian theology must as its basic function guide each believer as he or she responds personally to the perennial question: "Who do you say that I am?"...

CHAPTER TWO

Inexhaustible Mystery in Jesus

SPIRIT, WORD, AND POWER

Introduction

With the life of each Christian comprising an ongoing response to Jesus' invitation personally to know him, Cooke argued, theology's fundamental purpose is to provide resources for discerning that "word of God" as it arises in their interpersonal and societal circumstances. While the work of academic theology, then, continuously seeks accurate and apposite knowledge from revelation's ongoing history in Scripture, Tradition, and the vicarious experiences of earlier generations, at its most profound level, the theologian's task is focused with the believer on the person of Jesus. And this is Jesus not, as Kant and so much of modern theology would have him, as a moral exemplar from ages past to be reasonably emulated; rather, this Jesus invites the believer into an intimate companionship of freedom and mutual trust encapsulated in the questions, "Who do people say that I am?" and "Who do you say that I am?" Cooke repeatedly invoked those questions in both his writing and teaching. That scene in Mark's Gospel (8:27–30) is a characteristic source for Ignatian contemplation, wherein the retreatant does not study about Jesus but, rather, dialogues with him in a living friendship. Cooke's theological method, then, presumes both his own and his audience's primary theological activity of prayer—a conviction with roots in his early Jesuit formation.

On principle, the two years of novitiate were not to be a time of academic study, certainly not the pursuit of theology; that would come years later. We were to learn how to pray, to develop our "spiritual life."...But just as in high school, a few valuable elements of theological reflection were being provided during the two novitiate years. Reading about the lives of the saints—a regular part of the daily exercise of "spiritual reading"—laid the ground for ecclesiology and spiritual theology. Meditative prayer was a constant reflection on the reality of the divine and its impact on human existence. Of course, the experience of the thirty-day retreat, the full impact of the Spiritual Exercises of St. Ignatius, was in its own way the creation of a framework for thinking about God that would endure for years, undergoing changes and eventual "reform" only in my tertianship year....In a distinctive way, the Exercises constitute a Christology that flows into one's understanding of all the other elements of being a Christian, a Christology that for me evolved over years of meditative prayer and infused an experiential dimension into later technical study of Jesus of Nazareth.

Yet, basic as was the experience of the Exercises, I believe that something else occurred very early in the novitiate that has had as profound and lasting an influence on the way I have tried to do theology. The first book given me by the novice master for daily "spiritual reading" was a slim volume by a French Jesuit, Raoul Plus, entitled *God within Us* (1949). What it dealt with was God's *presence*, and it absolutely blew my mind. For weeks I read and reread the book until the novice master insisted I move on to another. As earlier described, I had grown up taking for granted that God existed and was at work wherever I was. But that God was "present" as described in this little book? For the first time, I had to probe the reality of personal presence as it involved God and deal with the implications of God not just "being there" but "being for." I have since come to think that at the heart of Christian theological developments during the past century has been the notion of divine presence, and for me personally, the principal element in my hermeneutic has been the presence of God through the presence of the risen Christ. Obviously, there has been a constant modification of the theological elements and ramifications of this early insight, but it has never ceased to be operative in my thinking....If authentic theologizing is a quest for the living God, then my two years of novitiate certainly qualified as theology. The deepest and most real awareness of God has always come for me in the context of prayer; reflecting academically on aspects of theology has often drifted into quiet contemplation.

While the person of Jesus thus figures constantly through-out Cooke's writings—in his theological anthropology, sacramental theology, ecclesiology, and theology of ministry—the preface to the one book he devoted entirely to the topic, God's Beloved, *encapsulates both the passion of his conviction and awareness of the historical-critical challenges it poses:*

For a Christian theologian, the fundamental question with which he or she must grapple is the one Jesus proposed to his immediate disciples: "Who do you say that I am?" Whatever response one gives to this question underpins and permeates his or her entire understanding of Christianity—indeed, his or her understanding of oneself, of human life, of human history, and of God. This question has assumed an urgency in today's world beyond what it has had for centuries largely because of Christianity's exposure to the rich traditions of other great world religions, and because modern science and technology have laid claim to be alternatives and more satisfactory responses to human needs and potential.

But if modern critical thought and scientific methodologies have challenged traditional understandings of Jesus, they have also provided the Christian theologian with tools to deal with and profit by the challenge....the scholarly research that has been achieved in biblical studies, in historical and sociological studies of Christian origins, and in the psychology of religious experience in order to understand a bit more clearly and accurately the reality that was Jesus of Nazareth.

More specifically, this book will focus on Jesus' own experience of the divine, on his awareness of God as his "Abba." The reason? Here, if anywhere, one can discern the distinctive understanding of the divine that Christianity claims to have derived from Jesus. In many ways, the undertaking is difficult, perhaps foolish, since it is obviously unclear whether it is possible for us in the late twentieth century to probe the awareness of someone who lived two millennia ago in a culture quite different from our own. Yet to admit total defeat is to concede that Jesus cannot ultimately be normative for Christianity as a way to God.[1]

That is quite a claim, susceptible to significant contestation, yet Cooke forged forward into a series of chapters that made the book a much fuller exploration of the possibilities he outlined in his 1987 articles on revelation: Jeremiah as paradigmatic of Israelite prophets, Jesus as eschatological prophet, and the Spirit as empowerment of his mission. Cooke argued at greater length for the "immediacy" of Jesus' awareness of God: in the mysticism of prayer, the prophet experiences a radical encounter with God in "undifferentiated simplicity," in a way unrestricted by the conventions of his socio-religious context yet necessarily interpreted therein. Explicitly citing the New Testament scholarship of James D. G. Dunn and the constructive christological work of Edward Schillebeeckx, Cooke identified this original divine awareness in the man Jesus with the Gospels' and Pauline attributions of his and the subsequent early Christians' address to God as Abba. Elsewhere, moreover, Cooke critically reviewed and taught Rahner's foundational theology, such that one can likewise sense in his argument for the fundamental importance of Jesus' immediate awareness of God the Rahnerian insistence on the sovereign freedom of the Holy Mystery (a term protecting the divine from all the accumulated idolatries symbolized by the name God) in its "unthematic" presence to humanity. Thus, while dedicating further chapters in God's Beloved to the first-century religious and sociopolitical Galilean context and Jesus' male identity therein, Cooke did so with the conviction that the uniqueness of Jesus' awareness of God affected the originality of the transformative prophetic message he brought to bear on them. Building on Dunn's work, Cooke concluded that the Spirit of God now empowers the sacramental-prophetic mission of the Church in its members, whose trust (faith) in their own experiences of prayer and praxes for justice rest on that of the crucified and risen Jesus.

---

1. Bernard J. Cooke, *God's Beloved: Jesus' Experience of the Transcendent* (Philadelphia: Trinity Press International, 1992), vii–viii.

Hence Cooke's argument for ongoing theological reflection on Jesus' experience of divine presence: the common humanity of the baptized with Jesus indicates our capacity to experience God's immediate presence in analogous fashion, while our ongoing quest for more accurate knowledge of Jesus' experience provides guidance for our individual and communal discernment of the "word of God" in our time. The firmness of that practical-theological conviction Cooke recalls acquiring through contemplative prayer during tertianship, while also indicating how essential to his theology over subsequent decades was time in class with students:

Perhaps the most important contribution to my doing theology that came from the months in Münster was the realization and acceptance of the *transcendence* of God. It came not by rational reflection but in the experience of prayer. I had to let God be God. Any attempt to understand the divine was futile. No ideas fit, not even the metaphysical insights that I so cherished. What remained was the awareness of presence that first came to me during novitiate with Raoul Plus's little book. What also remained was the realization that the only avenue open, at least for me, to encountering the divine was through Jesus of Nazareth, that he was/is truly "the Word of God," God's revealing, God's self-communicating. That has meant a years-long, never completed quest to answer the two questions that the Gospels tell us Jesus proposed to his disciples: "Who do people say I am?" and "Who do you say I am?" Nothing has contributed so much to that quest as the thirty-five summers when I was privileged to teach the course in Christology at Boston College's Institute of Religious Education…a precious opportunity to keep up with the current literature, to exchange understandings with a challenging group of adult students of widely diverse backgrounds and ministerial involvements.

While the affinity between Rahner's and Cooke's theologies may be readily inferred from the Jesuit formation and spirituality they shared in common (all the more due to Rahner's part in the revival of the Ignatian spirituality in early to mid-twentieth-century Europe), it is the book by the far more obscure Raoul Plus that Cooke repeatedly mentions. Drawing upon medieval and contemporary spiritual writers, notably both men and women, the French Jesuit's text is an extended invitation-cum-demonstration of how the believer can enter into "mental prayer" so deep as to feel a closeness, an affinity with divine presence "where realities are evident," the mysteries of the faith are "seen from within."[2] Cooke's affinity for Plus's spiritual theology, it turns out, lay in mystical experience reaching back to his youth:

One incident in the early years of my faith awareness and incipient theologizing, which was very much Christ-centered, I must note. It was an experience, the first of four such in my life, that I am still unable to understand though its impact remains with me. It happened early one afternoon when I was about ten. I had planned to take in a Saturday afternoon movie, something I rarely did. On the way, I passed our parish church and, on the spur of the moment, decided to park my bicycle by the church door and drop in for a very short "visit to the Blessed Sacrament." What happened then I could never describe much less explain. All I know is that "I was there," the movie completely forgotten, and it was hours before I emerged, just in time to get home for supper.

Aligned with devotion to the Eucharist and the heart of Jesus, the upshot of Plus's book is that all the baptized, not just vowed religious but very much the laity, are graced with varied capacities to receive God in immediate, supernatural friendship, such that one undertakes all aspects of life "with Him."[3] A perusal of the text, so "Jesuit" in its repeated three-point structure and guided contemplations of Gospel passages, discloses an array of concepts that, while in a pious register Cooke would leave behind, became characteristic of his theology: Word and Spirit of God, divine-human friendship, uncreated and created grace. Fundamental is his insistence that Christians are meant personally to know God in both immediate inward intimacy and mediated communal life, with the risen Christ acting as "Word of God" in the power of the Spirit who raised him beyond death to be united in friendship (communion) with all humanity.

---

2. Raoul Plus, SJ, *God within Us*, trans. Edith Cowell (New York: P. J. Kennedy and Sons, 1949 [French original, 1924]), 52, includes quoting of Robert Hugh Benson, *The Lord of the World* (London, 1907).

3. Plus, *God within Us*, 142, quoting Elizabeth of the Trinity.

Jesus, Divine Saving Presence in Human History

Insistence on the priority of the prophetic in the ongoing history of divine revelation, even as definitively identified with the person of Jesus, begs for some grounding of norms for discernment among the Church in any time and place. Two years after the publication of God's Beloved, Cooke incorporated key arguments from the book in a plenary address for the 1994 convention of the Catholic Theological Society of America (CTSA 24–35):

Jesus of Nazareth, Norm for the Church

I take the topic assigned to me as a base for our christological reflection, "Jesus as the norm of the Church," to be an attempt to focus our conversations here, and I will try to honor this focus. However, even this limited topic has at least two major methodological problems to contend with: (1) To what extent can we be assured that our understanding of Jesus of Nazareth is accurate, and (2) how can we restrict the discussion to the Jesus of two thousand years ago and prescind from Christian belief in the continuing human existence of Jesus as the risen Christ? With respect to the first problem, the historical reality of Jesus, limitation of time will require me to make choices among competing scholarly reconstructions of Jesus' life and activity and to do so without giving detailed arguments for my choices. Anyone familiar with the volume of recent publication about Jesus of Nazareth knows the extent to which even the most careful studies are subject to challenge by other competent experts. However, I believe that we share the judgment that attempts to deal with Jesus of Nazareth should employ the very best critical procedures, procedures that themselves must be subjected to constant criticism. Regarding the second issue, I can only say that, to the extent possible, I will focus on Jesus of Nazareth—and let me say at this point that I will be using the term *Jesus of Nazareth* to refer to that historical individual in his actual earthly career and experience. I believe that after essays like John Meier's in

78

Theological Studies,[4] we can proceed without too much hassle about terms such as *the historical Jesus.* Hopefully my use of the term *Jesus of Nazareth* can skirt that issue.

As you will see, I find it virtually impossible to avoid rather frequent reference to two thousand years of Christians' faith relationship to the risen Christ, for Christians' faith relatedness is to the risen Lord and not as such to the Jesus of two thousand years ago. Again, to reveal my own presuppositions, let me state at the very beginning my position regarding the resurrection as it touches Jesus himself: as far as I can see, mainstream Christian faith has consistently maintained that, in some fashion, Jesus of Nazareth continues to exist humanly and is present to the community of believers. I am aware that this understanding of Jesus risen is not universally shared among Christian exegetes and theologians today....

In good trinitarian fashion, I will deal with three topics. (1) The *memory* of Jesus has been a constant force in the faith awareness and life of the Christian community during the past two thousand years and remains such today. (2) God's Word, uttered in Jesus as God's parable, continues to function as a normative *word of revelation* in the life of the Church. (3) The lines of force by which God's Spirit worked in the life and ministry of Jesus of Nazareth provide the guideline for our own Christian life and ministry. I will add to this, in extremely brief fashion, my understanding of what it means to call Jesus the founder of Christianity.

1. The Memory of Jesus as Normative

It is a constant element of our experience that the memory of great persons, or the memory of persons close and dear to us, continues to influence us long after their death. Such memories touch our awareness of ourselves, affect the meaning we find in human life, inspire us to embrace certain ideals, and motivate us to certain courses of action. If recent TV programming is any indication, the memory of Martin Luther King or Robert Kennedy or Malcolm X continues to fascinate and attract millions of our fellow citizens. Certainly for millions of idealistic people, the

---

4. John Meier, "The Historical Jesus: Rethinking Some Concepts," *Theological Studies* 51 (1990): 3–24.

memory of the Central American martyrs works to shape their understanding of life and of what it means to be a dedicated and caring human being, and it alerts people to the power politics, shared by our nation, that oppress the poor of the earth. Hopefully that memory works also to help people evaluate the priorities governing our society, recognize the incompatibility of such oppression with Christian faith, and one day take effective action to bring about justice and peace. Such influential memories are intensified if the person in question had died in some heroic fashion, though the full resonance of their action is often difficult to define—as is the case with the memories that flood in for veterans visiting the Vietnam memorial in Washington.

For devoted Christians, the memory of Jesus of Nazareth exercises a special role. It is the memory of a teacher and prophet sent from God to help guide humans to their destiny; it is the memory of a great human who faced public repudiation and criminal execution rather than betray his witness to truth; but more than that, it is the memory of a beloved friend. This added element of deep human affection is reflected in the New Testament, especially in the Johannine tradition. Mary of Magdala is not the only one to refer to Jesus as *the Master* in a way that implies the warmth of deep friendship. Clearly, these early disciples of Jesus regarded his teaching and his example as normative of their own understandings, attitudes, and activity. The very emergence of Gospels testifies to the way in which Christians' own existence as individuals and as communities of faith was given intelligibility through reflection on the person and career of Jesus.

But such deeply human resonance with the remembered Jesus is not a phenomenon limited to those who had experienced Jesus himself in historical existence. Christian history is replete with examples: references to Jesus in the patristic sermons and baptismal catecheses, the warm human relatedness to Christ of women like Julian of Norwich or Margery Kempe or Teresa of Avila, or of men like Bernard of Clairvaux or Francis of Assisi or William Langland, or the devoted reflection of the mysteries of Jesus' life and death and resurrection that characterize Loyola's *Spiritual Exercises.* In our own day, even nonreligious media whose historical accuracy could certainly be questioned still draw from this memory images both consoling and disturbing—Pasolini's *The Gospel according to Matthew* or the more recent film *Jesus of Montreal,* and perhaps most touchingly *Godspell.* Somehow, recollections of this man, no matter how uncritical or even slanted their presentation, stir people and make it clear that beneath the surface of our human lives his memory still functions as an exemplar of what human life could and should be.

The memory of one not dead. All that we have said about Christians' remembrance of Jesus needs to be modified by the central element of Christian belief: Jesus is not dead, he is alive. This human figure, Jesus of Nazareth, is not simply someone of the past who is still with us in our cherished memories of him. Instead, he, the same Jesus of Nazareth, is believed by Christians to have passed through death into new human life, new life beyond the limitations of our space and time—a context of human existence that enables him to be present to people no matter where or when they are. The very notion of the Church, the community of believers, as "body of Christ" rests on the assumption that the ancient kerygma is true: "This Jesus of Nazareth whom your leaders put to death, he is not dead, he is alive and is Messiah and Lord" (Acts 2:22–34). Paul made clear to the Corinthian community the centrality of this belief, "If Christ be not risen, our faith is vain" (1 Cor 15:12–19).

Our memory of who and what Jesus of Nazareth *was* is an intrinsic element of our faith awareness of who and what he now *is.* The flip side of this is that Christians' belief today in the presence to them of the living Christ modifies in any number of ways their memory of Jesus' earthly life and death.

As generation after generation passed, there was the normal tendency to legendize the memory of the hero; and in the case of Jesus, because of the Christian faith that somehow Jesus' person touched the realm of the divine, mythic elements also entered the picture as early as the Gospels themselves. Along with this, various cultural contexts began to affect the manner in which Christians remembered the career and teaching of Jesus. As we all know, comparative studies of the Gospels themselves indicate the influence on the recollection of Jesus exerted by differing questions and problems in the communities that produced the Gospels. And even though the Greco-Roman "translation" of the Christ mystery rather early gained a monopoly on acceptable descriptions of Jesus, cultural reinterpretation of Christians' memories of Jesus continued as the West itself underwent evolution over the centuries. Not only were elements inserted into this memory, not only did the legendizing continue in teaching and liturgy and art, but some of what Jesus had been and done was conveniently forgotten or overlooked because it conflicted with the ideologies that controlled various historical periods.

In a way, it could not have been otherwise. If we are to consider Jesus as the fulfillment of what "human" is all about, that consideration is governed by what it means to be human for us in a definite cultural context at a particular point in history. If we are to honor Chalcedon's "true human, consubstantial with us in humanity," then Jesus must have been whatever it means for us to be truly human. So, if different cultures have understood differently what "human" means, they could not but remember Jesus in somewhat different ways. True, such differing memories would have always been formed by the Gospel narratives of a Jesus who lived as a Galilean in Second-Temple Judaism, but until quite recently, there was relatively little ability to discover how being human in Jesus' cultural milieu differed from peoples' assumption that "human" meant what they were.

Even within a particular cultural setting, Rome for example, there was not complete consistency in the way the memory of Jesus was handed on by various media—official doctrine, folk recollection, official and popular ritual, or iconography. Liturgy and popular devotion sometimes retain what theology and doctrine have forgotten or neglected. A historical witness to this tension came in the iconoclastic controversies, both those of the ninth century and those at the time of the Protestant Reformation, when the validity of pictorial remembrance of Jesus was challenged as inconsistent with accurate theology about Jesus. Again, we might note that this tension is to be expected, for—to take but one instance—theology, precisely because it is *theology*, cannot but emphasize transcendent dimensions of the Christ mystery; whereas liturgy, because it is privileged point of contact between God and the daily lives of humans, logically stresses the here-and-now presence of Christ.

Because all these various influences can distort the memory of Jesus, sometimes rather seriously, there is constant need to examine and, if needed, correct or supplement what claims to be the "tradition" about Jesus. To take but one example: How justified is the way in which the notion of "kingship" has been applied to Jesus? Certainly, whenever kingship was attributed to Jesus, there were avowals that his kingship was unique; yet, there was a subtle implication that power structures in the Church that were characterized as "monarchical" were grounded in Jesus' kingship. In recent times, the constant need to subject such understandings to a "return to sources" has been immensely aided by development of critical historical and textual methods that have allowed us to recreate as never before the reality of Jesus' life and activity.[5]

This is all too familiar to you. I would like to point to another centuries-long effort to test Christians' memory of Jesus against the realities of his life. This is the enduring desire and felt need of devout Christians, ordinary believing people, to contact as far as possible the "real Jesus" by pilgrimage to the places where he lived and ministered. Anyone who has had the opportunity to journey to Palestine, to walk along the shores of the Sea of Galilee or follow the Via Dolorosa through Jerusalem's narrow winding streets, knows the unparalleled sense of Jesus' historical reality that comes with visiting the places where he actually lived. And even if one cannot actually visit Palestine, one can sense the enduring impact of these holy places if one reads the baptismal catechesis of Cyril of Jerusalem and hears him tell the catechumens how they can go down to see the place where Jesus was executed. One can imagine, too, the sense of contact with Jesus of Nazareth that came for thirteenth-century Christians when Louis of France enshrined in the Sainte Chapelle the supposedly authentic crown of thorns.

Beneath all this shifting memory of Jesus of Nazareth there is one lasting and all-important remembrance: *there was a Jesus of Nazareth who was (and is) one of us.* Much as we treasure the wisdom of Jesus' teaching, Christianity is not most basically a tradition of wisdom teaching; it is the acceptance of a historical personage and of the sequence of historical happenings through which God working in this Jesus offered salvation for the human race. For Christians faith is the personal acceptance of this Jesus as Savior. Jesus is "holy Wisdom," but he is divine Wisdom embodied. For this reason, the memory of Jesus, in so far as we can purify and carefully amplify it, is always a challenge to our beliefs about him. Our belief must always be revised in order to conform more

---

5. On recent christological developments and the impact of critical studies, cf. Monika Hellwig, "Reemergence of the Human, Critical, Public Jesus," *Theological Studies* 50 (1989): 466–80.

accurately to what he was and in the vision of Easter faith now is. And if that memory governs our belief about this Jesus as the Christ, then it also guides normatively our understanding of our-selves as Church and our activity as disciples of this Jesus.

2. Jesus' Continuing Function as Word

To move on, then, to my second point, the manner in which Jesus of Nazareth has continued to be Word of revelation and of creation throughout the Church's history. What we have said so far lays on us as disciples and friends a responsibility of fidelity to his teaching and example. However, a more profound element of his normative role enters the picture when we accept the ancient and traditional belief that this Jesus of Nazareth, *precisely as this Jesus of Nazareth,* is in distinctive fashion God's own creative Word.

In talking about Jesus as divine Word, I think it important to sustain, as far as possible, the more *functional* approach to think-ing about the divine that characterized the religious traditions of Israel and that characterized Jesus' own Galilean/Jewish under-standing of God. That such an emphasis on the functional under-standing of *logos* is not only biblically accurate but relevant to our contemporary ways of thinking has been recently highlighted by George Tavard when he suggested translating the Johannine *logos* as "discourse" and then linked this to elements of present-day communication theory.[6] For Israelite faith, Yahweh was the God who acted and made self known in the events of their history. As for New Testament usage, recent study has come to near con-sensus that, for Jesus, the term *the kingdom of God* meant "God's reign," the continuing saving action of God in the history of his people.[7] Jews of Jesus' day, including Jesus himself, stressed the question "What is God doing?" rather than the more typically Greek philosophical question "What kind of being is God?"

God's Word, then, is God's continuing self-gift in self-revelation; it is not an aspect of God but, rather, to use our inadequate human way of speaking, an activity of God. Jesus' human existing embod-ies this divine activity; his existing as this distinctive human, Jesus

---

6. George Tavard, *The Vision of the Trinity* (Washington, DC: University Press of America, 1981).

7. Cf. Norman Perrin, *Jesus and the Language of the Kingdom* (Philadelphia: Fortress Press, 1976).

of Nazareth, was God's speaking, God's revealing of self incarnated. This divine speaking did not begin *with* Jesus of Nazareth—the early verses of the Epistle to the Hebrews makes this point explicitly—but in some way this centuries-long divine activity came to focus and realization in Jesus. While this points to a unique role in salvation history, it also places the historical Jesus of Nazareth in the broader context of the divine self-revelation that embraces the totality of God's self-giving in creation and human history.

The divine Logos works in the entirety of created reality, and though Jesus is this Logos, his human embodiment of God's Word is not by itself the only created expression of that Word. All that is, and especially all that is truly human, exists as sacrament of God's creatively loving presence.[8] This is not to detract from Jesus' uniqueness, for in unparalleled fashion, his life in the Galilee of two thousand years ago was acknowledgment of the God who truly is, that is to say it was priestly worship in the most basic sense. Who he was and what he did as Jesus of Nazareth sacramentalized, more than it *incarnated*, God's self-communicating Word.

As early as the traditions that led to the Gospels, Christianity has seen Jesus of Nazareth continuing the word of revelation spoken in the history of Israel. In a special way it has seen the continuity linking Jesus with the great charismatic prophets of the Israelite dispensation. But as the first decades of Christian reflection wrestled with the "something more" that characterized Jesus, they went beyond seeing him as the ideal prophet, the eschatological prophet, the embodiment of the history of prophetism, and came to view him as the very Word itself. While in various ways the lives as well as the oracles of Israel's prophets pointed symbolically to the God worshiped by the people, Jesus' life in all its facets was truly God's parable, a parable that spoke in living metaphor not only about God but also about the struggle of God's love in the encounter with reluctant human freedom.

If this is true, then only the concrete reality of Jesus of Nazareth is God's unique Word—not any interpretation or explanation or description. Not even the privileged witness of the New Testament literature, important a word to faith as it is, is the primary

---

8. This involves more than the sustaining action of God, which, obviously, must be coextensive with created reality. Creation is radically a divine *self*-sharing that can only find realization in personal presence to people of faith.

word of revelation, for beneath it lies the disciples' experience of Jesus and beneath that lies the reality of the Jesus they experienced. What grounds all the explanations and interpretations of Jesus is the reality of Jesus. But I believe that we must take yet another step: beneath the actual experience of Jesus lay the functioning of the divine Word which even Jesus could not understand without interpreting it in his own cultural context. Even for Jesus' privileged consciousness of God and of being God's Son, God and God's self-revealing Word which he was did not cease to be mystery. The heuristic moment of our theological reflection cannot stop with Jesus of Nazareth but must go beyond, to the divine mystery in itself, but it cannot faithfully go beyond and in doing so ignore this Jesus who still now functions as God's self-revealing Word.

The inexhaustible mystery that Christians have pondered for two millennia and which today defies our attempts to grasp it as fully and clearly as we wish is none other than what God did and does in this human who lived and died as one of us and passed through death into fulfillment of human existence that we hope to share as our destiny. So, if the Christian community, the Church, seeks to understand God a bit less inaccurately and relate to this God a bit more faithfully, that understanding and devotion must be grounded in and criticized by the real Jesus of Nazareth. Trying to discover who and what he was is the ultimate "return to sources." The gospel that Jesus preached by his very being remains as a challenge to the faith of the Church; it is always a challenge to conversion, *ecclesia semper reformanda*.

The real Jesus of Nazareth was the locus of the divine saving presence to human history; he was *Emmanuel*, and he was that precisely in his human self-giving, in his own personal presence to those with whom he associated, in his sharing of his and his Abba's Spirit with those he encountered. This sharing continues in the life of the Church and obviously adds an important element to the memory of Jesus we earlier discussed. One significant aspect of the Word that God spoke in Jesus is that this Word was spoken in and through the experiences that made up the life of Jesus. Recalling those experiences reveals the dynamics of divine-human interaction that continue today. For example, the frustrations that Jesus faced in his prophetic ministry spoke of humans' capacity to frustrate the saving influence of God's Spirit, for Jesus' uncompromising sharing of his insight into God and his loving concern for people was limited by the extent of his auditors' openness to him. The less than desirable response to the gospel that Jesus experienced was a manifestation of the limitation placed by creatures on the unlimited divine gifts of truth, love, and existence.[9]

To make the transition to the Church of today—the risen Christ's functioning as God's Word today cannot be essentially different from his being God's Word as Jesus of Nazareth. Indeed, the Word he was then remains the privileged window into the mystery of the transcendent God we seek and worship. Hence, the importance, difficult as the task is, of reaching back to discover the reality of Jesus, the prophet from Galilee, so that he can continue to function for us as God's own Word.

To add one element, only briefly, for it is an immense topic in itself. The continuing function in history of Christ as the divine Word occurs obliquely, perhaps it would be more accurate to say "sacramentally," in the lives of those faith-filled disciples who reflect and translate Christ's self-giving and transforming presence to them. They are, in the words often repeated in patristic literature, "images of the *Imago Dei*." They are the exemplary "hearers of the Word," through whom the risen Christ can continue to communicate the divine self-giving. Examining this historical process of Jesus functioning in resurrection as Word, present to those of faith, is central to the largely unaccomplished task of constructing a *Christology*. And coming to appreciate the word spoken in the life of the Church is itself intrinsic to the discovery of Jesus of Nazareth, for the experience of authentic Christian faith is a hermeneutic that enables us to discover the deeper dimensions of the career of Jesus of Nazareth as it did for those early disciples who produced the New Testament literature.

To summarize what I have been trying to say about Jesus functioning as Word: hearing accurately the Word that Jesus was

---

9. Most basically, God's creative contribution to created reality is the continuing "gift" of existing, existing that in itself is fuller than created reality can express. Creatures' contribution to this process is precisely limitation, formation that involves definition/limitation/identity-distinct-from-God. The dynamic reality of existing always struggles against such limitation; existing has a finalistic thrust toward greater expression. This is the source of ongoing evolution and of evolving history. At the personal level of creation, this is a question of Truth/Word trying to find more enlightening and life-giving expression to consciousness and Love pushing toward union-in-distinctiveness, toward the openness to receiving divine love that is creation's main manifestation of love of God.

and is functions normatively to enrich and critique the faith of the Christian community, for the hope and worship of that community are directed to the God revealed in Jesus. We do not have any other God than the God Jesus called *Abba*. Christianity's image of God, its naming of God, its worship of God stand always under judgment by Jesus' experience of God. To move on, then, to my third point:

3. God's Action in Jesus through Their Shared Spirit

One thing that careful study of the New Testament has taught us is that the christological perspective of the early Church was clearly *theological*—they viewed the events that constituted Jesus' human career as God's activity in and through Jesus. God has saved us in Jesus as the Christ. John's Gospel, for instance, recognizes this by having Jesus say, "The Son can do nothing by himself; he does only what he sees the Father doing; what the Father does the Son does" (5:19). More general is the insight shared by all the traditions that the empowerment of Jesus to function as prophet and healer comes from God's own healing and life-giving Spirit.

In speaking this way, we are again forced to situate Jesus' ministry in the broader context of God's activity in the whole of creation and history, for the mystery of God's creative Spirit pervades the whole dispensation of divine loving self-gift. There may well be a unique and paradigmatic enspiriting of Jesus, but the mission of God's Spirit is not limited to this human. Having said that, we need immediately to make a most important qualification: it would be correct to see God's Spirit working in a context wider than the influence of the risen Christ were it not for the fact of Jesus' own relatedness to that wider context. Jesus' own existing and identity as the risen Christ involves a relatedness to all other humans; he is truly the human for all others. His risen existence makes sense only in terms of his sharing with his brothers and sisters that Spirit by which he lives—that is the basic finality of his Passover, without that purpose resurrection as it now is could not be. While the manifestation, the "contact" if you will, of God's creative Spirit working in Jesus was severely limited during Jesus' earthly lifetime by the bounds of space and time, that limitation no longer prevails after Jesus' death, at least as far as the Christ himself is concerned.

At this point let me break the logic of my treatment, for, even though it is not the focus of my paper, some mention should be made to recent efforts to develop a Spirit Christology.[10] This is not the place to describe recent approaches to this issue, much less to debate the advantages of any particular position. However, I believe that four personal observations can be made, observations that may well be challenged in our later discussions:

1. Some of the proposed advocates of a Spirit Christology seem to me to make too great a separation between the functioning of God's Spirit and of God's Word, to make it a matter of either/or. The scriptural perspective, on the contrary, sees the two realities of God's Word and God's Spirit as inseparably interdependent. No doubt theological reflection has neglected the role played by God's Spirit in the person and career of Jesus and in the continuing soteriological role of the risen Christ; but this function of the Spirit needs to be integrated with classic Logos Christology rather than treated as an alternative or a complement.

2. While it is true that the scriptural view of God's Spirit stresses the notion of God's outreaching, creative power, the same can be said in slightly different fashion of the biblical theologies of God's Word. That divine Word is proclamation, but it is also creatively effective of what is proclaimed. "God said, let there be light; and there was light." It is word of command, but as revelation unfolds, it becomes clear that it is more appropriate to call it word of invitation, for the heart of the word spoken is the Word of God's self-giving love—and at that point we are dealing with God's Spirit of creative love, for it is the granting of that Spirit that speaks God's self-gift.

3. Use of language such as describing God's Spirit as the intermediary linking Father and Son can

---

10. E.g., Philip Rosato, "Spirit Christology: Ambiguity and Promise," *Theological Studies* 38 (1977): 423–46; David Coffey, "A Proper Mission of the Spirit," *Theological Studies* 47 (1986): 227–50.

be misunderstood to suggest a need to bridge the distinction between them by the Spirit—the image can be that of a bridge, and a bridge implies a gap that needs to be bridged. However, the implication of New Testament texts is that there is a total coincidence of Father and Son in the one Spirit. The Spirit that sources Jesus' own human existing, impels and empowers him to healing ministry, and that which animates him in risen existence is God's own Spirit.

4. It seems to me that, quite understandably, there has been the tendency to read back into the early Christian understandings the insistence on Spirit being a distinct hypostasis that characterizes the fourth and fifth century trinitarian disputes. Have we not come to treat God's Spirit as a third divine "someone"? Have we not somewhat forgotten that "the Holy Spirit" is none other than Christ's Spirit at the same time that this Spirit is God's Spirit?

This Spirit, Christ's Spirit, continues to work in history, specifically in the lives of the faithful who make up the Church, empowering them as disciples to co-minister with Christ to the emergence of God's kingdom. But this movement of Christ's Spirit, of God's Spirit in Christ is not basically different in its direction, in its eschatological orientation, than it was in the earthly career of Jesus, so that that empowerment and Spirit-guidance of Jesus of Nazareth provides normative insight for the Christian community as it tries in each period of history to discern the impulse of God's Spirit in its life. In trying to get some grasp on the reality of this, I have found it helpful to use the notion of "trajectory" that has proven fruitful in recent study of the New Testament and early Christianity.

The notion of trajectory, for example, in the case of a shell shot from a cannon, implies that the forces that will bring the shell to its target are already at work as the shell leaves the gun's muzzle, and implies also that if one were able at that moment to know all those forces as well as the elements against which the shell would have to work as it moved toward the target, one would be able to predict the path, the trajectory, of the shell. Applying this to the case at hand: if one could discover the entirety of the divine force at work in Jesus as his earthly life passed into resurrection, one would know the eschatological orientation of God's Spirit as it invited humanity toward its destiny. And it is precisely this orientation, to the extent to which we can discover it, that is ultimate norm for our existence and behavior as individual Christians and corporately as the Church.

Clearly, this is not a new idea; every age of the Church has felt the need to discern the movement of Christ's Spirit in its midst. What I wish to highlight is the manner in which the historical career of Jesus is the privileged witness to this trajectory, to the direction in which God's Spirit is working to lead reluctant humanity to its destiny, a direction that we as the Church must honor as the guide for our own decision making and ministry. Whatever we truly contribute to the betterment of human life, to realization of the reign of God, cannot be other than sacramentalization of God's own Spirit at work in history.

But it is not just the historical reality of Jesus of Nazareth points the direction in which our activities of evangelizing and healing must move. Observing the Spirit's creative power working in Jesus tells us also the *manner* in which that Spirit continues to move in our lives. Both Old Testament and New Testament Scriptures see God's Spirit as God's *power*, the power of creation, the power of life, the power of loving self-gift that produces both new being and new life. It is this divine *dunamis* that, as we saw, worked in Jesus, sourcing his very existence as a human, leading him to this public ministry, and empowering him to teach and heal as prophet and legate of Wisdom.

However—and the point needs stressing—this divine power is radically other than the power by which humans ordinarily try to shape their lives and their history. Jesus of Nazareth possessed neither economic nor political nor official religious power; in those realms he was an ordinary human, one of the powerless of the earth. More importantly, he explicitly rejected any such power as the means by which to bring about the reign of his Abba. As he teaches his disciples (in the twentieth chapter of Matthew) the rulers of civil society govern by domination, but it is not to be so in his kingdom. Instead, he will have power in the lives of people precisely by his loving them and by his witness to truth, even unto death. It could not be otherwise if he was to be faithful to the

Spirit that his Abba shared with him, for that was God's creative love, the Spirit of truth.

Clearly, at this point we encounter one of the most important challenges posed by Jesus of Nazareth to the institutionalizing of the Church: how is power exercised in the Church? That some institutional elements must be part of the Church's historical existence is obvious; the question is, which institutions? Among these institutional elements, there must be some forms of structuring and governing the activities of Christian communities. Paul's letters already make it clear that such governing of communities is itself meant to be rooted in the activity of Christ's Spirit, for true Christian governing is itself a charism (Rom 12:7). Having said that, we must also insist that such governing is not meant to be domination, not meant to divide the Christian community into powerful and powerless, not meant to control lives and faith by fear or ambition or ideological repression or distortions of truth. That such perversions of power have occurred in the Church's life needs no proof; perhaps it was inevitable that some of this occured—to underline their existence is not my purpose. What needs to be said clearly is that such an abusive understanding and exercise of power can find no support in the career of Jesus—the Spirit of God did not move him in this way to effect the salvation of humanity; and the Spirit's movement today in the Church is not other than it was in Jesus.

In summary, then, I believe we can say that Jesus of Nazareth in his human existing and activity is normative for the Church's understanding of God and therefore of its faith and worship, normative of the Church's ministry as it works to bring about God's reign, and normative of the institutions by which faith and hope and love are served and nourished throughout history. To know the real Jesus of Nazareth is to know more deeply and more accurately what we are meant to be as Christians.

Finally, what does it mean to say that Jesus of Nazareth is "the founder of the Church," a question that is much discussed today as we compare Christianity to other great world religions and Jesus to figures like Muhammad or Gautama the Buddha? I believe that critical study of the New Testament indicates that Jesus of Nazareth had no intention of starting a new religion, nor did the earliest Christians see him as starting a new religion—indeed, Christianity is not to be a religion, even though worship of the God revealed in Jesus is central to its existence. Jesus, I believe, understood his mission as one of fulfilling what his Abba, the God of Israel, had for centuries been doing. And with the breakthrough experience of Easter, the primitive Church realized that what had begun with Jesus was not a new religion, but a new humanity, indeed, a new creation. Christianity is meant to be a new way of being human, a way of being human that is governed by the truth revealed in Jesus and empowered by God's Spirit of love in our midst. Such a humanity, such a Church, is still a dream, but Acts 2 tells us that with the gift of the Spirit we are to dream such dreams, the same dreams that animated Jesus of Nazareth. To the extent that we effectively share those dreams, Jesus will be normative of the Church in our day.

Jesus founded the Church by freely and unreservedly, in his life and in his dying, opening himself to God's self-gift in Word and Spirit. From that living and dying there emerged a trans-formed humanity shaped by that Word and animated by that Spirit; and there emerged a community of believers dedicated in faith and discipleship to bringing about that new humanity.

God's Spirit, Love's Power

Spirit as the power of Word is the theological (trinitarian) principle for Cooke's sacramental anthropology, an anthropology irreducibly entailing individual human personhood, inter-personal friendship, and social, communitarian life. For this reason Christianity is not meant narrowly to be a religion but, rather, a way of being human, a new creation sacramentally realizing divine love in human sharing. That creativity comes by the power of God's Spirit, yet only in prophetic tension with the range of ways humans exercise power. Cooke organized his next to last book, Power and the Spirit of God: Toward an Experience-Based Pneumatology, *along a trajectory start-ing with the forms of human power most alienating from the divine (force and fear), through several with varied potential (office, law, fame, wealth, nature, imagination, and creativity), to the powers most amenable to the divine power revealed in Scripture and Tradition (symbol, word, thought, and ritual). The latter, symbolic cluster especially mediates the divine Word's power in creation and salvation, the love that is the Spirit:*

Communication to humans of divine selfhood, achieved in the mystery of God's Word embodied in creation and especially in Jesus of Nazareth, is a process of word power. However, the very communication of this creative divine Word has as its objective to share with humans God's own Spirit, God's compassionate mind-edness toward humans, God's love creative of their personhood. Proclamation of God's Word carries that Spirit and conveys it, or else it is spiritless and abstract "revelation" without power (PSG 134–35).

"Love," the fifth and final part of Power and the Spirit of God, *concludes as follows (PSG 168–77):*

The Power of Love[11]

It is precisely in theological examination of love as power that one touches on the basic question: What truly is ultimate power? Taking as a very general notion of power "the ability to achieve a particular goal," theology begins with the issue of the divine goal for humanity—what is the intent, the will, of God for humans? In one form or another, theological responses are variations on Irenaeus's famous remark: "The glory of God is the human person fully alive." Today, we would probably rephrase that in psychological terms: the fully alive person is the truly mature person; and we would extend that to human societies as well. The will of God, the goal of the divine creative/redemptive activity, that is, of divine providence, is that humans, individually and in communities, should realize as fully as possible their potential as persons.

Current reflection on human maturity leaves little doubt that the measure of maturity is a person's capacity to love and that one acquires this capacity most importantly through loving and being loved. Professional psychology would examine maturity in terms of a person's ability to deal with relationships—which is saying basically the same thing. Here we may be in the midst of a "revolution" in psychology: whereas the basic thrust of Freudian

---

thought is that one attains to autonomy (and presumably to maturity) by freeing oneself from dependence on relationships, some current reflection (e.g., Jean Baker Miller and study at the Stone Center) insists rather on preserving, cherishing, and deepening key relationships....[12]

Christian Reflection on Love

Stress on the primacy of love in the Christian Scriptures is undeniable. Beginning with the teaching and ministry of Jesus himself, the law of loving concern for others dominates the perspective of Christianity on humans' relation with God and, derivative from this, humans' relationship to one another and to themselves. The Johannine tradition, in particular, places authentic human love at the very center of faith and discipleship. "This is my command, that you love one another as I have loved you."

While such statements may be the distillation of two generations of Christian reflection on Jesus' person, activity, and teaching, they clearly are grounded in the manner in which Jesus himself related to others, both to his close friends and to the wider group of humans who entered his life. In addition, they reflect the extent to which the earliest Christians placed love and friendship at the heart of desirable human behavior, beyond strict ethical demands.

But did Jesus regard love as power? Perhaps this question as such never occurred to him. However, it seems undeniable that in his public ministry, he felt himself empowered by God's Spirit, empowered to act lovingly as he did. His parables reflect his awareness that the healing/saving power, God's Spirit, to which he bore witness in word and deed was that of love, unconditional divine love. Furthermore, his own compassion and concern for those he encountered, especially for the marginalized, were the sacrament in which he experienced his Abba's love for those people. And he experienced the power of that love, the power of his Abba's Spirit, to heal.

Even more directly, as the scene of the desert temptations indicates, Jesus realized the conflict between his own empowerment

---

12. Jean Baker Miller, *Toward a New Psychology of Women* (Boston: Beacon Press, 1986). Also her essay "Women and Power," in *Women's Growth in Connection*, ed. J. Jordan et al. (New York: Guilford Press, 1991).

and the empowerment that would have come with earthly wealth or political influence. In his "kingdom," the power to be exercised was not that of the rulers of this world but the mysterious power of self-sacrificing servanthood. Greater love than this no one has, to lay down one's life. So, it does seem rather clear that Jesus in his ministry lived with the constant awareness of the battle taking place between two "powers," the power of God's Spirit that was the power of love, and the powers of "this world."

The Battle between the Power of Love and the Power of Evil

If one follows through on the biblical worldview of a battle between God and evil, it is possible to see the "love dimension" of the Spirit as fundamental power. Sin, the most basic of evils, is essentially the denial of the love that is appropriate to any given situation; it need not be only hatred, for apathy and irresponsibility also qualify. It is precisely because of this absence of love as creative of life that evil can only be healed by the "insertion" of love into the situation. This was graphically illustrated in the ministry of Jesus: at one level, his response to the various forms of evil he encountered—hunger, disease, ignorance—was to counter them and work for a betterment of the human situation in question. But as his public ministry progressed, he apparently became increasingly aware that there was a deeper level to evil that could be overcome by only one power, a self-giving love that was willing to sacrifice physical life itself. What this implies is that the divine love, the Spirit, working in and through Jesus' self-giving love, is the very heart of salvation.

The earliest memories that fed into the Gospel narratives retain the disciples' awareness of Jesus' friendship. Though it is a composite of many memories about Jesus, the "last discourse" in John's Gospel conveys in almost palpable form the love Jesus felt for his friends, even though he was aware of their weakness and inability to support him openly in his final ordeal. And like a parent with his or her children, as he faced death, he longed for them to love one another. "A new commandment I give you, that you love one another, even as I have loved you" (John 13:34). Though the last discourse does not explicitly link power and love, it does link loving friendship with God's/Christ's Spirit, a linkage that continues into the Johannine stories of Jesus' Easter appearances and giving of the Spirit.

What seems clear is that Jesus' immediate disciples and the first generations that produced the Christian Scriptures possessed a developed theology of love as power, a theology that focused on God's Spirit and that was expressed in servanthood. Matthew 20:26, the third temptation in the desert, Acts 2, and Philippians 2—related to one another, these passages attest to the power exercised by Jesus as the Suffering Servant. But this Jesus, raised to glory because of his servant "obedience" even unto death (Phil 2), was God's embodied Word, spoke in his own human freedom the "mind," the Spirit, of his Abba.

While there is no explicit linking of "Spirit" and "love" in the remembered teaching of Jesus, his own attitudes and behavior, grounded as they were in the Spirit, spoke undeniably about the divine love. The Spirit that Jesus shared with his Abba was sacramentalized in his dealings with people—the power that moved Jesus was his Abba's love, for this was the deepest level of his relationship to God.[13]

Although the earliest generations of Christians were focused on love, divine and human (e.g., Paul's constant refrain "Have concern for one another," 1 John's "Little children, love one another"), the influence of Platonic thought in the Mediterranean basin gradually turned the discussion of God's power at work in salvation from the affective to the intellectual. From the third century onward, God's activity was described in terms of "illumination."[14] In trinitarian reflection, it was not until the latter half of the fourth century, that is, after Nicaea, that attention was paid in the conciliar creed to the character and influence of the Spirit. Not that awareness of the Spirit was totally lacking—the notions of the "sphragis" imprinted on a Christian by the Spirit, of the sanctifying power of the Spirit in the baptismal water, of the Spirit's endowment of an

---

13. On the Spirit's action in and through Jesus, especially after the resurrection, cf. Thomas H. West, *Jesus and the Quest for Meaning* (Minneapolis: Fortress Press, 2001), 225n25.

14. However, it is good to remember that in Platonic and especially Neoplatonic circles, "illumination" involves more than just rational thought. This is particularly true of Augustine and the Augustinian tradition. Gilson in *The Christian Philosophy of St. Augustine* (New York: Random House, 1960) remarks that "the Augustinian doctrine…refuses to separate illumination of the mind from purification of the heart" (p. 31). In that same volume, Gilson has a lengthy exposition (pp. 77–96) of "illumination" in Platonic and patristic thought.

ordinand were already present in second-century theology—but the dominance of Logos was already well established.

As Christianity moved out of its Semitic origins and into the Greco-Roman-Platonic-Stoic thought world, the cultural dominance of patriarchy overwhelmed it. The conflict of love and patriarchy was not immediately recognized or felt, nor did patriarchy totally triumph, but a combination of developments—clergy divided from laity, monastic asceticism, suspicion of sex and passion leading to celibacy as an ideal—made love "second rate" as an influence on "educated" Christian faith and theological reflection. On the contrary, intellectualism/rationalism as characteristic of the male *imago Dei* fitted into patriarchal cultural domination. This stress on the intellect is strikingly apparent in the influential writings of Pseudo-Dionysius, where the symbolic theurgy central to the system functions primarily in the realm of hierarchically ordered intellectual activity—illumination, ecstatic insight, and so on. Dionysius does preserve the Platonic notion of the overarching impact of the Good, but human personal relations do not enter at all into the process of human striving for "perfection." Symptomatic of this is the total lack of reference to women in the Dionysian corpus.

Still, the belief persisted that love of God is the supreme expression of Christian faith and life. The Spirit was recognized as the power that would lead the Christian to this "perfection," the Spirit of life that animates the baptized with a share of divine life. There was overwhelming stress on the development of the individual Christian and on the influence of the Spirit in leading the person to that which is the acme of "perfection," that is, agape. The influence of Paul's writings was key to much of this development. While Paul is explicitly concerned about the well-being of communities, there does not seem to be much theological reflection on the role of the Spirit as divine Love forming Christian communities. For centuries, even up to today, spiritual theology and most of the reflection on "grace" are focused on the faith life of the individual. An obvious exception to this remark is, of course, the prominent but unappreciated role of the epiclesis in eucharistic celebration.

Christian writing in the patristic period and the Middle Ages provides ample evidence that love remained a focus in Christian teaching about virtue, salvation, perfection, imitation of Christ, and grace. There is considerable dispute, however, about the exact understanding of love that prevailed in those centuries. This disagreement came to a head in the mid-twentieth century with a flurry of debate triggered by Anders Nygren's *Eros and Agape*, Pierre Rousselot's *Probleme de l'Amour au Moyen Age*, and C. S. Lewis's *The Analogy of Love*.[15] What emerged from the discussion was a greater appreciation of the diversity of Christian views about love prior to modern times. Though all admitted the necessary contribution of both thought and affectivity, leading theologians and theological traditions placed relatively greater stress on one or the other. However, as a result of studies like those just named, there emerged a question that is still open to debate: Was, as some allege, the warmth and intimacy associated with romantic love lacking prior to the troubadours? Was God's love for humans and human agapic love for one another as well as for God to be understood in terms of responsible concern, altruism, and unselfishness but without the feelings associated with eros?

What stands as a challenge to this entire discussion is the experience of mystics throughout Church history. Certainly, the experience of a given mystic was deeply influenced by the prevailing cultural understanding of love, influenced also by the particular spiritual tradition that she or he had inherited. However, there was a prevailing experience of intimate relationship to Christ and God that lay at the heart of mystical contemplation throughout the centuries, a feeling that at times found expression in explicitly erotic language. There was a knowledge of the heart that was admitted to be superior to purely rational understanding.

An intriguing tribute to the continuing tradition of love as central to Christian spirituality is the way in which it "infiltrated" the Dionysian influence. That the writing of Dionysius and in particular his *Mystical Theology* exerted a major influence on medieval spiritual theology and theology thereafter is beyond dispute. Moreover, that influence is most evident in the currents of mysticism that are notable for their stress on affectivity—the Cistercians, Bonaventure and other Franciscans, the Victorines, Mechtilde, Julian, and so on. The Dionysian image of the overflowing abundance of the divine goodness is pervasive in medieval

---

15. See Martin D'Arcy, *The Mind and Heart of Love* (New York: H. Holt and Co., 1947) for a review and commentary on this debate.

spiritual literature and is consistently interpreted as the overflow of divine love. Yet, in Dionysius himself, there is a striking absence of reference to love. Instead, there is what Paul Rorem refers to as the "relentlessly intellectual approach to union with God and his [Dionysius's] omission of any reference to love in the *Mystical Theology*."[16]

Where, then, does the entrance of love into the Dionysian tradition come from? Obviously, the biblical texts are an immediate candidate; but no doubt the influence of Augustine, specifically the affective side of the Augustinian heritage, was also responsible. Probably the most powerful influence was the actual spiritual experience of the mystics and theologians concerned, their experience of intimate relationship to God, the experience of loving and being loved.

Postmedieval centuries saw such classic Christian reflection as Francis de Sales's *The Love of God*, John of the Cross's *Living Flame of Love*, Teresa of Avila's *Interior Castle*, and the final "Contemplation for Obtaining Divine Love" in Loyola's *Spiritual Exercises*. With all their distinctiveness, these writings maintain a fundamental alikeness that is characteristically Christian. They all see human destiny achieved in love of God; they all see the possibility of attaining such love as dependent upon God's prior loving of humans; they all see love for God necessarily finding expression in humans' love for one another. Along with many other expressions of Christian spirituality, they manifest a certain pre-Freudian innocence in their healthy positive regard for warm human friendships.

At the same time, in certain circles, often in seminaries and religious communities, there developed a suspicion of human friendships, especially what were considered "particular friendships." Some of this may have been connected to concern about homosexual relationships, but the more common worry was that such friendships could detract from a person's total love for God or could threaten the overall concern of members of a community for one another. It was also linked at times with a false understanding of celibacy, as if commitment to celibacy demanded renunciation of deep human friendship. Theologically, this has been offset more recently by increased appreciation of the sac-

---

16. Paul Rorem, *Pseudo-Dionysius* (New York: Oxford University Press, 1993), 223.

ramentality of friendship, the insight that genuine love between humans is the most basic symbol of the presence of a loving God in human life.

Love and the Spirit of God

Throughout the history of Christian understanding of love, there is a constant linkage of love with God's Spirit, therefore with the divine exercise of power. At times, the Spirit is simply equated with divine love. At other times, the name *Gift*, that is, the expression of love, is seen as proper to the Spirit. Indeed, the reference to the Spirit as divine love is so constant and pervasive that it is, for all practical purposes, taken for granted in Christian doctrine and theology. However,...the manner in which this is modeled in people's understanding is manifold.

During the patristic and medieval periods, the Spirit was seen as the gift of divine love, and theological detailing of this Gift was in terms of the various charisms granted by the Spirit. The medieval summas, such as that of Thomas Aquinas,[17] based their treatment of the Spirit's "mission" on an explanation of the gifts given to humans by the Spirit, the gifts listed in Isaiah 11 and by Paul in 1 Corinthians 12. However, what was always viewed as the fundamental gift was, to quote Paul in Romans 5, "The divine love poured into our hearts through the Holy Spirit which is given to us." What is especially relevant to the topic of this book is that all these "gifts," including the Spirit as Gift, were regarded as empowerment of the human subject.

Speaking of divine gift giving inevitably raises the question of God's creative activity as self-giving and the link of *Creator* Spirit with the Spirit as *gift*. Perhaps it is in viewing God's action of creating in terms of the creative power of love that one can make some sense of the kenosis that occurs in creation.[18] Seemingly in contradiction to God's infinite power, creating involves a divine relinquishing of absolute power; for the reality of creatures that exist with their own distinct being implies randomness in the universe. This "independence" is much more evident if human creatures possess genuine power of free self-determination. But it is characteristic of

---

17. Cf. Aquinas, *ST*, I-II, q. 68.

18. On the kenotic aspect of creation, cf. John Haught, *God after Darwin* (Boulder, CO: Westview Press, 2000), 53–54.

the power exerted in love, in this case the creative loving of God, that it influences the beloved with respect for the otherness of the beloved. God's creative loving is not dominating.

Long before the Middle Ages, the Spirit was linked with divine love. In the East, Didymus taught that the Spirit is within the Trinity the Gift of Father and Son and is the great Gift to humans in the process of sanctification because the Spirit is Love.[19] Basil of Caesarea in his treatise on the Spirit, though reflecting almost totally the intellectualism characteristic of the Platonic tradition, saw *Gift* as a name proper to the Spirit.[20] In the West, Augustine in particular referred repeatedly to this link. Yves Congar mentions the frequency of Augustine's reference to Paul's citation of Romans 5.[21] So, while, in the patristic and medieval periods, the principal focus in theological speculation about the divine Spirit had to do with the trinitarian relationship of the Spirit to Father and Son, there was a constant accompanying reflection about the Spirit's effect on human life in the mystery of "grace." So strong was this linkage that the Middle Ages witnessed an ongoing debate as to whether the Spirit caused grace or whether the Spirit *was* the grace.[22]

With the classic Reformers, the role of the Spirit as transforming love was overshadowed by the Spirit's work of supporting the power of the Word, particularly the biblical word in its witness to the saving activity of Christ. Justification came through imputation of the justifying act of Christ, and sanctification was achieved in attachment to Christ. Even in nineteenth-century liberal Protestantism, despite its emphasis on religious experience, no role in human transformation was assigned to God's Spirit as Love.[23] An important qualification to this negative judgment needs to be added: namely, the widespread influence of the various forms of Pietism. Embracing such diverse phenomena as the Moravian Brethren, American and English Methodism, and French Jansenism, the Pietist impulse brought to the fore the religious sentiment believed to flow from the animating presence of the Spirit.

---

19. *On the Holy Spirit*, 28. Probably to be dated around 370–80.

20. See *On the Holy Spirit*, written about 375.

21. Yves Congar, *I Believe in the Holy Spirit*, vol. 3 (New York: Seabury Press 1983), 90.

22. See the article of Michael Schmaus in *Encyclopedia of Theology*, ed. Karl Rahner (New York: Seabury Press, 1975), 647–48.

23. On Protestant approaches to pneumatology, cf. Gary Badcock, *Light of Truth* (Grand Rapids: Eerdmans, 1997), 86–123.

Though its influence waned in Europe, Pietism produced a lasting effect in Pentecostal developments in the United States.[24]

In Catholic circles, the postmedieval traditions of mysticism, which included Teresa, Francis de Sales, Ignatius Loyola, and John of the Cross, reflected the same stress on Christ's redeeming role but maintained also the teaching of the Spirit's mission as divine Love. Relatively little attention, however, was paid to the role of the Spirit in the dogmatic theology that was taught in post-Reformation Catholic seminaries.

Recent developments in pneumatology have been deeply influenced by research and reflection on the life, death, and resurrection of Jesus and the resultant "Christology from below." Intrinsic to this christological development has been examination of the role in Jesus' career of the empowering presence to him of God's Spirit, God's love.[25] In some circles, this has led to suggestive proposals of Spirit Christology.[26] Some theologians like Heribert Muehlen, Piet Schoonenberg, and Walter Kasper have more explicitly directed their reflection to the role of the Spirit. Karl Rahner, by contrast, apparently gives little direct attention to the Spirit, but this is deceiving. Actually, the Spirit's operation underlies the entire Rahnerian vision of the divine "gracing" of humanity that is central to Rahner's theological anthropology.[27]

At the same time, pneumatology has been enriched by the shifts in thinking about the Church, not just in theology but in the practical religious experience of the "ordinary" faithful that followed, for one thing, on Vatican II's description of the Church as "the people of God." Much of this has found expression in a widespread interest in "spirituality," in various forms of "the charismatic movement," and in a renewed sense of personal relatedness to God in response to the divine gift of love.

---

24. Cf. F. Ernst Stoeffler, *Continental Pietism and Early American Christianity* (Grand Rapids: Eerdmans, 1976); Ronald A. Knox, *Enthusiasm* (New York: Oxford University Press, 1950). The latter focuses on seventeenth- and eighteenth-century European developments.

25. Cf. Bernard Cooke, *God's Beloved* (Philadelphia: Trinity Press International, 1992).

26. Cf. Walter Kasper, *Jesus the Christ* (New York: Crossroad, 1976), 245–68, and Roger Haight, *Jesus, Symbol of God* (Maryknoll, NY: Orbis Books, 1999), 445–66.

27. A brief but helpful account of the pneumatological contribution of these and other contemporary theologians is provided by Badcock, *Light of Truth*, 124–211. On the fundamental theme of "grace" in Rahner's theology, cf. *A World of Grace*, ed. Leo O'Donovan (New York: Crossroad, 1980).

Summary. In a sense, if one thinks of "love" as the affective movement toward "the good," love deals with the ultimate exercise of power, that is, the motivations that lead humans to action. These motivations flow from the perception of something or some person or some activity as good; so, influence on people's values and perceptions is an exercise of power beyond any other.[28] Other forms of power—threats of violence, physical control, bribery, and so on—are exercised precisely to motivate people toward one or another course of action. Whether admitted by everyone or respected in a person's actual judgments, there is no good beyond a beloved friend. Consequently, friendship possesses a certain ultimate power to motivate, a power that at least theoretically overshadows the attracting power of anything else in human experience. There are striking instances of this, instances in which a person will give up wealth, political power, and public esteem because he or she has fallen in love and values the beloved above all else. It is because friendship has this basic power that it is the most fundamental sacrament of God's Spirit of love. It is true that some men and women judge wealth or earthly power as supreme goods and sacrifice personal relations to obtain material goals. Yet, there is a common sense judgment of most people that to forego human friendship is a tragic loss.

Seen from a theological point of view, love, ultimately the out-reaching "expression" of divine love that is God's Spirit, is the most powerful of powers. It is the power that breaks the cycle of violence in Jesus' dying and rising; it is the creative source of the power of nature, life power overcoming death; it is the power bonding humans together in the eschatological community that is the final destiny of human life; it is the prophetic power already working in history to achieve that relating of humans to one another in justice and peace that is the "reign of God." It is the bond of friendship, the pearl of great price for which humans are willing to confront the criticism and disdain of "the wise of this world" who place greater weight on the achievement of wealth and political power.

Although he no doubt would not want his own life story singled out as a "striking instance" of love's overriding power,

---

28. On the power of feeling and its relation to meaning and value, cf. West, *Jesus and the Quest for Meaning*, 25–28.

*Cooke's account of his departure from the Jesuits and mar-
riage to Pauline Turner—with all the consequences entailed
over the rest of their lives—testifies to the hard-won wisdom
behind those concluding paragraphs to his chapter on Spirit
and love. His reputation and career ("public esteem," above)
paid a price more than once, yet he was true to the "word"
prayerfully discerned in their experiences. The following passage, concluding the long "Marquette" chapter of his memoir,
follows on Cooke's description of how alienated from both the
Roman Catholic clerical system and, sadly, the local Jesuit
leadership (over racial issues at Marquette) he had become.
His account of the crisis bears not only on his ecclesiology and
theology of ministry (see chapter 4, below) but also reflects the
strong identification of the Spirit with truth advanced throughout the text of his "Experience-Based Pneumatology."*

What intertwined with and complicated the decision to
resign from the clergy was something else that occurred, not only
altering the pattern of my life but also deeply affecting my theology. I came to love Pauline as a "significant other." No doubt it
could be called "falling in love," but that would not aptly describe
the years-long growth of a relationship that for both of us was agonizing at the same time that it was enriching.

We first met when I arrived at Marquette, and she was a graduate student....Pauline was finishing up her work for an MA in English literature. As soon, however, as we moved toward the MA in
theology, she enlisted in that program, the one layperson in the
midst of a talented and forward-looking group of women religious,
of whom some became her lifelong friends. To defray the expense
of further graduate study, she was able to obtain a position as graduate assistant. With funding being so meager for our new graduate
program, Pauline served as informal secretary for the department.
Soon after we launched the new undergraduate curriculum, we
were able to obtain funding for two young male graduate teaching assistants, who along with Pauline, constituted the teaching
staff that worked with me in providing classes for 2,400 first- and
second-year students. Along with that daily cooperation, she
functioned as liaison for my contacts with the graduate student
community. She was elected head of the graduate student association and was very active as such. When the civil rights campaign

began two years later, she was in the thick of things and immediately enlisted me to work with the faculty group, with Father Jim Groppi, and a bit later with the African American activists.

Working daily together it was inevitable that we became friends, sharing interests and hopes. Although the love between us deepened over several years (albeit we both realized early on that it was a unique bond), for years there seemed no possibility that we would go on to marriage. We both cherished my role in the Jesuit order, we both were committed to the projects in which we were engaged at Marquette, we were both committed to working together in the ministries of the Church, all of which would be threatened if I left the clerical state. By 1968, however, several things began to change, making some decision about our relationship unavoidable. There was the tension with the administration after my role in the threatened black students' strike, joined to a growing criticism and opposition by conservative elements in the city. As for Pauline, although by this time she was an assistant professor respected and influential among the students and active within the faculty, it seemed unlikely that she would obtain tenure. She was pursuing doctoral study part-time, lacking the financial resources to continue full-time, and thus did not yet have her doctorate. Besides, her participation in civil rights activity did not endear her to many in authority within the university.

That meant more than a year of agonized prayer and decision into which fed all the disillusion with the Vatican, all my awakening to the evil of clericalism, all my deepened identity with the laity with whom I worked. Could I leave all I still hoped for at Marquette and, more broadly, could I leave the Society of Jesus that I deeply loved and that had been my home for thirty years? On the other hand, could I simply walk away from a person who had given her entire life to helping me carry out my mission at the university, whom I loved uniquely as a friend, and with whom I shared so much of my relation to God? Together we made the decision to move on, to find a new context in which we could continue working together....

We knew that the decision we made would be painful, and it was. Bluntly, we found ourselves ostracized by many with whom we had worked for years. We were resolved to continue to work together for the same goals we had and to do so as far as possible within the spiritual world of the Catholic Church. For that reason, we went through the official processes of the Vatican, though we did not see that it made sense theologically. What can it mean to be *reduced* to the laity? We hoped that on our part the prospect of Catholic/Christian ministry would not be blocked. Actually, it has been often blocked, and my own resources for doing theology in a truly scholarly fashion have been diminished because I never again had the privilege of working with doctoral students in a Christian university. On the other hand, a world of ministry with and for laypersons opened up for us, a world "ripe for the harvest" that most likely would not otherwise have become our service to the Christian community. Looking back, I have never questioned the decision we made forty years ago.

Still, to say that the decision was painful cannot begin to describe it. For thirty years, very happy years, the Society of Jesus had been my home. Large numbers of its members had been my closest friends, my brothers, whom I still regard as the finest group of people I have ever known. Sadly, during the Marquette years, none of my classmates or friends in the order lived there; they were spread over a number of other Jesuit communities. However, I had dealt with many of the younger Scholastics and become a bit of a model for them, such that I knew my resigning from the order would disappoint and puzzle many of them.

I anticipated that many others, women and men to whom I had given retreats, with whom I had worked to change the orientation of the Church before and after Vatican II, would feel misled, even betrayed. While it was far from easy to leave Marquette and all I had worked to accomplish there, I realized that it was good for the theology department that I move on. It had long been too much of a one-person operation, and the newer persons coming into the department were restless to take responsibility and makes changes to fit their ideas. I knew, too, as I described earlier, that a barrier had grown up between the university's administration and me, which was not good for the development of the theology programs.

Though some considered the distinction self-serving and artificial, for me the "resignation" was not from priesthood but from clergy. The commitment that came with my sacerdotal ordination remains, above all the ministry to clarify and intensify people's involvement in eucharistic liturgy. Though I cherished the role of eucharistic leader, missed it terribly, and miss it still, I knew that the Eucharist did not belong to me, that it was more important that the liturgy be celebrated authentically than that I personally lead it. In contrast, I did not find it at all difficult to leave the clerical state. My historical research as well as experience of life in the Church had long convinced me that clergy was not a beneficial development in the life of Christianity. I knew that many others of the ordained felt uneasy about clerical perks while nonetheless profiting from them, as did I.

Unfortunately, several publications and other agencies tried to enlist me in the campaign opposed to clerical celibacy, which was becoming prominent just at that time. I was asked to attack celibacy as unnatural and an impediment to psychological health. While I did not favor celibacy as an imposed condition for presbyteral ordination, and still do not, I respected celibacy as a spiritual charism that enriched the lives of many dedicated and mature persons as well as the Christian community. What I could neither accept nor continue in was clericalism, though I have always respected many of the ordained dedicated to unselfish service of their fellow humans.

To make the transition from Marquette practically feasible, I had obtained a year's research fellowship at Yale Divinity School, where I had a number of friends. My reception there was gracious, and the Divinity library held all the resources, both primary and secondary, I needed for the basic research that eventuated in my *Ministry to Word and Sacraments*. In the course of that year, Pauline and I went ahead with the decision to marry, obtained the dispensations from Rome that would enable us to work in Church structures, if we so wished, and were wed in mid-May. Fortunately, this was during the pontificate of Pope Paul VI....

But what future lay ahead? No Catholic college or university would hire either of us to teach, and the possibility of a Catholic teaching at a non-Catholic denominational or secular institution was only beginning to develop. At that juncture a welcome invitation came. The department of theology at the University of Windsor in Canada was planning to initiate a doctoral program and, knowing what I had accomplished at Marquette, thought I could be of assistance with their project. So, at that point we became immigrants.

CHAPTER THREE

Sacraments

MYSTERY OF FRIENDSHIPS, HUMAN AND DIVINE

Introduction

Cooke's memoir account of his resignation from the Jesuits and departure from Marquette illustrates his personal knowledge of how great a price people will pay for love and, in that, how revelatory of the Spirit's power is the living of truth in love. He nonetheless also saw in that crisis with Pauline a huge impact on the way he did theology going forward. One dimension entailed their approaching ministry as a team, a couple—a very practical way. But another was the sacramental theory he would develop as fundamental to his systematic and pastoral theology.

But what did all this have to do with my development as a theologian? Simply put, it did not negate any of my previous views, except perhaps in the area of ecclesial authority. Rather, it reinforced and deepened my understandings of God, thereby putting all my theological reflection in an expanded context....

No insight humans have with regard to the character of the Transcendent is more real and more traditional than that "God is love." Love, however, is something that is known in a manner that transcends the cognitive. Mystics have referred to it as "the language of the heart." One could express this somewhat more technically by saying that friendship/love is the primary and most

109

basic sacrament of the divine. That implies that human loves are more than just parallel to God's love, more than the most appropriate metaphor of God's relation to humans. Instead, God's Spirit transforms and empowers human loving, making God present to those open to loving. And it is in the experience of loving and being loved that humans most basically know the divine, at least implicitly.

I have been blessed lifelong by the experience of love, beginning with my family and continuing with a wide circle of friends thereafter. God's love has always been an intrinsic force in that experience. I knew what it meant to love long before I met Pauline; I have always loved people. So, my relationship with Pauline did not fill a void in my life, but it did introduce a dimension of love beyond what I had known earlier. For a time, it seemed to be in competition to other loves, such as my love for the risen Christ, but this—to my surprise—was resolved in prayer. I know that some persons attributed my leaving the clergy to my having abandoned prayer in the midst of intense activity. Such was not the case. Actually, it was in the deepened context of love that I realized the most central element in my theologizing about Christian sacraments: human friendship is the most fundamental sacrament in a human's life. What meaning can it have to say that God loves me if I do not know what it means to love? It is in the atmosphere of God's love being sacramentalized in my own experience of love that I have tried to theologize about the God revealed in Jesus.

> Cooke's preference for discussing the person and mission of Jesus in sacramental rather than incarnational terms would appear to have followed from the personal spirituality he developed, holding simultaneously the otherness and complete freedom of the divine as nonetheless immanent, creative, "poured out" in the narrative histories of human lives. The sacramental dimension lies in the capacity of human experiences, and especially the sharing of lives in interpersonal and communal bonds of friendship, to be revelatory of the unseen God.

The Fundamental Sacramentality of Friendship

The love Cooke realized in his friendship with Pauline, leading to their marriage, was a peak experience that reoriented his theology. He came to consider friendship as the basic human sacrament and, for Christianity, marriage as its paradigmatic form. The effect included his looking back to his parents as sacraments of God to each other, their children, and their wider community. His boyhood narrative also demonstrates how friendship is an inclusive term for all life-giving interpersonal relationships, whether parent with child, aunt with nephew, teacher with student, older youth looking out for the younger, age group peers, and so on. Due to limitations of space, the following extract includes only his family memories from that period:

Perhaps the most important theologizing came in observing my parents' religious attitudes and behavior, my mother's Marian devotion, my father's commitment to justice, the concern both of them had during those days of the Great Depression for the poor who surrounded us. Their interest in social justice took on very practical forms. My father was a dentist, an excellent dentist whom two dental schools had tried to recruit for their faculties. Most of his patients were poor, and in those Depression days it was common for him to be paid in potatoes or eggs or not at all. Venison was one of the most common means of payment, because our city bordered on the Menominee Indian reservation and native Americans, many of them my father's patients, were allowed to hunt year round. Perhaps most importantly, in caring for those less advantaged than us, my parents were always considerate of their human dignity. Many a time I would be sent out at dark to leave bags of clothes or groceries at the doorsteps of folks who never knew where the goods came from and never had to express a gratitude that would be sincere but demeaning.

One of the important influences in my growing years was my mother's sister, Bernadette. Dette came to live with us shortly after her graduation from high school. She did not have the opportunity at that point to attend college, but she managed to get employment in the First National Bank, no small achievement in those Depression times, and in just a few years—by the time I entered high school—had risen to vice president. She was a talented businesswoman, but her heart was not given to that. Music, especially piano, was her first love, and as a related form of recreation, ballroom dancing. Rather hidden, something else was happening. Dette was feeling the call to enter religious life, needless to say to my mother's delight. As she mentioned this to a few friends and family, her music teacher, a School Sister of Notre Dame, took for granted she would join that community. Much to her disappointment, Dette chose to join the Dominicans at Sinsinawa, Wisconsin, becoming Sister Armand. She never regretted it. Despite bad health, she went on to gain her MFA degree in piano, spent years teaching music, playing organ in the various places to which she was assigned, taking care of finances for whatever convent in which she lived, and died much too young.

Dette always kept in touch with me, and as I entered high school, she sent a gift, a small book that contained the New Testament and *The Imitation of Christ*, attributed to Thomas à Kempis. For four years of high school, I faithfully followed her advice by reading from those two each day. Little did I realize at that point that it was focusing my faith ever more along christological lines and pointing to the spiritual need to remain detached from the attractions of "the world." I was laying some of the groundwork for the Ignatian spiritual theology that would later shape my life. *The Imitation* did, however, propose an excessively negative judgment on "the world" that later years would have to correct.

Much more could be said about Bernadette's influence, but one thing related to her needs mention, as it has always flowed into my ecclesiology, namely, my realization that full membership—full holiness, if you will—was not confined to the ordained or the vowed religious. My mother always felt that her spirituality was second rank, that she would have come closer to God if she had entered religious life as Dette had done. I knew instinctively that that was not true. All my mother did was raise five boys with a healthy and truly Christian outlook on life; provide support and love for her husband and work with him as a coequal in local social justice activity; nurture our parish community as sacristan, organist, and informal counselor for the young assistant pastors; and spend at least two hours a day in prayer.

One further thing must surely be mentioned. In sharing with us boys their faith and its implications, my parents did so in a context of freedom. Each of my brothers, Paul and Armand, who have already joined my parents in life beyond, David and Tom, who with their families live today in California, was encouraged to be distinctively who they were, academically and religiously. But we were very much an identifiable family. Certainly, religious fidelity was a fundamental dictate of our life situation; that was the way things were meant to be. Being Christian was not an imposition but an invitation and privilege, not a burden but a gift. We were not pressured to embrace our Catholicism; it was simply assumed, even as we entered adolescence. Things were less complicated and dealt more with basics in those days of economic depression and war, before expansion of movies and then television. The normal processes of passing into adulthood surely marked my adolescent years, but my parents helped me to be grateful, happy, and self-determining.

What was most important in all this parental influence was not the accuracy of their Christian belief, though it was accurate and mature, but the fact that all the words and religious practice dealt with reality. The God to whom we prayed actually existed; the risen Christ was really present in the Eucharist; there really was a providence guiding our lives. Later in my theological career, when I would become conscious of the role of religious experience as starting point for theological reflection, I came to appreciate how my early years of living faith in our family had provided an invaluable dimension of doing down-to-earth theology.

Doing down-to-earth theology: the unpretentious phrase captures how Cooke understood his mission of developing a "theology of the laity." Nonetheless, the designation he recounts acquiring early on in his years at Marquette was "sacramental theologian." Cooke's theology—both in his pastoral-educational work and early publications—became centered on situating the sacramental in daily human life, with Church rites, especially the Eucharist, catalysts for interpreting God's presence therein. Coupled with this was a theology of grace, grace as relational, as the symbolic expression of God's down-to-earth relationship with and through people. For this reason, Cooke came to propose that sacramental theology, rather than starting from baptism, consider deeply committed friendships, with marriage as their paradigm, the fundamental human and, thus, Christian sacrament. The argument appears in the most widely read of his books, Sacraments & Sacramentality *(S&S 80–91).*

Human Friendship: Basic Sacrament

In the traditional short definition of Christian sacrament, the third element is a brief statement about the effectiveness of sacraments: "Sacraments are sacred signs, instituted by Christ, *to give grace.*" Sacraments are meant to do something. What they do is essentially God's doing: in sacraments, God gives grace. We will devote the remainder of this book to studying how the various Christian sacraments give us grace, beginning with the sacrament of marriage. Before looking at the sacramentality of human friendship and of marriage in particular, it might help to talk briefly about the kind of transformation that should occur through sacraments.

In trying to explain what sacraments do, we have used various expressions: celebrants of sacraments "administer the sacraments" to people; people "receive sacraments" and "receive grace" through sacraments; sacraments are "channels of grace." The official statement of the Council of Trent, which has governed Catholic understandings for the past four centuries, is that "sacraments contain and confer grace."

The traditional understanding of grace and sacraments would include at least the following. The grace given was won for us by the death and resurrection of Jesus. Without depending upon misleading images such as a "reservoir" or a "bank account," it seems that there must be some way that the graces flowing from Jesus' saving action are "stored up" so that they can be distributed to people who participate in sacraments. The grace given in sacramental liturgy is, at least for baptized Christians, a needed resource if people are to behave in a way that will lead them to their ultimate destiny in the life to come.

Beneath all such formulations—which we are all familiar with in one form or another—lurks a basic question: What is this "grace" we are speaking about? It is all well and good to say that we receive the grace we need when we come to sacramental liturgy, and that we receive it in proportion to our good will. But what do we have in mind when we use this word *grace*? We have already begun to see that *sacrament* should be understood in a much broader sense, one that extends far beyond the liturgical ceremony that is the focus of a particular sacramental area. Now, with grace also, a deeper examination leads us to the conclusion that grace touches everything in our lives; it pervades everything we are and do.

This book's final chapter will deal in detail with the reality of grace, but some brief discussion of grace at this point may help us to understand better the effectiveness of the various individual sacraments as we study them. In trying to get a more accurate notion of grace, it might help to remember a distinction that was sometimes made in technical theological discussions, a distinction that unfortunately received little attention and so was scarcely ever mentioned in catechetical instructions about grace. This is the distinction between "uncreated grace" and "created grace."

"Uncreated grace" refers to God's graciousness toward human beings; "created grace" refers to that special ("supernatural") assistance God gives to humans to heal and strengthen them and to raise them to a level of being compatible with their eternal destiny. For the most part, our previous theological and catechetical explanations stressed created grace as a special help that enabled persons to live morally good lives, an assistance to guide and support them when they faced temptations. There was also a frequent reference to "the state of grace," the condition of being in good relationship to God and therefore in position to move from this present life to heaven, rather than to hell. But there was practically no mention of uncreated grace.

During the past few decades, there has been a renewed interest in and study of grace. We have learned to pay much more attention to uncreated grace, that is, to the reality of God who, in the act of self-giving and precisely by this self-giving, transforms and heals and nurtures our human existence. Along with this new emphasis on God's loving self-gift as *the* great grace, there has been more use of the notion of "transformation" to aid our understanding of created grace. Under the impact of God's self-giving, we humans are radically changed; this fundamental and enduring transformation of what we are as persons is created, sanctifying grace.

In various ways, sacraments—in their broader reality as well as in their liturgical elements—are key agencies for achieving this transformation. Although the effectiveness of the different sacraments is quite distinctive, each area of sacramentality touches and changes some of the significances attached to human life. As these significances are transformed, the meaning of what it is to be human is transformed; our human experience is therefore changed, and with it the very reality of our human existing.

This process of transformation is what we now turn our attention to, hoping to discover what sacraments are meant to accomplish in the lives of Christians.

Sacrament of Human Friendship

Explanation of the individual sacraments traditionally starts with baptism. Apparently it is the first sacrament Christians are exposed to, and the one all the others rest upon; it is the one that introduces the person to Christianity, etc. However, as we attempt to place the sacraments in a more human context, there is at least the possibility that we should begin with another starting point. Perhaps the most basic sacrament of God's saving presence to human life is the sacrament of human love and friendship. After all, even the young infant who is baptized after only a few days of life has already been subjected to the influence of parental love (or its lack), which in the case of Christian parents is really the influence of the sacrament of Christian marriage.

Sacraments are meant to be a special avenue of insight into the reality of God; they are meant to be words of revelation. And the sacramentality of human love and friendship touches the most basic level of this revelation. There is a real problem in our effort to know God. Very simply put, it seems all but impossible for humans to have any correct understanding of the divine as it really is. God is everything we are not. We are finite, God infinite; we are in time, God is eternal; we are created, God is Creator. True, we apply to God the ideas we have drawn from our human experience; we even think of God as "person." But is this justified? Is this the way God is?

Some fascinating and important discussion of this problem is going on today among Christian philosophers, but let us confine our approach to those insights from the biblical traditions. As early as the writings of the first chapter of Genesis (which is part of the Priestly tradition in Israel that found final form around 500 BCE), we are given a rich lead. Speaking of the Creation of humans by God, Genesis 1:27 says that humans were made "in the image and likeness of God." That is to say, somehow the reality of human persons gives us some genuine insight into the way God exists. But the passage continues—and it is an intrinsic part of the remark about "image and likeness"—"male and female God made them." This means that the imaging of God occurs precisely in the relationship between humans, above all in the interaction of men and women. To put it in contemporary terms, some knowledge of the divine can be gained in experiencing the personal relationship of men and women (and one can legitimately broaden that to include all human personal relationships).

The text provides still more understanding, for it points out that from this relationship life is to spread over Earth; humans in their relation to one another (primarily in sexual reproduction, but not limited to that) are to nurture life. And humans are to govern Earth for God; they are to image and implement the divine sovereignty by this nurture of life that is rooted in their relationship to one another. As an instrument of divine providence, human history is meant by the Creator to be effected through human community, through humans being persons for one another.

Implicit in this deceptively simple biblical text is a profound statement about the way human life is to be conducted. If life is to extend to further life, either by creating new humans or by creating new levels of personal life in already existing humans, it will happen on the basis of people's self-giving to one another. And, if women and men are truly to "rule" the world for God, they will do this by their love and friendship, and not by domination. To the extent that this occurs, the relationship of humans to one another will reveal the fact that God's creative activity, which gives life and guides its development (in Creation and in history), is essentially one of divine self-gift. Humans have been created and are meant to exist as a word, a revelation, of God's self-giving rule; but they will function in this revealing way in proportion to their free living in open and loving communion with one another.

Whatever small hint we have regarding the way God exists comes from our own experience of being humanly personal. Our tendency, of course, is to think of the divine in human terms, even carrying to God many of the characteristics of our humanity that obviously could not apply directly to God; for example, changing our minds as to what we intend to do. Excessive anthropomorphism has always been a problem in human religious thinking and imagination; we have always been tempted by idolatry. Even today, when our religious thinking has been purified by critical and scientific thought, we still fall into the trap of thinking that God exists in the way we think God does. This does not mean, however, that we must despair of ever knowing God. On the basis of biblical insights (like those in Genesis 1:27 and even more in New Testament texts grounded in Jesus' own religious experience), we can come to some true understanding of God by reflecting on our own experience of being personal.

For us to be personal—aware of ourselves and the world around us, aware that we are so aware, relating to one another as communicating subjects, loving one another, and sharing human experience—is always a limited reality. We are personal within definite constraints of time and place and happenings. Even if our experience as persons is a rich one, through friends and education and cultural opportunities, it is always incomplete. For every bit of knowledge, there are immense areas of reality I know nothing about; I can go on learning indefinitely. Though I may have a wide circle of friends, there are millions of people I can never know; I can go on indefinitely establishing human relationships. There are unlimited interesting human experiences I will never share. In a sense, I am infinity but an infinity of possibilities, infinite in my incompleteness. Yet, this very experience of limitation involves some awareness of the unlimited; our experience of finite personhood points toward infinite personhood and gives us some hint of what that might be.

God Revealed as Personal

What lets us know that the divine is indeed personal in this mysterious, unlimited fashion is the fact (which as Christians we believe) that this God has "spoken" to humans; God has revealed not just some truths about ourselves and our world, but about God's own way of being personal in relation to us. God in the mystery of revelation to humans is revealed as someone. What this means can be grasped by us humans only through our own experience of being human together. In our love and concern for one another, in our friendships and in the human community that results, we can gain some insight into what "God being for us" really means. These human relationships are truly insights into God, but not just in the sense that they are an analogue by which we can gain some metaphorical understanding of the divine. Rather, humans and their relationships are a "word" that is being constantly created by God. In this word, God is made present to us, revealing divine selfhood through the sacramentality of our human experience of one another.

One of the most important results of this divine revelation and genuinely open relationships to one another is the ability to trust reality. This might seem a strange thing to say, for reality is a given. Yet, the history of our times has been one of growing uncertainty and strong distrust of the importance and goodness and even the objective reality of the world that surrounds us, especially the world of people. Great world wars, among other things, have made many humans cynical about human existence and have made many others unwilling to admit that things are as they are. There is abundant evidence that our civilization is increasingly fleeing toward fantasy, taking refuge in a world of dreams, so that it does not have to face the real world. It is critically important, perhaps necessary for our sanity, that we find some basis for trusting life and facing reality optimistically and with mature realism.

Most radically, a culture's ability to deal creatively with reality depends on its view of "the ultimate," of God. We must be able to trust this ultimate not only as infinitely powerful but also as infinitely caring, as compassionate and concerned. The only ground, ultimately, for our being able to accept such an incredible thing—and when we stop to reflect, it is incredible—is our experience of loving concern and compassion in our human relationships. If we experience the love and care that others have for us, beginning with an infant's experience of parental love, and experience our own loving concern for others, this can give us some analogue for thinking how the ultimate might personally relate to us. Jesus himself drew from this comparison: "If you who are parents give bread and not a stone to your children when they ask for food, how much more your Father in heaven."...

Experiencing love in our human relationships makes it possible for us to accept the reality of our lives with a positive, even grateful attitude. And this in turn makes it possible for us to see our lives as a gift from a lovingly providential God. If we have friends, life has some basic meaning; we are important to them and they to us. What happens to us and them makes a difference; someone cares. If love exists among people, there is genuine, deep-seated joy, because joy shared by people is the final dimension of love. If this is our experience of being human, then our existence can be seen as a good thing and accepted maturely and responsibly.

All this means that our experience of being truly personal with and for one another is sacramental; it is a revelation of our humanity at the same time that it is a revelation of God. This experience of human love can make the mystery of divine love for humans credible. On the contrary, if a person does not experience love in his or her life, only with great difficulty can the revelation of divine love be accepted as possible. Learning to trust human love and to trust ourselves in it is the ground for human faith and trust in God.

To say that human love is sacramental, especially if one uses that term strictly (as we are doing), implies that it is a mystery of personal presence. Obviously, in genuine love, there is a presence of the beloved in one's consciousness; the deeper and more intimate the love, the more abiding and prominent is the thought of the beloved. To see this as truly sacramental of divine presence means that human love does more than make it possible for us to trust that God loves us. The human friendships we enjoy embody God's love for us; in and through these friendships, God is revealing to us the divine self-giving in love. God is working salvifically in all situations of genuine love, for it is our consciousness of being loved both humanly and divinely that most leads us to that full personhood that is our destiny. Such salvation occurs in our lives to the extent that we consciously participate in it, in proportion to our awareness of what is really happening and our free willingness to be part of it.

It is instructive to note that when Jesus, immediately after being baptized by John, was given a special insight into his relationship to God as his Abba, the word used in the Gospel to describe his experience of his Father's attitude toward him is the

Greek *agapetos*, "my beloved one." This was the awareness of God that Jesus had, an awareness of being unconditionally loved, an awareness that became the key to human salvation. And John's Gospel describes Jesus at the Last Supper as extending this to his disciples: "I will not now call you servants, but friends."

Marriage, Paradigm of Friendship

Among the various kinds of human friendship and personal love, the one that has always been recognized as a paradigm of human relationship and love, and at the same time a ground of human community, is the relation between husband and wife. There is considerable evidence that humans have never been able to explain or live this relationship satisfactorily, basic and universal though it is. In our own day, there is constant and agitated discussion of the way men and women are meant to deal with one another, and there is widespread talk of a radical shift taking place in the institution of marriage. As never before, the assumptions about respective roles in marriage are being challenged. Marriage is seen much more as a free community of persons rather than as an institution of human society regulated for the general benefit of society; equality of persons rather than respect for patriarchal authority is being stressed. And with considerable anguish in many instances, people are seeking the genuine meaning of the relation between women and men, and more broadly the relationship of persons to one another in any form of friendship.

Questioning the woman-man, and especially the husband-wife, relationship is not, of course, a new phenomenon. As far back as we can trace, literature witnesses to the attempt to shed light on this question. What complicates the issue is the merging of two human realities, sexuality and personal relatedness, in marriage, a merging so profound that people often are unable to distinguish them. We know, however, that in many ancient cultures, there was little of what we today consider love between spouses; marriage was a social arrangement for the purpose of continuing the family through procreation. In not a few instances, there was so pronounced a cleavage between love and sexuality that the wife was considered the property of her husband, and she was abandoned if she proved unable to bear him children. If men sought human companionship, they sought it outside the home. Apparently, the marriages in which something like a true friendship existed between wife and husband were relatively rare.

Sacramentality of Marriage in Israel

In ancient Israel, an interesting development began at least eight centuries before Christianity. Surrounded as they were by cultures and religions that worshiped the power of human sexuality, the Israelites assiduously avoided attributing anything like sexuality to their God, Yahweh. At the same time, these neighboring erotic religions were a constant temptation to the Israelites; the great prophets of Israel lashed out repeatedly against participation by Israel's women and men in the ritual prostitution of the Canaanite shrines. In this context, it is startling to find the prophet Hosea using the example of a husband's love for his wife as an image of Yahweh's love for his people Israel.

Apparently, Hosea was one of those sensitive humans for whom marriage was more than a family arrangement; he seems to have had a deep affection for his wife, Gomer. The love was not reciprocated; his wife abandoned him for a life of promiscuity with a number of lovers; perhaps she became actively involved in some situation of shrine prostitution. At this point, Hosea was obliged by law to divorce her, which he seems to have done. But then "the word of the Lord came to Hosea," bidding him to seek out and take back his errant wife. And all this as a prophetic gesture that would reveal Yahweh's forgiveness of an adulterous Israel that had gone lusting after false gods.

Once introduced by Hosea, the imagery of husband-wife becomes the basic way in which the prophets depict the relationship between Yahweh and the people Israel. Tragically, the image often has to be used in a negative way. Israel is the unfaithful spouse who abandons Yahweh to run off with "false lovers," the divinities of the surrounding fertility religions. Yet, despite this infidelity on Israel's part, Yahweh is a merciful God who remains faithful to his chosen partner. "Faithful" becomes a key attribute of this God of Israel. Yahweh is a faithful divinity who keeps promises to Israel. And the husband-wife relation becomes in the prophetic writings an alternative to the king-subject relation that the rulers of Israel and Judah (for their own purposes) preferred as a way of describing the covenant between Yahweh and Israel.

Our particular interest, however, is not the manner in which the use of the husband-wife imagery altered Israel's understanding of the covenant between people and God. Rather, it is the manner in which, conversely, the use of this imagery began to alter the understanding of the relation between a married couple. If the comparison husband-wife/Yahweh-Israel is made, the significance of the first couplet passes into understanding the significance of the second couplet, but the significance of the second passes also into understanding the first.

The understanding the people had of their god, Yahweh, and of Yahweh's relationship to them, the depth and fidelity of his love, the saving power of this relationship, slowly became part of their understanding of what the marriage relationship should be. Thus, a "Yahweh significance" became part of the meaning of married relatedness. The sacramentality of the love between husband and wife—and indirectly the sacramentality of all human friendship—was being altered. It was, if we can coin a term, being "yahwehized." The meaning of God's relationship to humans became part of the meaning of marriage, and marriage became capable of explicitly signifying and revealing this God. This meant that human marriage carried much richer significance than before; it meant that the personal aspect of this relationship was to be regarded as paramount; it meant that the woman was neither to be possessed as property nor treated as a thing; it meant that marital fidelity was expected of both man and woman. Thus the "institution of the sacrament of marriage" begins already in the Old Testament.

Marriage as a Christian Sacrament

With Christianity, another dimension of meaning is infused into this relation between wife and husband, the Christ meaning that comes with Jesus' death and resurrection. Several New Testament passages could be used to indicate this new, deeper meaning, but the key passage probably is the one in Ephesians (5:21–31) that traditionally forms part of the marriage liturgy.

Be subject to one another out of reverence for Christ. Wives, be subject to your husbands as to the Lord. For

123

the husband is the head of the wife, just as Christ is the head of the church, the body of which he is the Savior. Just as the church is subject to Christ, so also wives ought to be, in everything, to their husbands. Husbands, love your wives, as Christ also loved the church and gave himself up for her....In the same way husbands should love their wives as they do their own bodies. He who loves his wife loves himself. For no one ever hates his own body, but nourishes and tenderly cares for it, just as Christ does for the church, because we are members of his body. "For this reason [in the words of Scripture] a man will leave his father and mother and be joined to his wife, and the two will become one flesh."

In dealing with this text, it is important to bear in mind what the author of the epistle is doing. As so often in the Pauline letters, the purpose is neither to challenge nor to vindicate the prevailing structures of human society as they then existed. Just as in other cases, the Pauline letters do not argue for or against an institution like slavery. The passage in Ephesians takes for granted the commonly accepted patriarchal arrangements of family authority without defending or attacking them; in a patriarchal culture, all authority is vested in the husband-father. However, Ephesians insists that in a Christian family, this authority structure must be understood and lived in an entirely new way. The relation between the risen Christ and the Christian community must be the exemplar for a loving relationship between the Christian couple.

This text contains a rich treasure of sacramental and christological insight that has scarcely been touched by theological reflection. Mutual giving of self to one another in love, not only in marital intercourse but also in the many other sharings that make up an enduring and maturing love relationship, is used in this passage as a way of understanding what Jesus has done in his death and resurrection. He has given himself to those he loves. His death was accepted in love as the means of passing into a new life that could be shared with those who accept him in faith. Jesus' death and consequent resurrection was the continuation of what was done at the supper when Jesus took the bread and said, "This is my body [myself] given for you." Ephesians 5 tells us that we are to understand this self-giving of Jesus in terms of the bodily self-giving in love of a husband and wife, and vice versa, that we are to understand what this marital self-gift is meant to be in terms of Jesus' loving gift of self in death and resurrection.

One of the important things to bear in mind in studying this text is that Jesus' self-giving continues into the new life of resurrection. Actually, his self-giving is intrinsic to this new stage of his human existence. The very purpose and intrinsic finality of his risen life is to share this life with others. The risen Lord shares this resurrection life by sharing what is the source of this life, his own life-giving Spirit. For Jesus to exist as risen is to exist with full openness to and full possession of this Spirit. So, for him to share new life with his friends means giving them his own Spirit. What emerges from this Spirit-sharing is a new human life of togetherness, a life of unexpected fulfillment, but a life that could not have been reached except through Jesus freely accepting his death. So also, a Christian married couple is meant to move into a new and somewhat unexpected common existing, which cannot come to be unless each is willing to die to the more individualistic, less unrelated-to-another, way of life that they had before.

Christ's self-giving to the Church is more than the model according to which a man and woman should understand and live out their love for each other. The love, concern, and self-giving that each has for the other is a "word" that expresses Christ's love for each of them. The fidelity of each to their love is a sign that makes concretely credible their Christian hope in Christ's fidelity. In loving and being loved, each person learns that honest self-appreciation that is the psychological grounding for believing the incredible gospel of God's love for human kind. In their relationship to each other, and in proportion as that relationship in a given set of circumstances truly translates Christ's own self-giving, the couple are a sacrament to each other and a sacrament to those who know them.

In this sacramental relationship, a Christian man and woman are truly "grace" to each other; they express and make present that uncreated grace that is God's creative self-giving. Although there certainly is mystery in this loving divine presence, it is revealed in the new meanings discovered in the lived relationship between Christian wife and husband. The trust required by their unqualified intimacy with each other and the hope of genuine acceptance by the other, which accompanies this intimacy, help bring about a new level of personal maturity. But this trust and hope are grounded in the Christian faith insight that open-ended love can lead to new and richer life. Perhaps even more basically, a Christian couple can commit themselves to this relationship, believing that it will not ultimately be negated by death. Instead, Christian hope in risen life supports the almost instinctive feeling of lovers that "love is stronger than death."

Psychological studies have detailed the ways a truly mature married relationship, one that integrates personal and sexual love, fosters the human growth of the two people, and it is not our intent to repeat such reflections here. But these same studies point also to the indispensable role that continuing and deepening communication with each other plays in the evolution of such a relationship. In a Christian marriage, the communication is meant to embrace the sharing of faith and hope in that salvation that comes through Jesus. The Christian family is meant to be the most basic instance of Christian community, people bonded together by their shared relationship to the risen Jesus.

All of us can think of marriages where this ideal has been to quite an extent realized, where husband and wife have over the years supported and enriched one another's belief and trust in the reality and importance of Christianity. Various challenges can come to Christian faith, if it is real faith and not just a superficial acceptance of a religious pattern. These challenges can change shape over the years, they can come with suffering or disappointments or disillusionment or boredom, they can come to focus with the need to face the inevitability of death. At such times of crisis, when faith can either deepen or weaken, the witness of a loved one's faith and hope is a powerful and sometimes indispensable preaching of the gospel.

Perhaps the most difficult thing to believe over the course of a lifetime is that one is important enough to be loved by God. Nothing makes this more credible than the discovery of being important to and loved by another human. The fidelity of one's lover—not just in the critically important area of sexual fidelity but also in the broader context of not betraying love by selfishness, exploitation, pettiness, dishonesty, disinterestedness, insensitivity—makes more credible the Christian trust in God's unfailing concern.

One could go on indefinitely describing how a Christian couple "give grace" to each other because the contribution to each other's life of grace (their being human in relation to God) involves the whole of their life together. The sacrament of Christian marriage is much more than the marriage ceremony in the Church; that ceremony is only one important element in the sacrament. Christian marriage is the woman and the man in their unfolding relationship to each other as Christians; they are sacrament for each other, sacrament to their children, and sacrament to all those who come to know them. The meaning of what they are for each other should become for them and others a key part of what it means to be a human being.

Before ending this reflection on the sacramentality of Christian marriage, it is good to return to what was said earlier: all genuine friendship, and in a particular way the friendship between people who share faith in the God Jesus revealed, is sacramental. While marriage, because of its society-recognized pledge of life-long fidelity and its creation of new human life, does play a paradigm role for friendships, deep friendships also play a paradigm role in reflecting the personal relationship that marriage should be. It is important for those who, for one reason or another, are not married to realize that the essence of marriage's sacramental power, the transforming power of human love, is open to them also in proportion to their mature care, concern, and affection for others. Married and single are meant together to form one community of friends....

Cooke authored Sacraments & Sacramentality *during his early years on the Holy Cross faculty. The original (1983) edition quickly realized widespread use as a textbook in colleges, universities, and even some seminaries, along with strongly positive reviews in journals, with many lauding as "innovative," "fresh," and "insightful" his argument for friendship as the point of departure for "a broad-based 'sacramentality' of human life." Critical feedback, nonetheless, included people's objection to his identifying "Christian marriage" as "basic sacrament." Indeed, those terms comprised the title and subtitle of the chapter, reprinted immediately above, that in the book's revised edition, he would change to "Human Friendship: Basic Sacrament." Cooke explained in the preface to the*

127

second (1994) edition, "In the earlier volume I had suggested that [Christian marriage], rather than baptism, was the initial sacramental exposure of a child born into a Christian family. Readers seemed to find this suggestion appealing, but not a few of the unmarried objected to giving marriage a paradigm role when I went on to treat human friendship as revelatory of God's loving and transforming presence to women and men."[1] Among his own personal and professional experiences during the decade between the first and revised editions of the book contributing to his expanded notion of the sacramentality of "deep friendships" was increased exposure to women's relationships and concerns:

One area of my theological growth during the Holy Cross years…happened during a sabbatical year, the only one that I had in a long teaching career. At that point, Pauline was in the midst of doctoral studies at Episcopal Divinity School (EDS) in Cambridge, sharing in a new program in feminist theology that had been set up by a friend of hers, Elizabeth Schüssler-Fiorenza, who encouraged her to pick up her discontinued graduate studies and gain the doctorate. So, we moved for a year to the EDS campus. Fortunately it possessed an excellent library that allowed me to pursue my own research.

Apart from the library, the distinctive area of my learning had to do with an expansion of my understanding of homosexuality. Much earlier in my career, during the Marquette years, I had consistently counseled men who were homosexually active and had been apprehended by the police. At that time, homosexual activity was a penal offense in Wisconsin, with the first offense mandating psychiatric treatment and the second, imprisonment. At that time, most psychiatrists considered homosexuality curable. When a cure did not happen, they generally classified it as a religious aberration and advised the men to approach someone at Marquette. Guess who. As a result, I had developed an insight into the gay community and acceptance of the phenomenon long before the contemporary, somewhat more enlightened public openness emerged. But I had never directly encountered lesbianism, though I knew about it abstractly. That changed during the Cambridge year.

---

1. Bernard Cooke, *Sacraments & Sacramentality*, rev. ed. (Mystic, CT: Twenty-Third Publications, 1994), v–vi.

Episcopal Divinity School was widely known within Episco-palian circles as accepting of homosexuality. For the large num-bers of lesbians in its student body, EDS was a safe and friendly place. So, the majority of Pauline's fellow students as well as sev-eral faculty members were openly lesbian. During that year, I came to know many of these women, even accompanied Pauline to some of their social gatherings, where I was without exception welcomed, and discovered that homosexuality among women was a very different phenomenon from that of gay men. That experi-ence was an invaluable asset in subsequent years as I, like so many others, have had to develop a mature and honest attitude toward homosexuality and recognize heterosexism as discrimination unjustly diminishing many people in our society.

Mentioning Pauline's study for her doctorate at EDS brings to mind the broad range of theological learning that has resulted for me because of her work in feminist thought. I have not only become acquainted with a wide range of literature and a number of first-class theologians but also discovered a whole way of theol-ogizing that would otherwise have remained unknown to me. The first chapter of Pauline's dissertation was an in-depth explanation of a feminist hermeneutic. As she was developing that chapter, I profitably shared a good deal of her reflection.

Eucharistic Celebration: Fostering Love in Community

Cooke's perspective on friendship, as presented in Sac-raments & Sacramentality,[2] *is fundamentally human and mystical and, in that sense, sacramental. Also fundamental, as with all Christian theology, is his recourse to the biblical con-tent of revelation: in making the case for Christian marriage, a*

---

2. For additional examples of his work on the sacramentality of friendship, see Bernard Cooke, *Power and the Spirit of God: Toward an Experience-Based Pneumatology* (New York: Oxford University Press, 2004), 165–68, 183–89; *The Future of the Eucharist* (New York: Paulist Press, 1997), 42–47; *The Distancing of God: The Ambiguity of Symbol in History and Theology* (Minneapolis: Fortress Press, 1990), 5–7, 178–80; *Christian Symbol and Ritual: An Introduction*, with Gary Macy (New York: Oxford University Press, 2005), 55–68; and *The Eucharist: Mystery of a Friendship* (Dayton, OH: G. A. Pflaum,1969).

paradigm for deeply committed friendships, as sacramental of divine love, Cooke enlisted Paul's Letter to Ephesians, thereby presuming the reality of the Church as the body to which Christ has joined himself as one. The formation and fostering of a community of friends, bound with Christ as no longer master but friend, is the ongoing activity of sharing (of communio, of koinonia) that constitutes the Church.[3] As a historical body comprised of many (bodily) members, the Church is the sacrament of the risen Christ who now lives and acts in the world as life-giving Spirit. The redemptive, salvific effectiveness of the Church, both in fostering the identity of its individual members and forging bonds of friendship in service to one another and all humanity, can only come about through embodied practices of sharing—sharing in a vision, sharing a value system, sharing a mission, and all of this empowered through sharing in a communal spirit (the Holy Spirit).[4] While the process of baptism initiates people into this life of Christian community, it is the celebration of the Eucharist that both expresses and deepens the bonds of love meant to take ongoing practical form in the life of the community and amid the wider world. The following extracts from an article on Eucharist, charity, and Christian unity Cooke wrote for the ecumenical journal Diakonia (DIA 309–25) are representative of his advocacy for the ritual activity of the Eucharist—the mutual presence in assembling, proclamation of the word, sharing at the table— as the irreducible symbolic (thus, sacramental) necessity for the Church to realize its vocation as sacrament of God's reign.

Charity and the Eucharist[5]

Let us begin with charity and its relation to that unity which is meant to characterize the Church, the people of God. Clearly we are referring by "charity" to that kind of human love which is meant to join men together in openness, self-giving, and practical

---

3. See Cooke, *Sacraments & Sacramentality*, 71–73; and Bernard J. Cooke, "Body and Mystical Body: The Church as *Communio*," in *Bodies of Worship: Explorations in Theory and Practice*, ed. Bruce T. Morrill (Collegeville, MN: Liturgical Press, 1999), 39–50.

4. See Cooke, *Sacraments & Sacramentality*, 123–33.

5. Published in the 1970s, the copyrighted material reproduced here does not meet contemporary standards for gender-inclusive language. *(Ed. note.)*

concern for the other's well-being—and precisely in the context of the Christian expression of such affection. Clearly, too, we are dealing with the mature love that is grounded in and specified by faith in Christ as the risen Lord. This is not to say that Christians have a monopoly on true charity, but only to limit our discussion to that manifestation of love that takes place within the context of a community sharing faith in the gospel of Jesus Christ.

In such a context, the charity that members have for one another contains as an integral element an identification with one another as fellow believers in and disciples of Christ: their shared adherence to Christ binds them personally to one another. Accepting one another's faith, they can assume an identity of view regarding the most basic facets of human existence and destiny and therefore find the kind of support and sympathy that true friendship promises. Again, on the basis of each one's acceptance of sonship relative to God the Father, an authentic familial spirit colors their human regard for one another, in a deep and proper sense they are brothers and sisters.

Moreover, the very objective that binds them together into common apostolic activity is love for men. The most basic command given them is that they love, love one another and together love the men and women who make up their world. This is their common mission, given to each upon his acceptance into Christian community through baptism: by their loving concern for their fellow men to be the sacrament of the Father's own redeeming love in Christ.

Such love lies at the very basis of Church's life. The Church is a community of lovers. Christ himself first and foremost. And just as Christ's unstinted gift of self to others for their redemption is the heart of his saving mystery of death and new life, so also the Christian community which makes his redemption effectively present in human history cannot do so otherwise than by unselfishly spending itself for the betterment of men. Since the very nature of love is to be personally unitive, it follows immediately that no element of unity in the Church is more profound and constitutive than is the charity of the community. It is almost tautological to speak of "the charity of the community," since Christian love of the people *is* their community; it is their sharing of self with one another, so that their very being as persons is in common.

Obviously, then, charity is more basic and essential in the unity of the Church than are any external structures. This is not to resuscitate the notion of a structureless Church, nor to suggest that faith and charity by themselves would suffice—for, as we will see a bit later, the very existence of charity in the Christian people demands some institutional forms. But it cannot be denied that there is a priority of value and necessity enjoyed by charity; it is the goal for which the structures of community life exist; it is the criterion against which their validity and effectiveness are to be measured. This is just another way of recalling that fraternal love is the ultimate law given by Christ to his followers.

While it might be superfluous to draw attention to it, since it should be obvious, it might be worthwhile to recall that the institutional aspects of the Church's life are directed not just toward fostering the charity of the individual members, but also toward intensifying the shared life of love which is a mark of the Church, its holiness as a community....

The Spirit: Bond of Unity

Ultimately, of course, the bond of unity within the Church is the Spirit communicated by the risen Lord to his body, the Spirit of love expressing in the followers of Christ a created witness to the love that binds Father and Son in unparalleled community. To bring it into being with ever greater depth of life and unity, the Spirit grants to the community those gifts—of prophecy, of teaching, of governing, of healing—that have sustained its communal existence from the earliest days of Christianity. But, as St. Paul reminds us so forcefully in the celebrated passage of 1 Corinthians, the greatest charism given by the Spirit is Christian love.

Vatican II, especially in *Lumen Gentium*, has emphasized for us the fact that the Church is basically people rather than an organization. Organizational bonds undoubtedly have their place, but never as ends in themselves. People can be organizationally unified, at times into a very tightly knit union, without forming authentic human community; this is the spectre of Orwell's *1984* that is beginning to haunt us even before the arrival of that date. The Church is not such; its unity is meant to be sacramental of that community of mankind under the fatherhood of God which Jesus established in his death and resurrection and which is constantly coming into being—as is the Church itself—through the power of the Spirit. In the last analysis, persons can be welded into deep and lasting community only through sharing of love; hence it is not difficult to see the basic and indispensable role of Christian charity in the unification of the Church.

Christian Love and Worship

Let us, then, pass on to consider the relation of Christian love to worship, so that we can later apply this more specifically to the act of eucharistic worship. Worship is acknowldgement of God by an individual or community. In the light of the revelation made in Jesus of Nazareth, Christians see authentic worship as taking place fully only when the true God, the Father of our Lord Jesus Christ, is knowingly accepted in faith. Moreover, because Christian faith is a practical personal acceptance of the mystery of Christ, it involves relationship to Christ himself, to the Father, to one's fellow Christians, and—at least potentially—to all men. This is just another way of saying that it involves love: one cannot acknowledge Christ as his brother unless he loves Christ; one cannot genuinely acknowledge the Father of Christ as his own Father unless he possesses the love that is proper to a son.

It is not just a case of love being a necessary condition for true Christian worship or an important element in it. If one truly loves within the context of Christian faith, this is itself acknowledgment of the Father and therefore worship. This is why St. Paul could urge the early Christians to make their entire selves a living sacrifice to the praise of God. Just as Jesus' own acknowledgment of his Father was not limited to the special ritual actions in which as a devout Jew he participated, nor to the final actions of Holy Week; so also the whole context of Christian life is in the truest sense worshipful. Not content with its own praise of the Father, the Christian community bears witness to the gospel, so that other men and women will be led to worship the true God. This witness is more than simple announcement of the gospel message. By its openness to men in their need, by its loving concern, the Christian community functions as a sacrament of God's own redeeming love. In loving one another and other men as well, Christians actually make effectively present in human history the reality of God's saving love. The Church's apostolic mission consists basically, then, in love that is fully and warmly human, but that is deepened in its range and effect because it is grounded in that love which touches human life in the death and resurrection of Christ. One can immediately see, even before any analytic consideration of the Eucharist, that its function of making present Christ's loving and redeeming act of death and resurrection does not stand by itself in isolation, nor does it claim totally unique power so to make Christ present. What it says in greater explicitness and solemnity the entirety of Christian life is meant to say—and, in ways we do not understand too well, all loving and genuinely human living is meant to say.

Sources of Charity

Since this pervading charity is so vital to the Church's unity and to its realization of its ultimate purpose of divine worship, it might be good in very brief fashion to examine the sources of charity in the Church. As already mentioned, when one is dealing specifically with Christian charity, he is talking about a love based on faith in the death and resurrection of Christ. This means that Christian charity is a conscious and positive response to the preaching of the gospel. Nothing less than genuine love is an apt response to the gospel, a full act of conversion.

What the gospel tells men is that God, the Father of our Lord Jesus Christ, so loved and loves the world of men that he sends his own Son and his own Spirit into the world for its freedom and fulfillment. The divine as revealed in Jesus Christ is not some impersonal transcendent infinitude. Though transcendent in the most profound sense, the God who reveals himself in Jesus of Nazareth is constantly present to men, transforming the meaning and purpose of their existence by his own loving gift of self to them. It is this divine gift of self in love that ultimately grounds that inner transformation of men that we call sanctifying grace; for it is in response to the absolute gratuity of this divine offer of friendship that men can respond by their own love, with a depth and fullness of selfhood that would be impossible without the divine initiative.

Christ himself in the culminating mystery of his death and resurrection is the sacrament of the divine self-gift. He is the living proof of the divine fidelity, and therefore the source of that hope that allows men to believe in the incredible gospel of God's love and to commit their lives and their destiny to this gospel. If this be true, then it follows that men must be exposed to the effective experience of the gospel if they are to develop into a community of love—they cannot believe, and consequently, cannot love in Christian fashion, unless the gospel is preached to them. While this obviously dictates much about the effort that must be made in the areas of effective preaching and religious education, it also says much about the need for effective Eucharistic Liturgy, for it is the Eucharist that supremely "proclaims the death of the Lord until he come."

It is by hearing in common the one gospel of death and new life, and in responding communally to its appeal for response in love, that the Christian people form a believing and loving community, truly one because there is only one Lord who is the object of their shared devotion, one Father to whom he leads them, one Spirit he grants to them.

Another source of the community's charity is the people's shared involvement in its mission, which we have already described as essentially one of sacramentalizing among men the redeeming love of God. Communities of human beings are united because of some common objective; in the instance of the Church, the unifying objective is its God-given mission which flows from the mandate of Christ and the indwelling power of his Spirit, the mission of loving and serving all mankind.

It is the nature of personal love to reach out in ever-increasing scope. In proportion as an individual learns to love anyone in greater depth and maturity, he is enabled to relate lovingly to others as well. Clearly, nothing is more difficult than to love with true maturity; actually, only Christ reaches this full ideal—he is the man for all other men. Yet, all Christians as individuals and the Christian Church as a community are meant to approximate this ideal. And as it does grow in its capacity to relate in love to all men, the Christian community grows in its own internal bond of affection and concern among its members. Its own life of faith and love is healthiest when the Church is self-forgetful and instead directed outwards toward the needs of men.

Thirdly, the community in love of the Christian people will develop and flourish in proportion as the individual Christians and the community as a whole enter more deeply into the mystery of Christ. It was into this mystery that the community initiates its new members in each generation through the mystery of baptism; it is into this mystery that the Church is meant to enter more fully as history evolves and moves toward the eschatological realization, when Christ will have fully prepared his bride for himself.

Certainly, in this area, one is dealing with mystery in the strictest sense, for this is the reality of the unity of God and man in Christ spilling over into the union of God and men in Christ. This is the mystery of that unity in life which Paul tries to express through the figure of the body, and the Johannine tradition through the figure of the vine. And no matter how dense the obscurity through which we grope for understanding of the unity of Christians with the risen Christ, it is unavoidably clear that he and he alone is our ultimate principle for union with one another. There is no way by which we can come into closer communion with one another than by being more closely bound to Christ. There is nothing that can so further the reunion of the Christian churches as that they and their individual adherents grow in their understanding of and devotion to the risen Christ. To the extent that we help bring our fellow Christians to deeper faith, we are inevitably hastening the desired day of reunion—and to the degree that we deprive them of the means of deepening that faith, we are postponing that day.

Every Christian has the right and the obligation of entering yet more profoundly into the mystery of Christ—by deepening and clarifying his understanding of Christ, by celebrating that faith and understanding in sacrament and so experiencing the central reality of the redemptive action, by personal communication with Christ in prayer, by broader participation in the life of that community which is the body of Christ. This right and responsibility he obtains through baptism, which is only a beginning, an initiation, that points ahead to growing personal identification with the risen Lord, to growing participation with him in the task of saving mankind. Parenthetically, we might reflect—since we are discussing the matter of intercommunion—on the grave reasons that must be present to justify any decision to bar baptized Christians from the kind of open eucharistic situation they may need in order to fulfill their baptism, i.e., the working of the Spirit. Whether we like it or not, we are part of that community which bears responsibility for the faith of all the baptized....

Quite bluntly, what is needed is large-scale conversion of our people, in all the churches, to genuine Christianity. The gospel must be preached in such a way that our contemporary Christians can really hear and understand it; without this, it is futile to hope for some magical infusion of love into the hearts of men. And one wonders how far the full preaching of the gospel can proceed if Christians are not exposed to the supreme proclamation of Christ's death and resurrection, the eucharistic action. Beyond this, Christian charity must find external expression if it is to grow and mature. Because it is an activity of human persons by which they relate to one another, it cannot remain a state of consciousness hidden and unexpressed within men; it must be stated so that humans can be aware of being loved by others and respond to that love. Yet, the nature of men as persons is not the only basis for saying that love among Christians must be externalized in order to grow; such externalization is demanded by the nature of Christ's redemptive activity in which the Church shares.

Christ redeems men by his act of human self-giving which is sacramental of the divine love transforming men. His self-gift finds its focal expression in his death and resurrection, but his in turn is sacramentalized through the love of Christians. In loving one another, the members of Christ's body contribute to the development of their human personhood, helping to heal the barriers of fear and distrust and egotism that stand in the way of that development. Even on the purely human level, this can be called a redeeming process, but in the mystery of Christ, it is much more: the very love of Christ himself and of his Father flows through this human loving to bring men to a level of self-realization otherwise unattainable.

Obviously, a Christian (or for that matter, any human) can only be helped and redeemed in this fashion by his brethren if he knows that he is so loved. This means that love must be given expression in word and deed; without this it remains blocked and inoperative, and eventually withers. To speak this way is not to reduce the work of redemption to simple psychological healing; but it is obvious that redemption, if it is to affect human persons as such, deals very largely with the psychological existence of man. It must take account of all the basic human factors of psychological need and development, but it must reach beyond them to include God's own activity of redeeming love. But to be effective, this too must find expression—not parallel with Christians' love for one another, but within that. This leads us inevitably to the Eucharist: the eucharistic action in which we share in Christ's own self-giving is the only adequate expression of our own Christian love for one another.

Eucharist and Charity

Let us, then, study more explicitly the relation between Eucharist and Christian charity. This is not a simple relationship, for the Eucharist is both manifestation of charity already existent and the source of further intensification of this charity. Not surprising, since it is the supreme sacramental translation of the Church's eschatological being, the expression of its pilgrim status, the Eucharist states the community's faith that it is already substantially redeemed, but also its hope that that redemption will find full future realization in the complete establishment of the kingdom of God. It professes the community's faith that it possesses the eschaton, for it is the celebration of Christ's risen triumph; but it is also the hopeful petition that the Spirit of the risen Lord work increasingly in its midst so that it share yet more fully in that triumph.

The Eucharist is essentially a manifestation of the charity that exists among the Christians who celebrate this action; it could not be otherwise, since it is a profession of their community with one another. Of its very nature, it is grounded in their assembly, their gathering together, their existence as the *ecclesia.* Symbolically, it proclaims the fact that these men and women accept identity with one another, identity in a shared view of life, identity in vocation and mission, identity in sonship. It says that their common action is grounded, not just in organizational unification, but in the deepest kind of personal communion. It says that they are God's own people, the sheep of his flock, whose gratitude for his saving action in Christ gives praise to him as Father.

Shared Love

What the eucharistic action is meant to express is the shared love of those present for Christ and the Father. It is the very essence of the eucharistic act to be in living symbol the act of Christ's self-giving. "This is my body which is given for you." Necessarily and simultaneously it is the action of the community accepting Christ's love by its response of love; for without this it would not be possible for the risen Lord to give himself to them. Even God cannot force his friendship on free beings....

As we mentioned earlier, the reality of Christians' common love of Christ and the Father is ultimately the mystery of the Spirit's presence in their midst. It is he who cries out for us, as we are without him unable to do, "Abba, Father." Only the Spirit, expressive of Christ's own sonship, can bear adequate witness to the sonship that links us Christians to one another as a family; only the Spirit can make of the eucharistic action an adequate worship of the Father....

So intimate is the link between the charity existent in a group of Christians and their manifestation of this in Eucharist, that the Eucharist lacks an essential element of its authenticity if this charity is absent. The stark attacks of the Old Testament prophets against the liturgy of Israel because it coexisted with social injustice and oppression finds its New Testament parallel in the saying of Jesus: "If you bring your gift to the altar and there remember that your brother has anything against you, go home first and be reconciled with your brother; then return and offer your gift." Eucharist is the celebration of community, of man's redemption from the alienation which is the very core of human sinfulness. It would be a lie, an affront to the holiness of God for a community to profess its love for one another, and for all men, when in reality it was torn by disagreement and enmity and misunderstanding. Obviously, some measure of these evils will exist, for the Church in history is a Church of sinners; but at least the assembled Christians must desire salvation from such division, which it does in eucharistic petition for the gift of the unifying Spirit.

Community in Charity

...True charity is concern for the good of others, and the Christian community, which manifests its loving concern for men, cannot do so without expressing its missionary intent to work for the redemption of the world. Hence, one of the aspects intrinsic to the celebration of the Eucharist is its function of concretizing for a definite community of Christians at a given moment in time the apostolate and commitment that are proper to them. This serves the purpose of clarifying for the bulk of the faithful the exact nature of the role they are to play as Christians and provides the occasion to crystalize their decision in this regard, a decision they all too often are reluctant to face....

One of the threats to the present-day activity of Christians in the task of bettering the human condition is that this becomes nothing more than participation in secular economic and political movements, that Christians forget the element of salvation through grace that must complement our purely human attempts to do good. This danger can be averted only if Christians remain exposed to the gospel and challenged by its values. To deprive them of the culminating proclamation of that gospel in the Eucharist would be to leave them without the necessary means to carry out their Christian mission.

Cause of Unification

Finally, then, let us look very briefly at the manner in which the Eucharist is not only manifestation of already existent unity in charity but the cause of further unification. Actually, we have already had to say much about this, because the very action of manifesting unity is that by which the unity is intensified. We are all familiar from our theological studies with the fact that there has been a constant teaching that charity is the fruit of the Eucharist. But until quite recently, there had been a long-standing tendency to understand that rather exclusively in terms of the increased sanctification of the Christians participating in the eucharistic action. However, now we are aware that we must lay more stress on the effectiveness of the Eucharist in fostering the growth of a loving community. We in the West are recovering some of the mentality that has characterized Orthodox theology in this regard, their insight that the Church is a community that is constantly being constituted in existence by the celebration of the Eucharist.

When we examine the evidence of the New Testament writings, this community dimension of the Eucharist's causality is quite clear. We have already discussed the manner in which the patristic texts touch on this matter, but I would like to highlight one aspect of this early testimony; while there may be little direct theological reflection on Eucharist as constitutive of community, the picture of the Church's actual historical emergence that is reflected in these writings points to the manner in which the eucharistic assembly did serve as the source of unification for the Christians of the early centuries.

While the action of Eucharist in forming community is certainly the work of God, and one cannot reduce it simply to the ordinary dynamics of human formation of community, it is equally true that this effectiveness of the eucharistic action is dependent upon the community consciousness of the Christians who celebrate this action. The experience of sharing in common their faith in the redeeming presence of the risen Lord is meant to bind Christians more closely to one another in loving identity. In every age, the Church is meant to live from the Easter experience....

Eucharist as Covenant Sacrifice

To argue (with Augustine) for the Eucharist's ultimate purpose as the transformation of participants into Christ—shaping free human beings into the pattern of Jesus' self-gift as love for others—leads to the conclusion that the sacrament's efficacy depends on input both human ("community consciousness") and divine (the Spirit's grace). The symbolic action of the eucharistic ritual, the proclamation of the word and responsive sharing in Christ's body and blood, sacramentalizes the grace of divine-human friendship generative of community in history. Sacrament functions here in terms of inner and outer, that is, Jesus' inner attitude and the symbolic/ritual "externals" comprising the only way he and his disciples, now the assembled eucharistic community, can deepen and share their awareness of divine love in their lives. As we saw in chapter 2, Cooke developed a decades-long theological reflection on the uniquely personal yet historically situated experience of Jesus as Jewish eschatological prophet. With regard to the Eucharist, the biblical category comprising the "external" form that such grace took for the Hebrews in history, and then in a radically new way in Jesus, was covenant. The theological themes of covenant and grace took hold of Cooke's theological imagination in Paris, steering his doctoral coursework in a biblical direction.

Shortly after I came to France, during the summer when I was relearning my French, I had decided to concentrate on the ecclesiology of the Church fathers. During my seminary years at St. Mary's, I had done some reading in biblical theology and had become intrigued by the notion of covenant, especially as that was developed in the first-rate book of Walter Eichrodt, demonstratively claiming that idea as the uniting thread running through the Hebrew Bible. So, why not see what the Church fathers did with that notion in their view of the Church? One difficulty: though I had a rather clear idea of how the Hebrew Bible handled this notion, I had no understanding of what the Christian Scriptures did. I would have to fill in that historical gap before doing serious work on the patristic period. Jean Daniélou was a leading patristic scholar with whom I hoped to work, so I approached him to ask for readings on covenant in the New Testament. His answer was surprising but honest: "I don't know of any such books. Why don't you go to your New Testament professor and ask him?"

That I did, and thereby hangs a tale. When I went to see the professor teaching the New Testament course, he began by assuring me that there was very little written about covenant in the New Testament, a statement that shocked me. However, as I began to plead my case, he became more and more interested and ended by insisting that I write my thesis on covenant in the Synoptic Gospels, offering to be my thesis director. He was approved as my director, and that hour-and-a-half conversation turned out to be the entirety of his direction. But from being a patristic scholar, I then became a scripture scholar of sorts. My controlling interest in Scripture was to equip myself to do systematic theology that would seriously incorporate the thought world of the Bible. And that happened. The work on my thesis was technically in redaction criticism, leading me into careful biblical theology. I learned to think biblically, not as completely as I wished but enough to challenge and complement the Greek modes of thought that so early shaped Christian theology.

The results of Cooke's doctoral dissertation eventually saw publication as a lengthy article in a 1960 issue of the journal Theological Studies, *"Synoptic Presentation of the Eucharist as Covenant Sacrifice." From there he continued to engage biblical texts to modify the Scholastic categories of*

*grace into a more relational and human-developmental reg-
ister, for which covenant remained central. The work came
together in his early book* Christian Sacraments & Christian
Personality *(1965), where in the first of four chapters on the
Eucharist, he redirected understanding of its sacrificial character from a narrow identification with the ordeal of Jesus'
passion to an appreciation of how this ritual meal (itself a
form of sacrifice) embodies the full range of ritual sacrifices
whereby Jews had come to live their covenantal relationship
with God. Published some fifty years ago, Cooke's treatment
of the biblical material remains sound,[6] while the details of
his theological reflection get at the heart of why the Eucharist
is the fundamental ritual sacrament for Christians' ongoing
relationship with God in Jesus (CSCP 117–31).*

The Eucharist as Sacrifice[7]

Sacrifice in the Old Testament

Ancient Notions of Sacrifice. According to the Mosaic traditions
that underlie the books of the Pentateuch, the Old Testament people came into existence as a unified group at Mount Sinai because
of the action of Yahweh in forming a covenant with them. This
covenant was formalized in a sacrificial act in which the blood of
a victim was shared between Yahweh and his people (Exod 24).
Thus, sacrifice is central to the approach of man to God in the
Old Testament....However, we must not think of sacrifice as something unique to the Israelites. Actually, in all the ancient religions
we know of, there was some manner of ritual act resembling the
sacrificial acts of Israel. We cannot determine with absolute accuracy the various purposes of the different mystery rites. Some
basic purposes can be recognized in almost all ancient religions,
including that of Israel.

---

6. In his second general textbook on sacraments, Cooke devoted a chapter to the Eucharist
as "Covenant Sacrifice," summarizing and simplifying the more detailed work he had
presented in the first, some two decades earlier. See *Sacraments & Sacramentality*, 108–14.
In a still later effort, with Gary Macy, serving an early twenty-first-century student audience
even less religiously literate, Cooke honed discussion of sacrifice to the ritual meal context.
See *Christian Symbol and Ritual*, 90–92.

7. Published in the 1960s, the copyrighted material reproduced here does not meet
contemporary standards for gender-inclusive language. *(Ed. note.)*

Perhaps the most fundamental objective of ancient ritual was to establish some contact with whatever powers controlled the forces of nature. Man tended to think of these ultimate powers as personal, and so he attempted to render such "divinities" present by the force of his religious ceremonial. This ceremonial used some sacred object (like a statue) to portray the god, or saw him as present in some sacred element (like ritual fire). In some cases, the ritual reenacted myths about the people's gods, and so "made present" those acts of the gods which they wished to guarantee.

With the god or gods present to him in ritual, man could now become united to divinity. This he did by offering gifts that would win favor and establish peace, or in some cases, appease an angry god and avert his harmful activity. In other situations, the ritual consisted of a sacred meal in which the divinity somehow shared food with the devotees. Having eaten together, the god and the people were united in a contractual bond.

Another meaningful feature of ancient rituals had to do with *sacralization*. The offering brought to the sacrificial act, and the people symbolized by the offering, were joined in the realm of the sacred, set apart as dedicated to the divinity. This making sacred could come about by lifting up the offering, or by placing it in a sacred spot (for example, upon an altar), or by the change effected through some force like sacred fire. Sacrificial dedication or sanctification seems to have been thought of as involving an entry into the realm of the sacred.

Again, all religious ritual implied an acknowledgment of an already existent religious relationship, or an attempt to establish relationship with a god. Sacrifice could serve to express the recognition of human dependence upon divine forces at work in nature. Or it could express a particular people's allegiance to their special protecting god. Or it might manifest the desire for reconciliation with some offended deity, thought to be showing his displeasure through some plague or disaster. The attitude of genuine personal thanksgiving seems to be missing. Are not the rituals that seem to be thank offerings really payments to the god of what was promised in earlier rituals of petition and bargaining?

Israelitic Notions of Sacrifice. On the surface, the ritual actions of the people of Israel appear similar to those of neighboring peoples. Actually more of the external ritual forms found among the Israelites were borrowed from Mesopotamia, Egypt, or Canaan.

However, there is a radical difference between Israel's religious ceremonials and those of other ancient peoples. This difference is clear in the externals of the characteristically Jewish festivals, but most importantly in their inner spirit and meaning.

Beginning with the experience of the exodus, the Israelitic expressions of faith are distinctive because their divinity, Yahweh, was unique among ancient gods. Because Yahweh was spiritual, not attached to any particular place, not immanent in the processes of nature, the whole notion of establishing contact and making him present drastically differed from similar concepts in other religions. Because Yahweh could not be represented (graven images were prohibited), Israel did not have a ceremonial re-presentation like that, for example, of the New Year's festival in Babylon.

What was represented in Israel's festivals was the *historical* act which lay at the beginnings of the people's existence and which was seen by faith to be the result of Yahweh's special intervention in history. In the course of the exodus from Egypt, Yahweh had made the covenant with his people at Sinai, a covenant that established Israel as a nation consecrated to this divinity. So it happened that sacrificial ritual during the Old Testament centuries never lost the central implication of covenant. The peace offerings celebrated on all the great feasts were essentially ceremonial reiterations of the Mosaic covenant; they were sacred meals shared by Yahweh and his people to express the union binding them together. Passover, Tabernacles, and the harvest festival all commemorated in their liturgical rites various aspects of the exodus experience of Israel.

Along with those peace offerings, in which the sacrificial meal was shared by God and the people in attendance, the Old Testament people also practiced the holocaust. As far as we can reconstruct the mentality of the ancient Israelites, it seems that the holocausts signified recognition of the sovereignty of this God who had brought their fathers out of Egyptian bondage into the land promised them. One can misinterpret the holocausts, seeing in the victim's destruction the essence of the act of worship. However, it seems that the Israelites did not think of the fires as something that destroyed the victim; rather, it was an action that *transformed* man's gift into the invisible element of fragrance that was thought pleasing to Yahweh. Moreover, it was Yahweh himself who transformed the offering, using fire as his instrument. The Israelites did not see fire itself as something divine, but like most ancient people, they did look upon it as a force especially associated with the divine, as Yahweh's own instrument, used by him to draw their sacrificial offering to himself. The fact that the fire sent up pleasing smoke to Yahweh was a sign of Yahweh's acceptance of the offering. When man consecrated his offering by laying it on an altar, Yahweh concurred by transferring it into a way of being more like his own.

When he came to the action of sacrifice, the Israelite thought of himself as bringing a gift to Yahweh. As a matter of fact, the Hebrew word *gift* comes closest to being the generic name for those Old Testament actions which we call sacrifices. Not that Yahweh needed the gifts that the people brought to the shrines. Especially in the later Old Testament centuries, Israel realized that all creation belonged to Yahweh, that he had need of nothing, and certainly not of the animal offerings made to him in the temple courts. However, the bringing of a gift had several meanings. It represented a self-offering, a desire to establish peaceful relations with God—or to reestablish them if reconciliation was necessary. Not only was the bringing of the gift filled with meaning, but Yahweh's acceptance of it, through the fragrant burning action of the fire, signified his divine good will toward Israel.

An interesting mentality, and one that Israel shared with other ancient peoples, is reflected in the offering of the first-fruits of the harvest and flocks. Apparently, according to nature, the earliest heads of wheat or the first bunches of grapes were thought to contain the whole life force of the crop. If this first, full, divinely given life was offered in sacrifice, the whole crop or vintage was rendered sacred, and a sacred people could then have sacred nourishment. Furthermore, the success of the rest of the crop was guaranteed because the entire harvest had been rejoined to its life source in the offering of the firstfruits. This notion of the offering of firstfruits to their divinity was so strong among some ancient peoples that they mistakenly sacrificed even their firstborn children. There are signs in the Old Testament that the people were not completely immune to this false idea. They had to be reassured by their religious teachers that Yahweh did not will human sacrifice. Instead, they were to offer to Yahweh the substitute gift of two lambs or two turtledoves.

In the later centuries of Old Testament history, especially in the strictly Judaic period that followed upon the Babylonian exile, the notion of *expiation* became quite prominent in the sacrificial ritual. The great annual feast of Yom Kippur (Day of Atonement) emphasized the people's reconciliation with Yahweh and the making of amends for the transgressions of the people. In addition, a whole array of sin and trespass offerings came into being. These served as liturgical reconciliations with God for individuals or the community. It seems that the historical tardiness of these expiatory sacrifices was at least partially due to the fact that a true sense of personal guilt and sin came into prominence only with the prophetic movement. Until men have seen their relationship to God as a *personal* reality, there cannot be that realization of sin which makes real religious expiation necessary or understandable.

Throughout the sacrificial ceremonial of Israel there runs the influence of Israel's God. Yahweh, who brought the people out of Egypt with power and a mighty right arm, is the divinity to whom each act of Old Testament ritual is directed. Yahweh's transcendence and spirituality impart their meaning to their actions and elevate them to a level not shared by other ancient religions.

Historical Commemorations. Most characteristic and unique in the religious rites of the Old Testament people is the *commemorative* character of their sacrificial acts. Their sacrifices involved, as an essential part of their meaning, references to the great events of Israel's history. But the ritual commemoration was more than mere remembrance of past happenings. It also provided, for those who participated in the ritual, an opportunity to share in the significance of the original happenings, to enter into their spirit and so pledge themselves as a continuing covenant people.

A most fascinating aspect of this commemorative nature of Old Testament liturgy is that it is a developing reality. While the commemorative significance of sacrifice remains essentially unchanged (it is always a recalling of the exodus), a deepening of understanding takes place over the centuries. Consequently, we find increasingly more detail and explication in the ritual itself. Cultural and historical influences have their impact, too, with the result that we find considerable accretion developing around the earlier and simpler ceremonial forms. What is notable in this complex process of liturgical growth is the influence of

Israel's concept of Yahweh and her recollection of his intervention in human history. By intervening, he radically transformed the new elements that came into the picture and made them part and parcel of the Old Testament world. In this process, the natural religious insights of ancient man, expressed and retained in his religious ritual, were brought into relationship with the truths of revelation and so transformed.

Christ's Sacrifice

Externals of the Last Supper. ...At the Last Supper, as they were gathered together with Jesus, the apostles were conscious of all these Jewish meanings of the Passover celebration. Christ's own awareness went far beyond theirs. He saw all the historical significances of the dinner. He also knew that this was the beginning of the new exodus....

One can see from the Gospel text that Christ's action of changing bread and wine into himself is clearly linked in his thinking with Moses' sacrificial action at Sinai. There Moses, after taking the blood of the victim and sprinkling it on the people, said, "Behold the blood of the covenant which the LORD has made with you in accordance with all these words" (Exod 24:8). The blood of the new covenant is not merely sprinkled externally upon the people; in a more sublime way, Jesus distributes the blood of the new covenant by giving his disciples the cup to drink. The parallel between Christ's words at the supper and those spoken by Moses at Sinai indicates that the Last Supper is the establishing of the new covenant in an act of sacrifice.

Christ's action was not simply a more intensified stage of the same covenant begun by Moses. It was, rather, the new covenant predicted by Jeremiah and Ezekiel, which was "not like the covenant which I made with their fathers when I took them by the hand to bring them out of the land of Egypt" (Jer 31:32). This was a new covenant in which the law would be written on the hearts of men instead of on tablets of stone. This was the new covenant which, in the minds of the prophets from Jeremiah onward, was to be effected when Yahweh came on the "day of the Lord" to bring salvation to his people.

Though the Gospel text is very succinct, there can be little doubt that Christ was conscious of this passage of Jeremiah when instituting the Eucharist. This was truly a new covenant, established in Christ's own blood and based on that new law which Christ himself is. Moreover, this new covenant fulfills the prophecy of Malachi that a new and spiritual sacrifice, a truly free inner offering of self, would mark the relationship of man to God on the day of the Lord.

Reflection on the relation of the supper both to Sinai and to the prophecy of Jeremiah leads us to conclude that Christ and the early Christians saw it as a sacrifice. Just as the old covenant had been enacted in sacrifice, this act of the Last Supper, which was the fulfillment and realization of Sinai, also had to be sacrificial. Besides, the words of Jesus when he speaks of his blood—"This is my blood of the covenant, which is poured out for many" (Mark 14:24; cf. Matt 26:28)—point to the ritual use of blood in the sacrifices of the Jerusalem temple. In the Septuagint, the Greek word used for "poured out" is the technical word for the pouring of the sacrificial blood upon the altar of the temple. Again, Christ's words when he changes the bread into himself indicate a sacrificial oblation: "This is my body which is *given for you*" (Luke 22:19).

From beginning to end, the Last Supper is a sacrificial action. It is not only, as is sometimes said in oversimplification, the act of Jesus changing bread and wine into himself; it is also the transformation of the entire feast of Passover with all it means. The Old Testament liturgy and system of sacrifice is radically transformed by being absorbed into the mystery of the new covenant. As we examine the action of Christ at the Last Supper, we can see that it fulfills the peace offering because the Last Supper is a sacred meal shared by God and the new chosen people; it fulfills the offering of the firstfruits because Christ is here being set aside in solemn consecration to his Father and is, as St. Paul tells us, the firstborn of creation, the firstborn from the dead....

Christ's Inner Attitude. When Christ was involved in the action in the upper room, what specified his consciousness, what was he aware of, what were the intentions which governed his activity? Fortunately, many indications are provided by his external actions. Even clearer are the words recorded in the Gospel narratives of this scene, and in St. Paul's First Letter to the Corinthians.

Quite logically, we argue from the externals, both gestures and words, to an understanding of Christ's consciousness at this moment....We wish to probe more deeply into the mentality of

Christ at this moment, because his human attitude during the action of the supper must be the model for all Christian participation in the eucharistic action and, therefore, for all Christian spirituality. There was, of course, only one state of consciousness in Christ. We can better understand its complexity by reflecting upon the way in which it was an attitude of obedience, worship, sacrifice, and thanksgiving.

An attitude of obedience. Scripture itself tells us that Christ's act in freely undergoing death was one of obedience by which he merited redemption for us and glorification for himself. Superficial understanding of this obedience sees it as conformity to an arbitrary law laid down for him by his Father. Something more radical is involved, namely, acceptance of the creaturely status bound up with his humanity. This involves admission of dependence upon a Creator God, as well as acceptance of those other factors of human life which bring man not just growth and development but also suffering, pain, and eventually death. Christ, in being obedient to his Father, was unreservedly accepting the lot which was his as a man. He did this in the concrete historical situation in which he found himself.

Christ's act of obedience involved an integral confrontation of reality. At no moment in his life was there the least compromise in Christ's acceptance of his human situation. As he approached the moment of his greatest difficulty, his passion and death, Christ solemnly consecrated to the Father this fullest expression of his earthly existence. The action of the supper expresses this inner obedience of Christ. Particularly significant are his changing bread into his body and his statement that he is putting himself aside as an oblation to his Father for the sake of men.

An attitude of worship. ...Christ's act of submission to the Father in obedience is worship. In worship, man acknowledges the sovereignty of God. In the Christian context, worship cannot be merely a matter of recognizing God as Creator. It must include recognition of God as Father. New Testament literature reveals how profoundly Christ's human consciousness and all his affectivity were directed toward his Father. The seventeenth chapter of St. John's Gospel describes Christ's state of consciousness at the Last Supper. Christ dedicated himself to the Father in reliance upon the Father's love, and completely accepted the role which he as the Son made man must play so that the Father might have other sons....

An attitude of sacrifice. Sacrifice as an attitude is very closely allied with worship. However, genuine sacrifice is more than interior acknowledgment of God. It must also include public manifestation of irrevocable dedication to this God. The internal attitude involved in sacrifice is what makes the externals of the act personally meaningful, truly significant. If in sacrifice we bring a gift and place it apart as belonging to God, then our internal attitude should logically and honestly be one of setting ourselves apart, a dedication of ourselves to the service of the God whom we worship. Christ was quite obviously sacrificing at the Last Supper because the externals of the supper were the externals of a sacrifice. By changing bread and wine into himself, he clearly set them apart from their normal profane use. His words, which accompanied this transformation, signify that this is his giving of himself to the Father. He was dedicating himself publicly and irrevocably to the task which his Father had committed to him, the task of encountering death and so destroying the mystery of evil.

Christ, in offering himself, had that internal attitude which is the heart of sacrificial action. This conclusion is confirmed by St. John's Gospel, which gives us such rich insight into Christ's consciousness at this privileged moment. Christ repeatedly voices his gratitude for the task which his Father had given him to do. He gives thanks for the reality of the Father himself. He thanks the Father for the fact that he, the Christ, is now approaching death and resurrection, is coming to the moment of his human fulfillment, the moment of his glorification. Hence, Christ's gratitude is made manifest by his actions as well as by his words. The early Christian community saw this in describing the act of Christ in this way. In recording what happened, the Gospel text says that Christ took the bread, and "when he had given thanks he broke it and gave it to them" (Luke 22:19). Christ obviously intends to situate this act in the context of thanksgiving. We can see, then, that the attitude of Christ at the supper is precisely that of sacrifice. Christ was submitting himself in gratitude to his Father, to render supreme worship to him by sacrificial gift (oblation) of himself in death and resurrection.

As we look at the concrete reality of Christ's choice at the Last Supper, we find that it was essentially a matter of his opening himself to a new way of life. He chose to relinquish the limited existence which we human beings enjoy in our present context of space and time, and open himself to a greatly amplified and spiritualized human existence. Since his experimental knowledge was just as human and limited as our own, Christ had no immediate experience of his coming death, nor of the new kind of life which was to be his. His willingness to commit himself to this passage through death into new life represented a profound expression of trust in his Father's providential care for him....

Another important element of Christ's interior attitude toward his death and resurrection is his acceptance of both *for the sake of men*. Christ said, "And for their sake I consecrate myself" (John 17:19). The action of the Last Supper is not just a matter of Christ *giving up* his life. More importantly it is a question of Christ *giving* his life to men, of giving himself as a living person so that men might share his life. Developing this idea, we see that the mystery of resurrection is not something that happens to Christ in isolation from the rest of men. Christ takes on new life. Christ passes into resurrection to bring men to that same risen life which he himself possesses. Christ's action of giving himself to his Father is simultaneously the action of giving himself to men as a source of their new life. There is no opposition, as a matter of fact there is no distinction, between these two acts of giving. It was precisely in order to give himself to men that the Father sent him into the world in the mystery of the incarnation. Christ's inner attitude is clearly one of sacrifice, not just because he accepts death but also because he willingly passes over into the new risen life which other men are destined to share.

In summary, the Last Supper is essentially a sacrificial action, a preeminently spiritual and personal sacrifice, the total self-giving of Christ in his humanity to the mystery of man's salvation in conformity with the Father's will. This sacrifice recapitulates and fulfills the sacrificial liturgy of the Old Testament and of all the natural religions of mankind. It is a sacrificial action because of the inner attitude of Christ who gratefully and obediently acknowledges the fatherhood of his Father. It is a sacrifice also in its externals, linked in their significance to the entire sacrificial ritual of the Old Testament....

Everlasting Sacrifice: The Christian Eucharist

Christ's Resurrection. Catholic belief in the Mass as Christ's continuing act of sacrifice is grounded in the mystery of his resurrection. Because he is in this new state, to which he passed in the mysteries of redemption, he is able to abide with his Church and continue his redeeming sacrificial action in her midst....

The New Testament says very little about this new way in which Christ lives as man. We know, however, that Christ's resurrection brought with it an increase in his human freedom. In his risen state, Christ lives in a dimension of human bodily existence, in which he is no longer limited by the narrowness of our space and time. Strictly speaking, the risen Christ cannot be said to be in any place in our world. It is more accurate to speak of him as being present *to* a place, since no spatial situation can either contain or limit him. Again, he is not limited by our time, but lives in a new context of sequential existence whose nature we will understand only when we ourselves participate in it in the next life. Freed as he is from such limitations, he is also freed from the inability to contact more than just a small group of human beings. He needs none of the techniques we have devised to extend the range of our communication with other human persons. Instead, his resurrected humanity makes it possible for him to be present to human beings wherever they may be in the entire range of creation.

This freedom from limitation in no way denies true bodily existence. We must not get the impression that Christ in his present risen state has only a semblance of a body. Rather, in a way in which we cannot fully appreciate, he is more thoroughly human, more integrally man in both body and soul than he was in the period which preceded his death and resurrection. The mystery of death and resurrection is not a denial of bodily existence. It is the passage to fulfillment of human life, the life of a spirit incarnated in a body. The Catholic Church has always firmly insisted that the risen Christ is truly and completely man. His human nature is perfectly integral.

Presence of the Risen Christ. This means that Christ is able to be present to his Church and to baptized Christians throughout the entire world. This presence, though invisible, is a presence of immediacy. Christ does not stand at a distance from his Church, as we learn from his reminder to his disciples, just prior to the ascension: "Remember, I am with you always until the end of the world" (Matt 28:20).

...Starting with the letters of St. Paul, the Church has used the image of the body to describe Christ's relationship to the members of his Church. Christ is the head, the members of the Church form his body, which lives by him and under his direction. The Church serves Christ much as the human body does the human spirit: it manifests the invisible Christ externally, locates him in a given context of space and time, and is the instrument by which he acts on the lives of men. The term *mystical body*, as applied to this mystery, indicates that the word *body* is not to be taken simply in a metaphorical sense, as in any ordinary societal grouping of men. The meaning of *body* in the mystical body lies somewhere between. In the Church, individuals retain their identity, and yet there is a truly vital principle that unites them in one life.

This presence of Christ to the members of his Church is not a static presence. Rather, it is a *dynamic* presence, grounded in his activity in their midst. He is actively present to them, and present to them precisely so that he can be actively present to the rest of mankind. In this manner, he carries on the work of redemption he began in his public life and achieved essentially in his death and resurrection. There are not two redeeming actions of Christ, one consisting of death and resurrection and the other taking place now in the Church. There is but the one redeeming act of Christ, starting at the Last Supper and continuing unbroken up to the present moment and unto the end of time. From the fact that Christ exists now risen and dynamically present to the Church, we can come to some understanding of Christ's present human consciousness. When we inquire into his present state of awareness and into the basic decision which flows from his human act of love, we find that this inner attitude is the very one that must lie at the center of all genuine sacrifice.

Eucharist as Reconciliation

The Eucharist is the mystical-sacramental means whereby the Holy Spirit empowers Christians to have in them the same mind, the same attitude as Christ Jesus (see Phil 2:5). Cooke's biblical theology of the Eucharist finds Jesus' inner attitude and outward gestures at the Last Supper to constitute the most fulsome of sacrifices, integrating in one ritual a profound worship of God at once personal and public. Jesus' inner attitude of love—obedient to his Father in self-giving for the life of humankind—continues in the humanity of his resurrected existence, such that those who participate now in the Eucharist are empowered for lives of obedience to the will of the God who is for the redemption and deliverance of humanity. The mystical interiority of the ritual celebration is for making women and men Christ's body in the world, ethically engaged in outward activity characterized by his reconciling love among people.

Pervading Cooke's memoir are indications of intimacy with Jesus nurtured by his life-long participation in the Eucharist. Throughout the chapters, as well, are indications of how inseparable that mystical devotion was from awareness of the needs of the poor and oppressed. Such awareness, necessitating action, he acquired with and from others, beginning with his parents and continuing through the chapters of his memoir. One entry recounts how Fr. Wehner educated Cooke and his fellow tertians on the priority of serving the poor in postwar Germany:

A key instance of the transformation of my personal understandings was Wehner's weeklong discussion of obedience in the Church. I will never forget his opening remark: "We must be careful not to confuse obedience with cowardice. The Germans in this room know what I am talking about." From other sources, not from him, I learned how he personally implemented this. There were one or two old retired Jesuits, definitely of the old school, who regularly reported to Rome that Wehner himself was engaged in pastoral work on weekends and that he allowed us tertians to become engaged in pastoral activity, whereas according to the rules, we were supposed to devote ourselves totally to study and prayer. As always, such reports triggered a rebuke from Rome. His response was direct: "In this postwar situation there are thousands of people in dire need. There are about thirty capable and eager young men here who can help meet this need. I cannot in justice block their work with the needy. I know this runs contrary to the usual regulations, but it seems to me that this is the only Christian course. I am perfectly happy to be removed as tertian master if you disagree with my judgment." His policy directly affected me. At the time, Germany was still divided into three zones of postwar occupation; we were in the British zone. For the entire British army in northern Germany, there was only one Catholic chaplain, whom I ended up assisting on weekends. That meant that I was responsible for a big base hospital and about twenty thousand troops.

Memories of his service as Catholic chaplain on a NATO command base (Fontainebleau) near postwar Paris included his reflection on the plight of prostitutes working in that vicinity:

Speaking of those trips to Fontainebleau each week reminds me of a subtle challenge to my doctrinal understanding of sin. On my 5:30 a.m. rail trip, I was invariably the only male in the car, all the others being prostitutes on their way to conduct business in the shabby hotels surrounding the train station. They were all young, late teenagers, who chattered lightheartedly with one another, even though they must have realized that some of them would be physically brutalized in the course of the day and that one or other would not return alive. In that context, what could the standard classification of their sexual activity as grave sin mean?

Highly consequential for the turn his religious vocation would take was his solidarity with African American students at Marquette caught up in the 1960s ferment for civil rights:

The decade of my teaching at Marquette was, of course, the decade of Vietnam and of the civil rights struggle. Milwaukee, being one of the most tightly segregated cities in the US, did not avoid the demonstrations and protests against the inferior schools and restricted housing imposed on the African American community. Fortunately there was relatively little violence, but hostility ran high, even in the university. At least as far back as Ralph Metcalf's winning Olympic fame while a student there, Marquette had been regarded in the black community as "friendly." The official position of the university was clear; Catholic ethical doctrine on social justice and human equality was honored in teaching and operational policy. Being composed, however, of humans caught up in the struggles and fears of the civil rights movement, the university could not completely avoid conflict.

To the school's honor, there was a sizable group of faculty that organized to further the civil rights of Milwaukee's black population, working with them in their campaign. But there were many others who were clearly of another mind, making it clear that it "was none of the university's business." Our theology department was in the first camp. Pauline Turner in particular was a prominent participant in the local efforts of the African Americans. Pauline went to Selma, Alabama, during the crisis there and managed to get herself arrested for involvement in the demonstrations against abuses in the school system, to the discomfort of some faculty who were unhappy about her being identified in the press as an assistant professor at Marquette.

My own participation in the struggle was taken for granted. The engaged faculty were all my friends, and the students expected the department to be in the leadership. We nonetheless made it clear that the African Americans were the leaders, while we were there actively to support them. Eventually, my identification with the black students in the university led to problems—but more of that presently. Involvement with the civil rights movement in Milwaukee meant going public, sharing in the demonstrations, many of them organized and led by Father Jim Groppi. It meant also helping the organized efforts of the black leadership in their campaign to change the city's policies on housing and schools. Certainly, I can claim no influential efforts on my part, which I definitely and deliberately subordinated to the emergent leadership of some very talented African Americans, a few of whom went on to national prominence. It did, however, teach me experientially much about the Church's mission and about the actual reality of the Christian community in Milwaukee.

As I just alluded, my links with "the black issue" at the university led me to a rather painful and life-altering experience. It happened toward the end of my years at Marquette and contributed to my leaving. Across the country, college students were demanding a change in academic policies and administration, sometimes with violent protest. Marquette was no exception. Though our students avoided the violence—burnt no buildings, smashed no computers—they did "occupy" the chapel, renaming it "the

Camillo Torres chapel." The local police responded by besieging the building, knocking down the main door, and detaining some of the protestors until university authorities intervened.

As for the African American students, they decided to threaten withdrawal from the university unless a list of their demands was met. Some of their demands were excessive and impractical—for example, that a large portion of the faculty and administration be immediately recruited as African American— but some of their complaints were justified and reflected attitudes of the country at that time. The protest took place in the spring, with some of the students on the verge of graduating, some even from graduate and professional programs. In most cases, their parents had undergone great sacrifices to provide for their educations. So, their dropping out of school at that point made no sense. Before they actually took action, they arranged a public meeting of all the black students and their supporters in the ballroom of the student union, a meeting that was to finalize their decision to resign from the university. To slow down the decision, two of us—myself and a Jesuit colleague, Bill Sullivan, who later became president of Seattle University—made an offer to the assembled crowd: put off your resignation for a week and allow the two of us to negotiate a settlement with the school's administration; if at the end of the week there has been no progress, we will resign along with you. Actually, the students were happy for the intervention; deep down they were uncertain about the whole affair, and so agreed with our offer. I began a long week trying to mediate a solution.

Faced with the student protest, the university administration panicked: an emergency committee was formed, drawn largely from the law school, all of them, i.e. the lawyers, members of the conservative John Birch Society. Heading the committee was a man who had recently come to Marquette as special assistant to the president, recruited because of his reputation as an expert in banking affairs, a man who had never before had any association with a Catholic institution or Catholic social teaching. At its beginning, the group immediately adopted a hardline approach. Fortunately, two of the Jesuits who were added to the discussion by virtue of their positions within the administration convinced the group to invite me to describe what was occurring among the black students, since by that time I had begun meeting with them day and night trying to help moderate voices prevail.

So, rather reluctantly I was invited, but as I began to describe the situation as I knew it, I was interrupted: Didn't I realize that the whole thing was a communist plot to infiltrate the university?... Most of the committee dismissed my account. The chairman turned to the Jesuit president of the university, an ex officio member of the group, and suggested I be asked to leave—which he did, and I did. Fortunately, that was not the end of the story. Gradually some compromises were made, some of the students' demands met, and the crisis passed without any of the students leaving the university. For me, it was the beginning of alienation from the administration, and painfully from several fellow Jesuits in the administration. One of them in a gathering of Jesuits soon afterward publicly accused me of "disloyalty" and "grandstanding."

Cooke's concern for the rights and equality of women emerged in that period, as well, but only grew through his ensuing vocational partnership with Pauline, whose theological work prioritized feminist issues, as they settled into the faculty at the University of Windsor, Ontario.

The first influence was the graduate seminar on the history of women in the Church that Pauline and I co-taught each year. Needless to say, much of this, a revelation, proved more than mildly disturbing. Practically all the students in the seminar were women, and as the course progressed, the deep discontent of intelligent women with the official Church became more and more apparent. The second influence on my "awakening" occurred during that same time, the first Women's Ordination Conference in 1975.

Windsor is just across the river from Detroit, where in its suburb of Southfield, this Conference was held, so it was taken for granted that Pauline would be an active attendee. I went along to observe what I suspected to be an important event. What happened in terms of the lectures and discussions was the extent and caliber of scholarship among Catholic women in North America becoming widely known, providing an unavoidable challenge to the second-class status of women in the Church. For me personally, it was an important experience, not just that there was interesting and important theology being done by women but that

159

there is a distinctive feminist way of doing theology to which I needed to listen and learn but that remains "other" to me as a man, requiring discourse between us.

Eucharistic life, then, is an ongoing transformation of attitude for others, an attitude like Christ's so vigilantly aware of people's suffering in sin and oppression, so actively committed to mercy for individuals and justice in societies. Joining the memory of Jesus with the power of his Spirit, the Eucharist is the Church's primary source and means of reconciliation, a theme Cooke worked out in a series of parish talks that became the monograph Reconciled Sinners *(RS 85–94).*

Eucharistic Reconciliation

When the liturgical movement began to gain momentum and some acceptance in the 1950s and 1960s, the focus in the United States was the annual Liturgical Week. If one goes back to examine the proceedings of those weeks and notices the topics discussed and the governing themes chosen for each year, an interesting fact emerges. While in the earlier years there was an almost exclusive attention to strictly liturgical matters, within a short time there was growing mention of the relation of liturgy to social justice.

In emphasizing this link between worship of God and concern for healing the alienations in society, the liturgical movement recovered one of the most basic tenets in the Jewish and Christian traditions, an element that for some time had been neglected.

At least as far back as the great prophets of Israel, one can find biblical statements about the emptiness of religious ritual performed by those who simultaneously exploit the powerless of society. Jesus of Nazareth continued this prophetic tradition and in his teaching stressed care of the poor and disadvantaged as the will of his Father. The last parable of Jesus contained in the Gospels describes "the last judgment" when all humans are brought before him for evaluation of their lives; and the basis of judgment is simply that of feeding the hungry and sheltering the homeless.

Earliest Christianity recognized the link between healing the divisions of society and celebrating the "breaking of the bread" (the Eucharist). In his first letter to the community at Corinth, written around the year AD 55, St. Paul criticizes severely those who would discriminate between poor and well-to-do when the community gathers for its eucharistic liturgy. As he says, this is a sin against the body of Christ—both the eucharistic body and the body that is the Church. In the Epistle to the Galatians, he states the basic principle that in the body of Christ there is no place for discrimination on the basis of power or wealth or ethnic origin or gender. Reconciliation is to be a characteristic of the Christian community, and its eucharistic gatherings are to celebrate and cement their union in Christ.

Meal of Reconciliation

The basic structure of the eucharistic liturgy, that of a meal, indicates the role it is meant to play as a celebration of reconciliation. Eating together has always been and still is a familiar way of indicating a union with one another and, if people had previously been at odds, their reconciliation. In the temple liturgy of the Old Testament period, the central ritual of the "peace offerings" was celebrated as a sacred meal in which Yahweh and his people joined to renew the covenant, a covenant that the people all too often violated. This "peace offering" was a key element in the religious experience of Jesus and his disciples from which early Christianity drew as its own rituals gradually developed.

Out of the meals when Christians quite naturally gathered to be with one another, to recall and celebrate what had happened in Jesus' life and death and resurrection, to praise Jesus' heavenly Father for this great act of salvation, there emerged very quickly the distinctive celebration we know as the Christian Eucharist. But as it emerged, the Eucharist remained essentially a community meal that ritualized their peace with one another and with God, a meal that gave thanks for the reconciliation achieved in Jesus' death and resurrection.

Even though, for many centuries, Christians tended to forget the meal character of Eucharist, partially because of theological and doctrinal concentration on the Eucharist as a sacrifice, the eucharistic action, the Mass, was always in its essence a meal, a sharing of food and drink—bread and wine transformed into Christ's gift of his own life-giving body and blood. In the past half-century, both theologians and liturgical scholars have realized again the central importance of the meal aspect of Eucharist; and this realization is beginning to have its effect on our understanding of and participation in the Eucharist.

As we become more conscious that our coming together for Eucharist is a gathering at the table of the Lord and at his invitation, we are at least implicitly more aware that we must do so as a family able to celebrate its unity and peace. For any Christian group to assemble for Eucharist when unresolved major divisions exist in the group is a charade; it pretends to be a celebration and pledge of forgiveness and reconciliation when the people gathered there intend no such thing. Such a Eucharist is as inappropriate as would be a Thanksgiving dinner to which family members came, hostile to one another, disliking and even hating one another, and with no intention of trying to make peace and heal the antagonisms that divide them. One would ask such a family why they bother to get together.

Anamnesis *of Jesus' Reconciling Act*

However, the Eucharist is more than an acknowledgment of reconciliation among a group of Christians, a celebration of their peace.

It is the root source of that peace. Eucharist plays this key role in bringing about reconciliation, because it is the *anamnesis*, the making present of Jesus' death and resurrection by which the final reconciliation was introduced into our human history. Paul among first-generation Christians lays greatest stress on this peacemaking aspect of Jesus' Passover. In several passages, he speaks of the way in which Jesus has broken down the walls of separation, has brought those whose sins alienated them from God once more into union with that God.

When we say that Eucharist is *anamnesis* of Jesus' death and resurrection, we are trying to say that the Eucharist we celebrate is more than a commemoration of Jesus' Passover, that it is more than the occasion on which the power of that saving action touches our lives. Eucharist is the mystery of Christ's presence in our midst. Presence is something that has to do with people being for one another and communicating with one another. What happens in Eucharist is that the risen Christ is himself present, sharing himself with his friends, saying to them through the transformed bread and wine that he exists to be the source of their personal life and growth. Eucharist is more than a recollection of Jesus' resurrection; it is that resurrection, for the resurrection is nothing other than the risen Jesus himself.

And because the risen Lord is present among any group of assembled Christians, forgiveness of one another is a characteristic of any group that identifies itself as Christian. Because the Christ in our midst forgives each of us, extends to each of us a love whose fidelity reflects his Father's love for us, no one of us can truly respond to that offer of Christ's friendship while at the same time refusing to be reconciled with anyone else to whom Christ is also bonded in love.

In a family, a child cannot genuinely and fully respond to a parent's love and at the same time remain unforgiving and alienated from a brother or sister. That which is the source of reconciliation in such instances is precisely the love of the parent for both of them. So, the common bond that Christians have to the risen Christ is the ultimate source of the reconciliation and peace that unites people into one family of God. And above all, when Christians gather together in Eucharist to share in the one body of Christ and to become thereby that body of Christ which is the Church, reconciliation is celebrated and deepened. Needless to say, the extent to which this happens is conditioned by the extent to which those participating in the liturgy are aware that this is occurring—a Eucharist routinely performed and empty of meaning will not signify nor achieve the reconciliation that should take place.

In the reconciliations that should take place within the Church itself, particularly the reunion of the various Christian denominations, it is important to remember that the only ultimate and adequate source of reconciliation is the risen Christ. Official actions, theological reflection, pastoral exhortation, all have their place; but in the last analysis, it will be Christian relationship to Christ, their acceptance of genuine discipleship, that will lead them to a concerned and forgiving acceptance of one another.

Epiklesis, *the Reconciling Spirit*

Essential as is the element of *anamnesis* in Christian Eucharist, it must always be accompanied by the transforming power of God that touches both the assembled Christians and the symbolizing elements of bread and wine. So, in all the liturgies of the Church, especially in Eastern Christianity, the *epiklesis*, the invocation of God's Spirit, has played a prominent role. In what is really a continuing Pentecost, the Eucharist celebrates and deepens the risen Christ's gift of his Spirit to his disciples.

In the invocation of Christ's Spirit that forms an element of the Eucharistic Prayer (formerly the Canon of the Mass), the assembled Christians pray that this Spirit will through the change of bread and wine change themselves into the one body of Christ. It is, then, the Church's most constant and focal prayer for true unity of the people of God. But it is a prayer that recognizes that the desired unity does not yet fully exist; there are still alienations of one sort or another that need to be removed; there is still need for a deeper and more encompassing forgiveness among the people who make up the Church; the family of God is not yet as committed to peace, even in its own life, as it should be.

Even psychologically, this eucharistic *epiklesis*, if it becomes a genuine expression of the community's desire for peace and reconciliation, will become a source of such peace. To wish to forgive and be forgiven is already the biggest step toward such forgiveness. To state publicly together that they share this wish, as Christians do in Eucharist, creates a basic understanding and attitude that can then lead to more complete reconciliation. Special liturgies of reconciliation, such as those we discussed in the previous chapter, have this same objective; but the eucharist as the *anamnesis* of Easter and Pentecost celebrates and fulfills what those other liturgies begin to achieve.

Eucharistic Peace

It is not accidental that the Eucharistic Prayer is followed by the Our Father with its petition "Forgive us our sins as we forgive those who sin against us," and by the sharing of peace among the assembled people. Peace is both the context and the fruit of eucharistic liturgy.

Peace when applied to Eucharist must be understood against the background of God's centuries-long working in history, first with Israel and then with the Christian Church. *Peace* in that context has a rather precise meaning, one that extends far beyond mere absence of conflict. It is a meaning that flows from the reality of *covenant.*

As the traditions of Israel that are distilled into the Bible tell us, Israel existed as God's people because God chose them and formed an alliance, a covenant, with them. It was not only the ordinary forces of social change and economics and political activity that explain their distinctive identity and role in human history; it was the bond established at Sinai that made and makes Israel Israel. For it was at Sinai, during the rooting experience of the exodus from Egypt, that through the mediation of Moses, the people accepted the divine election and Yahweh revealed that "you will be my people and I will be your God."

This covenant was, then, the formative bond, the special social contract, that linked the Old Testament people to God and to one another. Not that the people always remained faithful to the pledges of Sinai; more than once they needed prophets to remind them of the covenant, to lead them to conversion and to reconciliation with their God. But to the extent that the covenant was observed, particularly by honoring social justice within the life of the people, peace resulted. Peace, *shalom,* was the situation that existed when the relationships appropriate to the covenant, Israelites to one another and Israelites to Yahweh, were respected. When justice and concern for the poor and weak characterized Israelitic society, when ritual honor of Yahweh was sincere and from the heart, when kings ruled by true law and not by whim, when prophets spoke truth, then there was peace. For it was then that the Spirit of the Lord permeated the life of the people.

In the theology of the New Testament literature, Jesus himself is seen to be the new covenant; instead of a law and a contractual agreement, it is a person who bonds humans and God. And it is when humans accept in faith the self-gift of the risen Christ that friendship between people and their God is created by the sharing of a common Spirit. This is true peace. So, in the Gospel narratives about Easter, the risen Jesus is described as coming to his disciples with the greeting, "Peace be to you. Receive the Holy Spirit."

To the extent that Christians are open to this gift of Christ's Spirit, they are open to one another. This Spirit is the personal power of divine love, creative of community that is grounded in love, creative of people as they learn to love maturely. Those who live by this Spirit live in peace, even when the externals of their lives are disturbed by misfortunes and oppression and misunderstanding. They live at peace with themselves and with one another. They are genuinely reconciled to human life as it is, even while they work to change it into the kingdom of God.

Such is the peace that Christians are meant to pledge to one another in eucharistic liturgy when, between the Eucharistic Prayer and their communing in the body of Christ, they wish one another the peace of Christ. It is one of the blessings of recent enrichment of ritual within the Church that we are again able in Eucharist to express our wish of peace for one another. Like other liturgical revisions, though, the giving of the peace can be relatively routine and perfunctory, or it can have the meaning it is intended to have. When it is done carefully and as a natural and sincere human action, it is automatically a gesture of reconciliation. Whatever barriers might separate two people who exchange the eucharistic gesture of peace, the sharing of Christ's peace is an implicit pledge to overcome these barriers. Obviously, this needs to be explained to people so that they will understand what they are doing.

Celebrating One Another

When people are genuinely forgiving and reconciled to one another, they are content to deal with each other as they are. They can quite realistically recognize the shortcomings that others, and they themselves, have but at the same time be grateful for those with whom they are sharing life.

There are obvious advantages that come when one is surrounded in one's work and neighborhood and public involvements with people who are friendly and trustworthy. Beyond that is the benefit that comes when one is part of a genuine community. In such a group of people, one can feel at home, can share interests and activities, can find sympathy and support, can in the deepest sense relax and be oneself, can be at peace. Christian communities are meant to be such, and their community celebrations—the Eucharist in particular—should humanly and simply express their gratitude for the Christian sharing they enjoy.

Clearly, if people gathered together are happy to be together, grateful that they share in a true community of friends who care

166

for one another, they are basically reconciled with one another. Their celebration of reconciliation at a liturgy such as the Eucharist does not even have to make explicit mention of reconciliation. On most occasions, it would be more appropriate simply to realize that they are celebrating one another. The rituals of Eucharist would allow them to do what many people find embarrassing to do individually, to say how much they appreciate one another. If this is said, it confirms whatever forgiveness and reconciliation took place in the previous history of the group.

Daily Reconciliation

We might mention one last aspect of the Eucharist as the most important sacrament of reconciliation. Christian sacramental liturgies are not meant to be isolated religious events; they are somehow meant to deepen the meaning of our entire life. Most of the liturgies of sacraments, however, deal with special moments of Christian experience—being initiated in baptism, formally entering upon a more adult stage of Christian life in confirmation, being empowered for ministry in an ordination ceremony. It is the Eucharist that is the liturgy of our day-by-day attempts to live out the Christ mystery.

What should happen in our eucharistic liturgies is that with some regularity, such as each Sunday, the happenings of our lives are brought into contact with the gospel. As Eucharist proclaims the gospel, challenges to conversion, and points us in hope toward the final realization of our potential as the individuals we are, the relatively humdrum course of our lives takes on deeper meaning and the responsibilities of our particular situation become less avoidable. At the same time, hearing the gospel in the light of what is actually taking place in our lives makes Christian beliefs come to life; we understand what Christianity is by trying to be Christian.

Since the need for forgiveness and reconciliation is something that runs throughout our daily experience, usually in small ways, the regular celebration of Eucharist inevitably deals with this continuing reconciliation. Eucharistic liturgies can do this in very specific ways, treating the particular situation of a given group instead of expressing only a broad and general Christian attitude of forgiveness.

Naturally, for eucharistic liturgies to function in this way, the communities that celebrate Eucharist must understand that this is what is meant to occur and plan their liturgical celebrations to achieve this goal. This can happen in different ways—as part of the initial recognition of sinfulness and need for forgiveness, or as an element in the homily, or in conjunction with the prayers of the faithful, or along with the giving of peace, or as part of the explained meaning of receiving communion. What is important is that those creating and those participating in liturgy come to understand the intrinsic nature of Eucharist as a celebration of Christian reconciliation, of Christian peace.

In proportion as Christian celebrations of Eucharist do become liturgies of peace and forgiveness, they will act as sacraments, and therefore causes, of the peace which God intends for the entire human family. Then will the kingdom come, then will God's will be done.

CHAPTER FOUR

Church

MINISTRY AND TRADITION

Introduction

That Cooke's theological career developed around the sacraments and realized its highest academic scholarship concerning the history and theology of ministry, he attributed to his devotion to the Eucharist. Practice—and not just theory (theology, in a textbook sense)—of the Eucharist through personal and communal experience across continents and decades consistently moved him to reconsider the status and function of all the baptized in the life and mission of the Church. In his memoir, reflection on ordination to the sacramental priesthood during his seminary years leads into recounting the origins of his mission as a theologian of and for the laity:

Much of the third year at St. Mary's focused on our ordination to the presbyterate at that year's end. Inevitably that meant reflecting theologically and prayerfully on the sacrament of holy orders. I looked forward, above all, to the empowerment that ordination would give me to celebrate the Eucharist. After ordination, I cherished celebration of the Eucharist, whether privately or for a community, as the great privilege of my life. It would be years before I began to question some of the aspects of the theology of order as I understood it in 1952, particularly the role of the ordained person as the "presider" and not "the celebrant." I came to realize the extent to which understanding of "internal empowerment by ordination" depended upon the introduction of Aristotelian thinking during the twelfth century. Despite those questions—and I was not alone in raising them—the Eucharist has still remained at the center of my theological vision. I believe that Eastern theology is correct in seeing Christianity as constantly emerging from the Eucharist.

If the third year ended with the euphoria of ordination, the fourth began with a bit of a shock. Jesuit superiors gave me a new assignment. Instead of preparing to teach Protestant theology in the theologate (my assignment when sent to begin my studies at St. Mary's), I was to attempt to develop a theology for the laity. This was quite a novel idea in those days when theology was something males studied as a step to ordination. That laymen, to say nothing about women, would be interested in it or even think of it as a profession was unconventional. My assignment was triggered by dissatisfaction with college courses in religion, widely considered uninteresting by collegians and ineffective by their teachers. So the decision was made to do something about it, though ideas of a remedy were rare to nonexistent. A few experiments had been launched, mostly attempts to adapt seminary theology for nonseminarians, which clearly did not work. There were a few suggestive developments in Europe, where interest in creating a more vital approach to catechetics had led to periodicals like *Lumen Vitae* and to the pastoral theology movement triggered by Josef Jungmann's *Frohbotschaft*.

So, I shifted gears and turned my reading to whatever there was that seemed to promise insights into shaping theology to fit the needs and interests of the laity. What at first looked like a diversion from the center to the periphery of theological reflection proved just the opposite. It seemed rather clear that any relevant theology for the laity would have to engage their experience. Using experience as the springboard for theological reflection was—surprise, surprise—at the very heart of the theological revolution then taking place in post–World War II Europe. I had become aware of this revolution largely through my work as an editor of *Theology Digest*, and knew that it involved debate about the nature of faith as much more than a reasoning process, debate about the character of the Church as a community, debate about grace and salvation. All of this clearly impacted on any believer's understanding and practice of religion, independently of seminary training. Such elements of the "new theology," along with the understanding of Jesus' resurrection reflected in Durrwell's *Resurrection* and the emerging insights into divine presence and providence, could, if effectively communicated, basically alter people's understanding of God and themselves as Christians. The agendas for a theology of the laity and for nurturing the newest theological currents were largely the same, but how to achieve this in the repressive climate that had just produced the papal encyclical *Humani Generis*? One big advantage: for the moment no one at the Vatican took theology for the laity seriously enough to see it as a threat to "orthodoxy."

All this is clear to me now, but it wasn't as I began to think about a theology for the laity. I was uncertain what to do next, where to turn for the formal education that would forward the search and at the same time provide the doctoral training that would give me the necessary academic credentials to teach on the university level. Evidently, nothing in North America offered what I needed; perhaps Europe did....Somehow I would have to gain some fluency in one or two languages if I was to follow classes and converse intelligently with the people in Europe who had the knowledge I needed. The solution proved to be the most important year in my personal and theological development.

That closing sentence refers to Cooke's tertianship year under Fr. Karl Wehner's inspirational direction. Even before beginning the formal program, however, Cooke had a memorable pastoral experience with the laity during his initial months in Germany at the Jesuit house of philosophical studies in Bavaria:

My goal at Pullach was to spend the summer becoming conversant in German. It was a matter of learning the language or starving. I did gradually expand my vocabulary, became accustomed to the distinctive word order of the language, and overcame the mental block that German had earlier caused in me—all of this with the aid of the young Jesuit students who included me in their periods of recreation, invited me along on their picnics, and gently corrected my constant mistakes. Stumbling my way through the German language clearly did little to advance my theological acumen, but one experience did help lay the ground for later reflection on liturgy. I had been only three weeks at Pullach when the superior asked me to help out in a neighboring parish the following Sunday. Somewhat worried about my faltering German but erroneously assuming that the parish in question was only a short distance away, I consented. So, at 5:30 a.m. Sunday, I set out on a bicycle for a village called Warendorf. I discovered it meant cycling almost to the center of Munich, then taking a right turn for a few more miles and, miracle of miracles, I did arrive at the little parish church in Warendorf. The sacristan, the sister of the pastor, welcomed me with a chatter of which I understood not a word. I later found out she'd been speaking in the local Bavarian dialect.

So, I set out to begin Mass in the usual fashion at the foot of the altar when the congregation simply took the action away from me. Because of the difficulties of the Nazi period, German Catholics were granted some use of the vernacular, and the congregation that Sunday morning made the most of it. What I was experiencing, including listening to a layperson preach the homily, was something my theology led me to only years later: the community, and not the ordained presider, is the fundamental celebrant of Eucharist.

> *That little experience elicited for Cooke reflection on authority, tradition, Eucharist, and the status and role of ministers, ordained and lay, in the Church. His thought on all of those, including their interrelatedness, would later evolve dramatically during his dozen years at Marquette, where his development of theological education and pastoral formation for laypeople coincided with a breadth of lecturing, publishing, and consulting experiences. His memoir account begins with Marquette student liturgies, then broadens to the national scene.*

The liturgies were held in a little theater in the round established by the outstanding theater division of the English department. It was quite small, but that had the advantage of forcing people to become close as a community. There, long before Vatican II's Constitution on the Sacred Liturgy, we were implementing the mandates that document would generate. We celebrated in English, with various roles usually exercised by an ordained celebrant shared among the participants, and we incorporated art, current literature and music, and liturgical dance. Fortunately, we had rich resources to draw upon in the student body....The liturgies were carefully orthodox in essence but included many things not officially approved....Importantly, these eucharistic celebrations were profoundly engaged experiences of prayer, truly functioning as "the final word" in the theological understandings we were trying to develop in our classroom activity....

This local attempt to provide more appropriate eucharistic celebration for our students was part of a broader participation in the burgeoning liturgical reform movement in the country. A few years prior to my return from studies in Europe there emerged a small but dedicated American group aware of the liturgical reforms beginning in Europe [who] recognized the stagnant nature of sacramental practice in the Church, and began agitating for change. Crucial to their activity was their annual Liturgical Week, a gathering of several hundred "reformers" from all parts of the country to exchange ideas and celebrate the Eucharist in as innovative a fashion as then permitted. They advocated such "weird" notions as using the vernacular language rather than Latin, and were broadly dismissed by Catholic authorities across the nation. For the most part, they were concentrated in a few places, particularly St. John's Abbey in Minnesota and the Boston area, guided by a handful of pioneers including Virgil Michel, Gerald Ellard, Godfrey Dieckmann, Fred McManus, Bill Leonard, and Gerry Sloyan.

I quickly became active in this movement, giving talks at the annual Liturgical Week, privileged to know and appreciate the crusade for good liturgy and the leadership who were working to further it. Joining with other like-minded persons was an exhilarating experience that gave promise of a better day. That day was slow in coming, despite the papal encyclical *Mediator Dei*, which to a limited extent, legitimated the growing movement. Fortunately, some first-class historical and theological research by scholars like Josef Jungmann was feeding into liturgical reform, communicated in North America through such publications as *Orate Fratres* (later renamed *Worship*), with public awareness of the need for reform growing. For the moment, though, we could not dream of the breakthrough that would come with Vatican II. As I reflect, I am grateful that, as far back as high school, I was exposed to the earliest stages of the liturgical reform, through talks given by Gerald Ellard and our adoption of the *Missa recitata* for our daily school Mass. My later involvement in liturgical revision was inevitable. Today, reflection on the Eucharist remains the center of my theological outlook.

But much more was demanding my interest and activity. The 1960s was a decade of immense activity, ferment, and change, and this was especially true of the religious and theological world that included Marquette. This was the decade of the Vietnam War and the student activism accompanying it, a decade of explosive confrontation of racism and civil rights, and the decade that saw feminism come of age in the American church. These were the years that the Catholic Church in the US began to move slowly into ecumenical awareness and participation, the decade that not only witnessed the earth-shaking event of the Second Vatican Council but also the catechetical and liturgical ferment that preceded and fed into it, the decade that saw the anguish caused by the encyclical *Humanae Vitae,* and in the field of theology, the decade continuing the mid-twentieth-century theological revolution—perhaps the most basic shift in the history of Christian thought.

For better or worse, all of this touched my life and caught me up in an unrelenting schedule of activity: giving retreats, especially to groups of fellow Jesuits with whom I could share the new insights into the Spiritual Exercises I had acquired in Germany, frequent talks to women religious as they wrestled with the need to rethink and revamp much of their traditional lifestyle, membership in a small national group working to shape a new paradigm for faith formation, serving as consultant for two new series of religious textbooks, giving any number of talks at conventions, and publishing essays on changing understandings of such doctrines as resurrection and grace.

Such an energetic commitment to reform across all key areas of Church life (and of the Church's role in wider society) inevitably drew Cooke into collaboration with a full range of Church officials (regionally, nationally, and internationally), comprising contrasting positive and negative experiences of authority and ministerial leadership, to be recounted in a subsequent section, below. Sufficient for concluding this introduction to Cooke's theologies of Church, tradition, and ministry is to note his ongoing integration of those topics, grounding them in theologies of salvation (soteriology) and sacrament (sacramentality), and continuously rethinking them with students, faculty, and the wider faithful in a series of locations (geographic and cultural) over the next four decades.

Theologies of Church and Ministry

At the time Cooke left Marquette and the Jesuits in the late 1960s, he had begun work for the US Catholic Bishops Conference for a book on the theology of the priesthood, which was to be part of a series (including books on Scripture, ecclesiology, and other topics), a resource for practical and pastoral documents. That charge was rescinded after he resigned the clerical state, but questions of order and power in relation to the Church in its mission and ministries had established themselves as the focus of Cooke's historical and theological scholarship going forward into the 1970s.

On a most practical level, moving forward from his research fellowship at Yale and marriage to Pauline meant relocating to Canada for a decade, first on the theological faculty at the University of Windsor and then as a founding member of the religious studies department at the University of Calgary. While both appointments entailed the usual complement of teaching and service, Cooke's account of that chapter in his life pivots on the completion and publication of Ministry to Word and Sacraments *(1976), his massive, single-authored study of history and theology numbering some 650 double-columned pages.*

By the time I left Windsor, the manuscript for *Ministry to Word and Sacraments* was complete and in the process of publication. Working on that book crystallized my methodology as basically historical, nonclerical, and ecumenical....It was during my years in Calgary that the long publication process ended and the book finally appeared. The book garnered quite favorable reviews and proved largely instrumental in my return to the US professional theological community. It was also a factor in my receiving the John Courtney Murray Award, the Catholic Theological Society of America's highest mark of recognition. Shortly thereafter I was elected to the Society's board of directors, and soon after I joined the faculty at Holy Cross I was serving as the Society's president. Probably my chief contribution to the CTSA's advancement was supporting the admission and influence of women, as well as scholars from other denominations.

Comprised of five parts, Ministry to Word and Sacraments *examines history and constructs theology for what Cooke identified as five fundamental categories of ecclesial service: ministry as formation of community, ministry to God's word, service to human needs, ministering to God's judgment, and sacramental ministry. Primary among the five is the formation of community, for Christianity's fundamental character is as a people called and formed by God. In the following, Cooke moves into constructing the basic parameters for a theology of ministry on the basis of ecclesiology, specifically, what the Church's mission as salvation is and how unity, not uniformity, characterizes the bond forged by the Spirit of the risen Christ through ongoing tradition (MWS 190–97).*

Ministry as Formation of Community[1]

If a particular understanding of the risen Christ and of "salvation" is integral to one's soteriology, so also is the view one has of the Church and specifically of the Church's role in the process of Christ saving mankind. This will touch upon the manner in which one understands the relationship between "internal" and "external" aspects of the Church; but inevitably, a discussion about Christian ministry and its soteriological role must draw attention to the external aspects, the institutionalization, of the Christian community. And perhaps most basically, it must face the question, What difference does it make whether a certain agent of salvation or a certain course of saving activity is "official"? It seems difficult to countenance the notion that the divine saving action is tied to the exercise of jurisdictional power within the Church; yet centuries of Christian faith have seen this as a correct reading of "Whatever you bind on earth will be bound in heaven...." In this context, obedience to the Church, which has usually meant obedience to Church officials and to the laws they have enacted, is equivalently obedience to God, and therefore the condition for achieving one's destiny.

Certainly, one cannot dismiss the real function of the Christian community and its official leadership in the work of salvation;

---

1. Published in the 1970s, the copyrighted material reproduced here does not meet contemporary standards for gender-inclusive language. *(Ed. note.)*

to do so would be to reduce the Church to a parasitic and introverted existence. Yet, it seems self-evident that the leadership of the Christian community should be helping the members of that community to develop their own personal integrity and autonomy, and to grow in their own capacity to form conscience judgments appropriate to the situations of life. These leaders should not presume to be the conscience of the Christian people, providing a detailed listing of *dos* and *don'ts* that will eliminate people's need to make their own critical choices. Again, it seems quite apparent that the leadership of the Church should be encouraging people to confront maturely the realities of their world, which means facing the presence of evil and the tension of "worldly" values with the viewpoint of the gospel. Certainly, this requires prudent preparation of Christians for what is a difficult and challenging task; it also requires guidance and counsel during the actual conduct of Christian life. But it does not imply the kind of paternalistic protection from reality which denies to people the opportunity to exercise their Christian responsibilities.

History indicates, however, that it is all too easy for Church officials to drift into such a paternalistic understanding of pastoral care and for the bulk of Christians to accept, even welcome, such an approach. Hidden in this situation is a theological understanding of "salvation" which sees the Christianization of the individual as an almost magical process, a process in which his own activity is merely a condition that must be fulfilled so that God will bless and sanctify him as a reward. Accompanying such a view of salvation is an interpretation of "mediation" (obviously, mediation by those in official positions) that has consistently bothered thoughtful Christians through many centuries. It is an interpretation that stresses both in doctrine and religious practice the need for ordinary Christians to reach God *through* the activity of Church officials. Whether this view be right or wrong, it is quite clear that it conditions basically the manner in which one thinks about the role of the Church's ordained ministers.

"Models" of the Church

Not completely separate from the implicit soteriologies we have been discussing, but distinct and important enough to merit special attention in any discussion of Christian ministry and priesthood, are the "models" according to which Christians have viewed the Church. What lies behind the importance of these models is the controlling influence of sense experience and imagination on all levels, even the most "rational," of human consciousness. Historically, a number of models (military, political, medical, etc.) have shaped Christian understanding of the Church; often, several models have been simultaneously operative at a given point in history, or for that matter in the consciousness of an individual Christian. To describe them, however briefly, will aid us in clarifying and appraising the various ways in which Christian ministry has been understood.

One of the most basic, but also one of the most elusive, models for the Church is that of the "moral entity." Whether one uses an image such as "holy mother Church" or not, there is a certain personification of the Church as a protecting or directing agent that acts upon Christians and to whom Christians are to relate themselves in loyalty and devotion. This "moral entity" is not identified with the Christians who make up the Church, not even in their corporate Christian existence; rather, it has a certain identity of its own. This identity is real and powerful in the consciousness of Christians, so real and powerful that the bulk of Christians have lost for many centuries the sense of themselves being the Church: "the Church" is this other reality to which they are related through faith and religious practice. While this mythic figure of the Church first took on historically the character of "sacred personality," it quickly assumed characteristics of "legal personality." The Church came to be identified increasingly with its governing structures, an identification made both by rulers and by the ruled. It is both interesting and instructive to study the manner in which ordained ministers (particularly those in administrative activity) have often felt a greater concern about this "mythic Church" than about the Christian people who are the Church.

Another model which inevitably affects one's notion of the Church is the cosmological myth that is prevalent in a culture at a given historical period. One possibility is that one views the Church as an integral component of the cosmic geography; the other possibility is that the Church in its structure is paralleled to the structure attributed to the cosmos. There are instances of both possibilities in the history of the Church. Perhaps the clearest instance of this sort of thing, and certainly one of the most influential, was the

Dionysian image of the stratified (hierarchical) Church fitting into the larger stratified structure of the created universe. And as an instance of the manner in which attributes drawn from the cosmic myth are transferred to one's understanding of the Church, we might cite the recurrent (and futile) hope of "restoration." This dream of going back to the "good old days" before the French Revolution, or before the Reformation, or before the "Catholicizing" of the primitive Church is closely linked to the view that there exists some ideal structure for the world and the Church, that this ideal guided God in creating the world and in instituting the Church, that man in his capitulation of evil, has turned away from the ideal structure, and that we should work to restore things to the way they once were and really ought to be. Quite evidently, such a view of the world and of the Church is radically incapable of confronting the evidence that has driven modern thought to an evolutionary understanding of man and the world.

Still another model that has exerted major influence on Christian thinking about the Church is the political model. Christianity is not, of course, unique in transferring to religion the images drawn from man's political activity; many other religions have imagined that the "heavenly city" was conducted along the same lines as the "earthly city." Still, the application of the political image to the Christian Church has had a major impact on the historical evolution of ecclesiastical institutions and of theology about the Church. And this kind of "politicizing" of Christianity was carried still further as the Church acquired for many centuries the dubious privilege of being the "established religion."

Connected with this political model is the long-standing argument about the nature of authority in the Church. Is it permanently determined by divine institution to be monarchical, or can it adjust in certain historical situations (such as the twentieth century) to a more democratic form of governance? Actually, the Christian community may not be faced with such an "either/or"; it may well be that the course of action open to us is not a shift from one political model (monarchy) to another (democracy) but entirely away from a political model. There is enough evidence, both scriptural and historical, to suggest that such a shift would not only be permissible but even highly desirable.

Since mankind's political activity has almost always included the conduct of war, it is not surprising that the military model has colored Christian notions about the Church. The Christian community is God's army, pledged to waging for him a holy war against the forces of evil; the ordained ministers of the Church are the officers in that army. Historically, it has not always been clear whether Christians in a given context were fighting God's wars or whether they were enlisting God to fight with them in their own wars. But there is no question about the prominence and powerful influence of the image of the "crusade." Such an image may have attached to it a certain glamour and overtones of heroism, but its application to Christian life in the Church is more than dubious. It carries with it the isolationist connotations of the Church being a fortress that protects Christians on the inside from the evils of the outside world and from which these Christians sally forth to demolish "the heathen and the infidel."

The incompatibility of the fortress image of the Church becomes quite clear when we bring it into conjunction with a New Testament passage such as Ephesians 2:14, which speaks of Christ as "our peace, who has...broken down the dividing walls of hostility." Such incompatibility is less clear when we come to the monastic model; it also has implications of "walls," implications of "retreat from the world," and implications of stratification within the Christian community. But it is not clear whether such implications are intrinsic to formally dedicated religious community life or whether they have somewhat accidentally accrued to it in the historical evolution of religious orders. This much seems clear: such dedicated Christian communities have been and still are seen as attempts to live Christianity more intensely. Therefore, they should logically serve as models for Christian life as a whole, though at the same time the life of the community as a whole is a norm for what the dedicated religious communities should be. Historically, the application of the monastic model depended upon the actual structure and conduct of monastic communities, which were not always ideal and to some extent at least were rooted in truncated soteriology. Moreover, the application of the monastic model to the Church as a whole was a negative one. The monastic ideals and way of life were not meant for "ordinary" Christians, the laity were nonmonks and therefore not intended to pursue Christian contemplation, just as they were nonclerics and therefore intended to be receptive rather than active members of the Church. The "walls" of the monastic model have existed not only between the monastery and the world but between the monastery and the rest of the Church.

The use of one or another model is probably unavoidable in the Christian's thought about the Church, but an awareness of the distortion that such use introduces into our understanding should lead to two conclusions. First, if some model does promise to be helpful as an aid to formulating Christian insight about the reality of Christian community existence, then we should use it critically, knowing that we are involved with metaphor and must therefore be careful not to overapply the metaphor. Second, and more important, we should let the Christian community be what it is and not try to categorize it as something else. Our starting point in probing its deeper reality must be our experience of being the Church, an experience that we try to understand as accurately as possible by the use of "scientific" methodologies (whether sociological, or psychological, or phenomenological, or some other) and by studying the centuries-long experience of Christians before us. This experience, both immediate and vicarious, should provide our basic image of the Church. Such use of our own experience of participation in the Christian community as the model for understanding the Church is, of course, precarious. Our particular experience (of liturgy, Christian service, etc.) may not be adequate; it may even be traumatic and misleading. But only if our view of the nature of Christianity is grounded in our own experience can membership in the Christian community be interiorized and become part of the living faith of individual Christians.

The Theology of Ministry

If the "experiential" model is to be basic to our understanding of the Church (and elements in it such as its ministry), a historical-descriptive method by which one gains knowledge about the present reality of the Church through recapturing as far as possible the experience of Christianity's origin and evolution must play a central role in an ecclesiology. However, even if one attempts to pursue this method as objectively as possible, it is impossible to do so without theological presuppositions—more specifically in this case, without one or other of the soteriological stances we described earlier. There can be widespread agreement

181

that the Church finds its origin in the death and resurrection of Jesus of Nazareth, but at the same time, widespread disagreement as to the meaning of such a statement.

Taking the soteriological viewpoint that *resurrection* means that Jesus of Nazareth continues to live and work as Christ and Lord and that he is constantly present to the Christian community in a variety of ways, then the "originating" of the Church through the death and resurrection of Christ is an ongoing historical process. One can, obviously, single out the temporal beginnings of this process and refer to that as "the origin of the Church"; but it would be a mistake to limit to that brief period of history Christ's input into the existence of the Christian community. To take seriously the presence of Christ to the Church or the animation of the historically evolving Church by the Spirit of Christ is to admit that terms such as "institution by Christ" or *de jure divino* cannot be limited to the earliest decades of Christianity. Not just the first community of his immediate disciples but the Church in its entire historical development comes into being under the impact of the risen Christ and his Spirit.

Without taking any particular theological interpretation of either Christian faith or the Church, it seems apparent that the Christian community is dynamically constituted by a shared faith in Christ, by a shared experience of his continuing presence. This is ultimately the distinctive characteristic of the Church, that which differentiates it from other religious or social groupings. Yet, in any given historical situation, the sociological reality of the Church does not correspond totally to this a priori judgment. The common unifying attitude, to the extent that there is one, is a mixture of religious and ethical and social viewpoints in which the specifically Christian point of view can be overshadowed by opinions that are either unrelated or opposed to the basic traditions of Christianity. Not infrequently, the mentality of the Christian Church has drifted toward a legalistic and moralizing view of Christian community existence. Absorption with external structures and practices has drawn attention away from the unifying activity of Christ's Spirit. Even more paradoxically, the critical role of Jesus as unique mediator between man and God has been professed verbally but not honored practically. A critical aspect of this has been the way in which classical trinitarian theology has largely bypassed the historical reality of the man Jesus. The basic problem with such views is that they thwart the authentic existence and evolution of the Church. They tend to make it a religious group committed to a "revealed message" rather than a community formed by shared devotion to a person.

But if one does retain the insight of Christ's presence to the Church and his continuing gift of the Spirit, an insight that has never been completely absent from Christian consciousness, it is possible to speak meaningfully of the Church as "the extension of Christ in history," not in the sense that Christians are the successors of Jesus but in the sense that they are a sacrament through which he can still make himself redemptively present to human history. Retention or loss of this insight has played an important role in Christian understanding of ordained ministry. It has been quite common to speak of ordained ministers as "legates of Christ" or "representatives of Christ" or even "vicars of Christ." But these and similar designations can be understood within the context of the entire Church embodying and sacramentalizing the presence of Christ, or they can express the idea that the ordained ministry "carries on" for Christ here below, since he himself has gone up to heaven. The latter view, which is patently grounded in an image of Christ "going up to heaven" in resurrection and ascension, has had incredible influence on centuries of Christian thinking and has been the source of no end of theological and ecclesiastical conflict.

One of the less happy developments in the Church's self-understanding was the gradual limitation to the ordained clergy of the notion of actively representing Christ. Though intrinsically it was the entire community that was body and sacrament, the bulk of Christians (the laity) was early reduced to passivity within the life of the Church. This passivity found expression in the laity's role (or lack of role) in liturgy, in the retreat of laity from more active evangelical witness, and most basically in the laity's Christian self-image. Fortunately, in more recent times, there has been recovery of the understanding that the entire Christian community is the body of Christ, sharing in Christ's prophetic-priestly role, "ordained" in baptism to evangelical witness, to concerned service in the world, and to eucharistic worship of the Father in union with Christ.

During the centuries-long evolution of the Church, one of the critical objectives of Christians, and especially of Church officials, has been the preservation of genuine unity. However, though the effort to achieve or maintain a true community has pervaded the Church's history, the understanding of the unity that would be desirable has been drastically different from one historical period to another or from one group of Christians to another. In the twentieth century, as we struggle to clarify our goals in the effort of ecumenical reunion, we are living through one of the clearest instances of such differing views of "desirable Christian unity."

From the beginning of Christian history, there has been the recognition that sin and error are divisive influences and that they must be curbed if the Christian community is not to fragment. Without disagreeing with this basic insight into the need for some discipline in Christian doctrine and behavior, one can disagree with the manner in which such discipline has often been sought. There has been a recurring ecclesiastical policy that the key to the solution lies in increased centralization of authority and administration and in monolithic formulation of doctrine, submission to this formulation being obtained through the centralized Church government. Such an approach has had short-term success, particularly when Christians have believed their salvation to be conditioned by ecclesiastical jurisdiction. But it does not take account of the legitimate pluralism that exists in Christian insight and conscience, a pluralism that is not only unavoidable and therefore tolerable but that is positively desirable because it is an expression of the catholicity of Christian faith.

It would be presumptuous to suggest any ready and simple solution to the problem of obtaining genuine unity of faith without jeopardizing individual belief and freedom of conscience. Yet, it is clear that two elements must be part of any realistic and viable solution. There must be some form of "spiritual direction" that can guide Christians as they form their own understandings and conscience according to the most authentic insights and traditions of Christianity, and as the ground for such practical spiritual direction, there must be a developed pneumatology which can aid the Christian community (and its individual members) in the perennial and difficult task of "discerning the Spirit." No amount of threat or coercion by ecclesiastical officials, no amount of doctrinal decrees, can substitute for these two elements in obtaining genuine unity of faith within the Church.

In the complex dialectic that constantly brings into being a living community such as the Church, the inviolability of individual faith and freedom must interact with the corporate understanding and decisions of the community, and both individual and corporate faith of Christians at any given time in history must resonate creatively and compatibly with the faith of earlier Christian generations. This raises the whole question of "tradition," its nature, its limits, and the instruments of its operation. As in so many other questions that we have mentioned, there can be no hope of giving a definitive response, but it does seem that "tradition" and allied notions such as "apostolic succession" must relate most basically to the Christian community as a whole. Certain agencies, for example, the episcopacy, may have a specific function relative to the preservation, development, and transmission of the Christian faith; however, the process of tradition is not confined to any such agency (or group of agencies) but rather involves the complementary activity of the entire Church.

For most of the Church's history, the problem of fostering the appropriate kind of unity within the Church has been aggravated by the intertwining of ecclesial and civil interests and structures; the effort to maintain the unity of the Church has often been inseparably mixed with efforts to achieve political unity. Church and civil governments have frequently depended upon one another for support; each has expected the other to use its power to preserve the situation in which authority is respected and laws observed and unity thereby preserved. For many centuries, the interpenetration of the civil and the ecclesiastical was linked with the notion of the *societas christiana*, the view that there was the one Christian people with two complementary leaderships, civil and ecclesiastical rulers. Ideal as this notion of a unified society might seem, and it has not yet died for those who dream of a "restoration," both historical experience and theological analysis indicate that it is unworkable and undesirable. To give just one basic reason: the kind of unity proper to the Christian Church, a unity that is grounded in genuine communication of faith among Christians, cannot possibly come by law and government either civil or ecclesiastical. There is no easy way to achieve the unity of the Church, precisely because it is, and is meant to be, a living and evolving reality. Some tension among "competing" groups and goals and insights and values is inevitable and, if confronted positively and resolved in a spirit of genuine charity, a source of creativity and enrichment. Unification of the worldwide Church is desirable, but it should not be achieved in a manner that destroys the healthy autonomy of the local Christian community. Considerable pluralism in theological opinion, in liturgical expression, in styles of spirituality, even in doctrinal formulation, can be a sign of catholicity; but it must be accompanied by the basic agreement about faith and life which permits men and women to identify with one another as Christians. Or again, institutionalization is unavoidable and appropriate external structures can enable a community of people to express their corporate existence and achieve their corporate goals; but structures tend always to grow rigid and self-perpetuating, and so the Church must always work to maintain flexibility in faith formulas and religious practices.

As one reflects on the historical evolution of the Church and on the extent to which a truly fraternal community in faith has characterized that evolving experience, it becomes clear that one of the enduring divisions within the Church has been that between clergy and laity. Perhaps it would be better to modify that judgment and situate the division between rulers and ruled, for in many situations, the lower clergy have tended to identify with the people and form a community with them rather than with the ruling group in the Church. On the other hand, those in positions of power and authority have consistently identified with one another in a special fashion and formed a "community of rulers" within the larger community of believers. Quite early in the Church's history, this special status of the ruling group within the Church was canonized as being "of divine institution"; and even when, as in the Protestant Reformation, there were groups that refused the authority of these rulers and formed their own Christian communities, some form of division between clergy and laity quickly arose in these communities.

Without denying the obvious need for leadership in any community of human beings, nor the fact that different persons in the Church will have quite different degrees of commitment to Christianity and consequently different degrees of involvement in and responsibility for the activity of the Church, we can say that the understanding of authority in the life of the Church must be basically changed, that there is no place in the Church for "rulers," and that the clergy/laity division was to a large extent the deviation from the authentic ideal of Christian community, and no theological justification can be found for allowing it to continue. This does not deny the intrinsic need for specialized ministries in the Church, nor the need for certain individuals to be officially ordained for one or other of these ministries. What it does deny is the equation of designated (ordained) ministry with either "superior status" or "ruling."

Order in Church Ministry

Doctoral studies in 1950s Paris proved crucial to the formation of Cooke's critical perspective on ecclesiology and ministry. While this should not be surprising, given the fact that his Jesuit superiors sent him there in preparation for a theological career forming the laity, an unexpected and, indeed, unsettling counterpoint to his positively benefitting from the newly formed catechetical faculty of the Institut Catholique was his exposure to the brutal ecclesial politics the Vatican was exercising over theologians and pastors in France.

I gained so much from both the lectures and practical experiences at the *Catechetique*, but most valuable were the insights it gave me into the Church in France, into the dynamics of its stormy history, its ongoing conflict with Rome, as well as about the nature of the faith and ministry of the people. What was happening in France had not yet begun in the US, but experiencing it in France helped prepare me to understand what occurred in the US two or three decades later....Those were years when the tension between Rome and northern European theology swirled around the papal encyclical *Humani Generis*. That tension would find expression and partial resolution in the behind-the-scenes commission debates at Vatican II, but in the mid-1950s, it was still to a large extent a "witch hunt" directed against the *nouvelle théologie*. Teilhard had earlier been exiled to the United States. The Holy Office decimated the Jesuit faculty in Lyon-Fourviere by removing key faculty. Congar, Chenu, and Liégé at Saulchoir were under attack from Garrigou-Lagrange and his allies, and in Paris, it was a regular thing to have both Vatican visitors and *monita* warning French theologians and ecclesiastical authorities of dangerous ideas and liturgical experiments. While I personally was not as a student directly involved in this conflict, it was the atmosphere of Catholic life in postwar France. Quite simply it was the concrete experience of conflicting ecclesiologies, an experience that did much to destroy my earlier naiveté about the nature and exercise of authority in the Church.

The saddest part of this theological persecution was its damage to persons and stifling of creative thought. One case I experienced vicariously. George Morel, one of my former tertian companions in Germany, a brilliant philosophical theologian, was understudy to Henri de Lubac and slated to succeed him on the faculty at Lyon-Fourviere. When, however, a Vatican official came to examine the "dangerous" teaching of the French Jesuits, George defended de Lubac, causing Rome to bar him from teaching theology on a pontifical faculty. Reacting calmly, "It's all part of the dialectic," George went on to become a leading expert on John of the Cross.

> The Marquette chapter of his memoir conveys how Cooke's engagements as an expert theological consultant locally, nationally, and internationally exposed him to a succession of dispiriting encounters with clerical power in the Roman ecclesial system. These led to identifying clericalism (as distinct from the objective need for ministerial offices) as the fundamental problem afflicting the renewal and advancement of the Church's mission. His account exudes empathy for not only the laity but also the lower ranks of the ordained, themselves pastorally limited by, if not often quite alienated from, the hierarchy's clerically constricting agenda.

Although there was no clear focus to my theologizing on the issue of Christian ministry, much of what I was doing dealt with it, and the research I was doing led eventually to my *Ministry to Word and Sacraments*. As my research dealt more and more with the process of Christianity's origin and historical evolution, I was inevitably dealing with ministry, i.e., what were Christians doing? For better or worse, this along with my experience of dealing with authorities within the Church fed into a hermeneutic of suspicion that increasingly questioned the "official" descriptions of Christianity's history. I was certainly not exceptional in this regard. As far back as Duchesne in the late nineteenth century and continuing through a line of historians and theologians like Chenu and Congar, critical scholarship had been gradually demythologizing the standard histories of the Church and particularly of the papacy. Personally, as I was increasingly exposed to this scholarship, I passed from a naïve understanding of the Church to one that was realistic. This was reinforced by my experience of the Vatican witch hunt during the time of my study in France, even more by immediate observation of how things worked at the Vatican.

Before I go further in the narrative, let me interject a remark: as I experienced the operations of the top levels of Church authority, I gained a great deal of respect for many men who were part of this world, were aware of its many negativities, and yet were able to work in it honestly. One instance may illustrate the point. After Vatican II, it was necessary to follow up many of the Council's innovative decrees by practical directives for application. One of these areas was the Catholic Church's new attitude toward ecumenism. A directory for ecumenical activity was needed. A small working group, international in its membership and led by Cardinal Willebrands, was established to produce such a directory. We met twice for a week each time and managed to produce the required document. Several months intervened between the two gatherings, and when we came to Rome for the second section of the directory, we had not yet seen any reaction to the first we had written earlier. When we asked Willebrands about it, he smiled and said, "It was lost."

Then he explained that incredible remark. At that time, the Holy Office (now the Congregation for the Doctrine of the Faith) demanded that they screen any document produced at the Vatican, so our document had been sent to the Holy Office and promptly "lost." Willebrands assured us that it could not really be lost because, as was the regular practice, its delivery had been by bonded messenger, with a record of the Holy Office having received it. A week before our second session, Pope Paul noticed that our committee was on his calendar and asked to read our earlier document, at which point the Holy Office immediately "found" it.

So, we spent a second week of hard work in two groups, English-speaking and French-speaking, integrated the work of the two, and translated the result into Latin. We finished with a sigh of relief, but the chairperson of the committee assured us that there was one more step. Our document would have to pass through Holy Office inspection, so we needed to insert a few "red herrings," that is, statements that were clearly unacceptable. Authorities at the Holy Office would self-righteously discover the passages, delete them, and thereby approve our intended document.

This instance of senseless game-playing in order to affirm presumed power was harmless. But enough of the operation of ecclesiastical authorities, especially under Paul VI's successor, was so destructively cruel as to bother me. I had hoped the deplorable tactics witnessed in the days of *Humani Generis* had ended with Vatican II, but not so. The later papal abuse of the Jesuit general Pedro Arrupe, an exercise of raw power and illegitimate use of authority, I found deeply disturbing.

What eventuated for me—and I can only say was my personal reaction—was a judgment that the entire structure of clericalism that had dominated the life of Western Christianity from at least the eleventh century was a deviation from authentic Christianity, countered only by thousands of heroic individuals, both within and outside clerical circles, who lived out the gospel in tension with ecclesiastic power structures. Frankly, it did and still does seem to me that clericalism has been a deleterious force within the Church for centuries. That leadership is needed, that some public approval, "ordination," of designated leaders is helpful, that some structuring of authority is appropriate, yes. But that is different from "clergy." Clergy is not a sacramental reality but a social arrangement of privilege and division within the community of the baptized.

My discontent with clericalism and judgment that it had been a historical detriment to the Church did not come simply as a negative attitude. What was happening to me during the years of my life at Marquette was a slowly deepening personal identity with the nonordained that inevitably transformed my doing theology. Really, that was logical. The fundamental mission given me by my Jesuit superiors, for which I'd trained, was to present Christianity in a plausible way to laywomen and -men. To do that, I had to enter their world of faith, to understand and live Christianity "in the world," to be in a "secular" sense "contemplative in action." Very central to my shifting religious identity was the realization early in my years in Milwaukee that the Church was people and that I was one of those people. True, something had happened in my presbyteral ordination: I was designated and committed to serve people by dedicated exercise of Word and Sacrament. But I was not raised to a higher level, did not become a superior Christian, part of the inner circle. I truly admired many of the priests and bishops with whom I worked closely in those years, men who viewed their authority in terms of service, but I also observed and to some extent shared the "unreal" reverence for their "sacredness" and the many privileges accorded them. It finally came to the point when I could no longer see myself as a cleric, though at one level, I have never ceased to be a Jesuit.

Whether justified or not, my discontent with clericalism came to focus on the Vatican. I was quite aware that a huge and centuries-old bureaucracy was bound to operate at times in an abrasive manner. What bothered me was the cruelty with which several priests who had come to me for counsel were handled by ecclesial authorities. In one case, it led to a severe mental breakdown. Even more disturbing was Rome's patriarchal domination of women religious in the US. Some of the demands laid upon them by "visitors" from the Vatican would have been laughable had they not been so petty and disrespectful of those dedicated women's intelligence and professional competence. Thank God there were some fearless leaders among them who stood their ground to undertake the revision of religious life according to the vision of Vatican II.

During my last summer before leaving Marquette, I had one last chance to test the validity of my decision. I accepted an invitation from Maryknoll missionaries in Uganda and Tanzania to lecture on Vatican II and its implications for the Church in Africa. What I observed in the weeks I traveled around East Africa was the Vatican's broad effort to Romanize African Catholicism, a policy clearly doomed to eventual failure. In instance after instance, there was clear manifestation of European disregard for the equality and competence of the Africans. Fortunately, this was not true of the missionaries actually working with the people;

most of them disagreed with the attitudes and actions of authorities Rome imposed on the local church.

One happening said it all for me. That summer was a period of preparation for one of the early post–Vatican II synods of bishops. Many of the native African bishops wanted debate on clerical celibacy, a critical issue for Africa. Some of us were able to read Rome's response, a letter that had been smuggled out of a local chancery addressed to bishops in Africa, advising them not to raise the question. What I found completely unacceptable was the one-sentence closing paragraph: "Do not forget you are funded by Propaganda"—the Vatican agency financially supporting Catholic institutions in mission countries.

While Cooke's extensive historical research for Ministry to Word and Sacraments *sought to demonstrate the material, ideological, and theological conditions giving rise to and changing the various major types of service in the Church, he identified the clerical power system as the irreducible factor obstructing practical reform and renewal. In our own day, frank awareness of the controlling power of the clerical ranks over the life of the Church has come in Pope Francis's pithy exhortations that cardinals not rule like princes, bishops "smell of the sheep," priests not act as cruel judges but merciful pastors, and seminaries stop producing "little monsters" inflicted on the laity. But whereas Pope Francis's admonitions address clerical attitudes, Cooke's writings on the sacrament of orders essay theological justification for overturning the entire clerical system, reorienting ordained ministry to the sacramentality of the Church in its members. In an article for the journal of the Canon Law Society of America, Cooke consolidated his argument for how the question of sacramental orders bears fundamental implications for the saving mission and identity of the Church (Jurist 410–18):*

Fullness of Orders

Dogmatic Authority

To what extent, then, does Vatican II's Constitution on the Church contain normative teaching that sets the limits within which change of ministerial structure can occur in Roman Catholicism? First, the strict dogmatic issue must be settled by going beyond Vatican II itself: the Council fathers propose their text as teaching but not as solemn teaching.[2] In matters pertaining to relative powers in the Church, they rest upon Vatican I in large part; in matters concerning Christian sacraments, they draw from Trent.[3] So, the dogmatic status of texts from these two councils that carry over into Vatican II must be evaluated in their original *Sitz im Leben* as well as in their usage (or modification) by Vatican II. Secondly, in the delicate task of situating all this in the centuries-long history of Christian tradition and process of doctrinal development, the text of *Lumen Gentium* (and the process from which it emerged) provides relatively little assistance, since the utilization of biblical and patristic sources is governed by the proof-text mentality and takes little account of critical textual or historical methodologies.[4] Thirdly, the statements of Vatican II (and the understandings that produced them) rest on a number of theological and doctrinal presuppositions whose verifiability conditions the normative force of the council's teaching.[5] The remainder of this essay will be directed to reflection on some of these theological issues. Mere listing of them makes it evident that the understanding of "fullness of orders" lies close to the center of present-day ecclesiology and soteriology.

---

2. Foundation for the normative limitation on changes within the Church, if there is such, would have to be the element of "divine institution" of the episcopacy; and it is precisely on this point that the text (20) says, "This sacred synod teaches that by divine institution bishops have succeeded to the place of the apostles as shepherds of the Church." Cf. Karl Rahner, in *Commentary on the Documents of Vatican II*, ed. Heribert Vorgrimler, vol. 4 (New York: Herder & Herder, 1969), 191.

3. The Council text itself indicates this in the notes relating to the key sections of chapter 3.

4. As an alternative approach to many of the same texts, cf. the historical portions of my *Ministry to Word and Sacraments: History and Theology* (Minneapolis: Fortress Press, 1976), which try to give a contextual understanding of the biblical and patristic statements relative to episcopacy and Christian ministry.

5. Christian faith today is to be guided by the faith of earlier councils more ultimately than by the (historically relativized) expressions of that faith found in council statements. Trent's discussion of original sin and its removal by baptism provides a classic instance of the need to distinguish between the truth attached to underlying faith insights and the truth of those interpretive elements that influence a given formulation of that faith: contained in any Tridentine statement about baptism removing original sin is the understanding that there was an actual historical happening in which two historic personages, our "first parents," performed a gravely sinful act. The truth or falsity of this understanding clearly affects the normative role of Tridentine statements about baptism (and original sin); we are driven to seek the deeper norm of Tridentine faith in baptism as salvation from sin.

Theological Questions

1. Vatican II's approach to episcopal power brings us immediately into contact with the tension between differing "models" for thinking about the Church. Both New Testament scholarship and emphasis on the Church as a community that lives by faith have brought to the fore an "organic" model—the Church as Body of Christ, animated by the Spirit, growing into eschatological fulfillment by increasing participation in the new life of the risen Lord.[6] Yet, the "hierarchical" model, whether stressing its more political aspect or its "causation from above" aspect, is quite clearly that which controlled the bishops' understanding of themselves at Vatican II. Now, one need not, probably should not, opt for only one model as the way of thinking about the Church—the Pauline mixture of body/building/bride imagery indicates this. Yet, it does make a basic difference whether one views the Spirit as working "from outside" upon the community through the mediation of the hierarchy who to some extent stand above the faithful, or whether the Spirit is viewed as working from within the community and as "the mission of the Church," bringing into being those agencies (including the bishops) that are needed for the Church's life and priestly ministry. Again, it makes considerable difference whether one uses a "participation" or a *communio* model for understanding the sharing of Christian ministry.[7] And it does make a difference in appraising the normative force of official teaching about the nature of the Church to be conscious that these official statements are employing one or other model. Even if such statements do legitimately and rather accurately reflect the reality of the Church, they do not do so adequately.[8]

2. Interlocking somewhat with this shift in models is the dialectic between function and institutional structure, a dialec-

---

6. Cf. Avery Dulles, *Models of the Church* (Garden City, NY: Doubleday, 1974).

7. This is not to say that one identifies the missionary teleology of the Church with the Spirit; rather, the Spirit is the indwelling though transcendent principle of that teleology. On the NT roots of this view, cf. James D. G. Dunn, *Jesus and the Spirit* (Philadelphia: Westminster, 1975). It would make an interesting theological study to combine Dunn's insights with the various points of view expressed in the Canon Law Society's seminar on the Church as *mission* (published in *The Jurist* 39 [1979]: 1–288).

8. What this means is that the principle *ecclesia semper reformanda* has to be applied to the cognitive order, and that the complementarity intrinsic to genuine religious pluralism must be respected as an asset to faith.

tic that exists both in reality and in our view of that reality.[9] For a variety of reasons, recent theological thought has moved away from a long-standing attention to the structures and dealt more with processes. The change in approach has affected all facets of theological consideration, from trinity to eschatology.

The ecclesiological explanation one gives of the relation between form and function will ground any judgment about the continuity or discontinuity of structures such as the episcopate. Moreover, it will radically affect the way in which one interprets the historical evolution of tradition in the Church. Diversity of viewpoints on this matter underlies much of the Reformation and post-Reformation controversy about the nature of the Church and of its ministering agencies.

Because function and form are inseparable in the actual historical reality of the Church, the view one takes of their relationship conditions one's understanding of the Church's history.[10] And to that extent, it conditions the judgment one makes about the necessity or contingency of any particular ecclesiastical institution.

3. To make the last remark more precise, one could point to the ambiguity of *koinonia* in Acts 2: does it denominate the observable social reality of the early Christian community or the process of sharing that unites them?[11] Closer to our present discussion would be the multivalence of the key term *munus*,[12] which is the operative word in Vatican II discussion of the episcopal function. In itself *munus* can refer to a responsibility or function, whether societally stabilized or not, though it tends to denominate something fairly permanent.[13] It can, of course, refer to a

---

9. For an interesting and productive application of this dialectic, cf. the December 1976 issue of *Theological Studies*, especially the interacting articles of Roger Haight and Robert Sears.

10. For the most part, histories of the Church have concentrated on the structural elements and on official activities; there is surprisingly little historical study of the faith and prayer and inner spiritual life of the Christian people, even little study of the activities of evangelization or sacramental celebration. Even exceptions like H. Bremond's classic on the "French school" deal more with the more notable expressions of Christian faith and do not describe the spiritual state of the community as a whole.

11. Cf. R. P. C. Hanson, *The Acts* (Oxford: Oxford University Press, 1967), 70n42; Ernst Haenchen, *Apostelgeschichte* (Göttingen, 1961), 152–53.

12. The word *officium* occurs three times in the chapter (25, 26, 28), but with the meaning of "duty," not as an alternative to *munus*; what does occur as something of an equivalent for *munus* is *ministerium*.

13. *Oxford Latin Dictionary*, ed. P. G. W. Glare (Oxford: Clarendon, 1976), 1146.

publicly (even legally) established role and authority, in which case it can be translated "office."

This imprecision of *munus* carries over into present discussion of Christian ministry. For one thing, questions are being raised about the appropriateness of jurisdictional power in the Church, especially when this notion is applied to teaching and sanctifying.[14] Responding to such challenges (which obviously touch the Catholic episcopacy's claim to fullness of orders), some theologians, Karl Rahner among them,[15] stress the intrinsic need for structure and order in any ongoing human society. Such a response does not really come to grips with the issue. Granted that enduring human communities need some stable, even explicitly established institutions, including some recognized leadership roles, this need not involve jurisdiction. An educational institution, for example, only accidentally (for purposes of service and management) includes some jurisdictional functions and roles—though often this principle is forgotten as education becomes controlled and administrators conduct themselves as rulers. Essentially, achievement of a school's purpose and the leadership guiding that achievement are grounded in the knowledge possessed by the teachers and in their pedagogical skills; that is its own kind of authority, but quite other than official jurisdiction.

Given the difficulties involved in unifying the millions of humans who comprise the Catholic Church, it may be strategically prudent, perhaps practically necessary, to introduce some jurisdic-

---

14. Given the importance of the notion for the thesis of this present essay, it might be well to clarify the meaning of *jurisdiction* as used here. Basically, the historical use of the term grew out of the legal function of passing judgment, especially in Roman law. Christian ecclesiastical use broadened that meaning to the more general sense of "the power to govern." Morsdorf, in the article on jurisdiction in *Lexikon für Theologie and Kirche*, col. 1220, sees the Church usage as including the classic three functions: legislative, executive, and judicial (*Gesetzgebung, Rechtsprechung, Verwaltung*); and in his article in *Sacramentum Mundi*, ed. Karl Rahner, Cornelius Ernst, and Kevin Smyth (New York: Herder and Herder, 1969), 3:229, he points out that jurisdiction is intrinsically linked to office. So, it is quite clear that the notion of jurisdiction is one that belongs to a legal/ political model for the Church, i.e., to a particular context and manner of governing. There are many other ways of guiding and directing a community, even other ways of governing; jurisdiction (as we have just described it) is an appropriate way of governing the Church only if the legal/ political model is an appropriate way of understanding the nature of the Church.

15. See, for example, "Aspects of the Episcopal Office," *Theological Investigations*, ed. David Bourke, vol. 14 (New York: Seabury, 1976), 188: "The existence of this office is justified, rather, on the grounds that in the concrete it constitutes the legitimate and, in the long run historically speaking, indispensable way of ensuring the necessary continuity of the community of Jesus with its origins."

tional government into the Church's life. But if so, these institution-alized functions are not those through which the Church primarily attains its goals. It does the latter through other authority and other ministry: the authority and ministry of faith correctly understood, accurately communicated in teaching, and authentically witnessed to in sacrament. Some governing may be helpful in enabling the Church's ministry to the saving Word and Spirit of God; this governing is not the heart nor the source of such ministry.[16]

Without retreating from the view that some governing function may well be required in the Church—a charism of governing has been recognized from Christianity's beginnings as a gift of the Spirit to the community[17]—we might begin to stress more the need for unifying *leadership* within the Church. Such leadership is distinct from official administration or legal regulation, though there is still a widespread presumption in the Church that they are meant to coincide. At the same time, there is a centuries-old tension in Christianity, which has remained one of the principal sources of potential division, between the leadership of office and the leadership of sanctity.[18] Given the oft-remarked shift in the nature of leadership in today's world, the new modes and world-wide scope of communication which have qualitatively altered the manner in which the symbolic aspects of leadership can influence people, and the fact that in discussing episcopal fullness of orders we are dealing with a sacramental (i.e., symbolic) reality, it seems that we need serious and detailed theological discussion about the ministry of leadership within the Church.[19]

---

16. Obviously, this runs counter to the soteriological view that salvation can be effected precisely through *official* power.

17. Cf. 1 Cor 12:28.

18. I have tried to examine this issue at various points in my *Ministry to Word and Sacraments*, not just in the context of recurrent Donatism, but also as part of the differentiation between Latin and Eastern Christianity and part of a continuing tension between episcopacy and religious orders.

19. Such study would have to examine in depth the symbolic role of the bishops. This has already begun with recent reflection upon episcopal power as essentially sacramental. Karl Rahner has increasingly stressed this aspect of the episcopal function, which is significant in the light of his strong emphasis also on the juridical aspect of episcopacy. Cf. *Theological Investigations*, ed. David Bourke, vol. 12 (New York: Seabury, 1974), 44–45. This stress on the sacramental aspect is, of course, completely in line with Rahner's view of the Church's role as expressed in his *The Church and the Sacraments* (New York: Herder and Herder, 1963). On the evolution of Rahner's ecclesiology, cf. Leo O'Donovan, Michael Fahey, J. Peter Schineller, and John Galvin, "A Changing Ecclesiology in a Changing Church," *Theological Studies* 38 (1977): 736–62.

4. Any Catholic analysis of the sacramental aspect of ministry raises rather quickly the question of the priestly identity of the
hierarchy. Though *Lumen Gentium* speaks of the high priesthood
of the bishops as axiomatic, the history of the first two Christian
centuries raises serious questions about this claim.[20] But even if
one accepts the legitimacy of such an attribution, there is need to
ask what it means. On the basis of the classical explanation, the
priestly role possessed in fullness by the hierarchy consists in (a)
worship and (b) sanctification of the people.

Clearly, one's interpretation of episcopal priesthood rests on
a given understanding of the nature of Christian worship, above
all on a particular understanding of the eucharistic act. This is
not the place to suggest any given approach to eucharistic theology. But it does make a great deal of difference in our understanding of the bishops' high priesthood whether we see Eucharist as
an action of the entire community as body of Christ, or whether
we view it as the action of the celebrant attended by the people;
whether we see it as an enactment of a sacred somewhat hidden
mystery, or as the celebration of the community's daily experience of being humanly Christian.[21] Any claim to a privileged role
in Christian worship is, then, basically relativized by the nature of
the worship in question, and any theological insight into the bishops' high priesthood is conditioned radically by one's theology
of Christian worship. Again, the distinctiveness of the bishops'
power as sacred power is certainly affected by current theological
reflection on the relationship of sacred and secular, both in life
and in worship.[22]

The second element in Vatican II's description of episcopal
priesthood is the bishops' power to sanctify the faithful, particularly through administration of sacrament. Not only does the
understanding of this sanctifying activity rest on a view of the
way in which sacraments function; it rests on a particular soteriol-

---

20. Cf. bibliography accompanying pp. 523–53 in Cooke, *Ministry*.

21. Vatican II's constitution on the liturgy points toward increased emphasis on the human
aspects of eucharistic celebration; without denying an element of "mystery" in Christian
sacraments, it stresses the pastoral need for sacraments (especially Eucharist) to be easily
intelligible to people and to relate to Christians' daily lives.

22. Developments in "theologies of liberation" are perhaps the most striking example: it is
precisely in the domain of "secular" activity (political, social, economic involvement) that
the intervention of God's saving (sacral) action is seen to occur.

ogy. But, quite noticeably, a revolutionary development is taking place today in our soteriology—in our understanding of "grace," "divine providence," the presence of God to history, "resurrection," etc. For one thing, there has been renewed recognition that the individual person must be the principal human agent of his or her own salvation. This changing view of the reality of God's saving action in human life is already having major impact on Catholics' practical attitudes toward the ordained ministry; and probably the impact will grow.

One element of soteriology prominent in Vatican description of episcopal ministry is the notion that the bishop acts *in persona Christi* (*Lumen Gentium* 21). This expression has received various interpretations historically (e.g., the bishop is a sacrament of Christ, or is a legate of Christ); but all concur that the bishops, particularly as sacramental celebrants, somehow signify to the people Christ's own presence. Through the bishop, Christ makes himself salvifically present to the faithful; somehow the bishop embodies this presence.[23] However, such a view of the bishop acting *in persona Christi* has long stood in tension with the view that the liturgical celebrant acts *in persona ecclesiae*. This more ecclesial view of the celebrant's role has recently received increased attention and acceptance among Catholic theologians. Edward Kilmartin, for instance, in his 1975 article in *Theological Studies*, makes a convincing case for the position that the bishop sacramentalizes first and foremost the faith of the community.[24] Such a view points to those statements of *Lumen Gentium* that speak of the Church in its entirety as the sacrament of the risen Christ.[25]

This is not to deny a genuine sacramentality to the episcopate; it is just a question of what is salvifically signified. While this may seem an abstruse bit of theoretical distinction, it actually has great bearing on the objectives and therefore the practice of liturgical ceremonies. Vatican II apparently wished to link the

---

23. Though grounded in the theology of Augustine and Chrysostom, the formal theology of the *sacerdotium* (bishops and presbyters) sacramentalizing Christ's presence is largely a medieval creation; cf. pp. 575–82 in Cooke, *Ministry*.

24. Edward Kilmartin, "Apostolic Office: Sacrament of Christ," *Theological Studies* 36 (1975): 243–64. On the historical use of *in persona Christi*, cf. Bernard-Dominique Marliangeas, *Cles pour une theologie du ministere* (Paris: Beauchesne, 1978); also Cooke, *Ministry*, pp. 574–90, 609–10.

25. Cf. *LG* 7–8, 38–39.

episcopal office and episcopal power most basically to the sacramental order—the fullness of the sacrament of orders; it is the fullness that comes precisely with episcopal ordination. Since the Council, theologians have picked up this clue and given increased attention to the sacramental dimension of the episcopate. Not only is episcopal power rooted in sacrament; episcopal power is itself sacramental power, the episcopacy is meant to function as sacraments function.[26]

5. If this line of thinking about the episcopate is legitimate—and Vatican II seems quite clearly to support, even encourage, it—it means that the principal source of episcopal effectiveness lies in the bishops' operative significance, in what they symbolize to the Church as a whole and beyond that to the world. The power involved in such an exercise of ministry operates within the realm of faith, precisely that faith which makes the risen Christ and his Spirit present to and transformative of human life. Because the preservation of authentic faith, grounded in the original apostolic experience of Jesus as the Christ and evolving through centuries of Christian discipleship, is critical to Christianity's very existence, the bishops function as a central and sacramental witness to their collegially shared faith which in turn reflects the faith shared by Christians throughout space and time. Such a role involves real power, real authority; but it is the authority and power of faith (sacramentally expressed) in the Word and Spirit of God, the authority and power of religious commitment to the establishment of God's rule of justice and peace. Such a role is truly a unifying force in the life of Christian communities and in all exercise of Christian ministry; but it unifies in the way that key societal symbols (including symbolic people) integrate and dynamize human communities.

Such a role finds paramount expression in sacramental liturgy where the celebrant's profession of his (and the episcopal college's) faith activates, enriches, grounds, and unifies the faith of the assembled people, helping to shape them into an actively worshiping community that becomes in this act of liturgical worship more intensely believing, more thoroughly dedicated to

---

26. "In the bishops...our Lord Jesus Christ, the supreme High Priest, is present in the midst of those who believe....He is not absent from the gathering of His high priests, but above all through their excellent service He is preaching the Word of God to all nations, and constantly administering the sacraments of faith to those who believe." *LG* 21.

Christian ministry, i.e., more fully the body of Christ. The word *fullness* can be truly used to describe the sacramental power of the episcopate, because it is the collegial dimension of the bishop's witness (in liturgy as well as in other expressions of episcopal concern for the faith and life of people) that points to the faith of the entire Church. The special power exerted by the bishop comes from the public nature of his faith witness as a recognized (ordained) member of the episcopal college.

6. Any discussion about the "fullness of orders" and the claim of the bishops to possess such a fullness leads us inevitably to examine the origin of episcopacy as an institutionalized structure in the Church. In Catholic circles, this has for centuries centered around the doctrine (scarcely ever challenged) that the episcopacy is *de jure divino.* It was instituted by Jesus himself in the choice of his twelve closest disciples whose function and authority (i.e., office) the bishops inherit by unbroken historical succession. It all seemed so simple to prove: the New Testament literature testifies to Jesus' choice and empowerment of the Twelve; the Pastorals witness to handing on of office; and historical evidences to the process of succession are traced back to the first Clementine letter, Ignatius, Irenaeus, Hegesippus, and Eusebius. But things are not so simple and direct as they had seemed. Modern critical scholarship has raised a number of issues that Catholic teaching must honestly face if it is justifiably to maintain the claims it has made for the episcopacy's origin and authority.

Perhaps the most basic question raised for us by critical study of the historical evidence is, what exactly did Jesus do that might be seen as "the institution of the episcopacy"? It is highly unlikely that he actually empowered the Twelve with a discernible office in a religious community or even granted them authority as the basis for the emergence of such an office. As a matter of fact, though there is no possible verification in such questions, it is rather unlikely that Jesus himself thought of establishing an institutionalized religious body. Even if one maintains, as genuine Catholic belief does, that Jesus Christ did institute Church, the essence of such institution was his dying and rising. What preceded death and resurrection was somehow an integral element in Jesus' role (not just "preliminaries") and pertained to the action of institution, but the manner in which it pertained remains to be clarified—though we know enough to know that earlier simplistic statements should not be repeated.[27]

Also, historical study raises questions about the actual emergence of episcopal structures from the Twelve. Careful study of the New Testament gives us no basis for saying that any of the Twelve functioned as an *episkopos*; nor is there any foundation for the contention that the various episcopal sees came into existence by branching off from sees begun by Jesus' own apostles. At the very least, Catholic explanations of the present episcopacy's links to the Twelve will have to be modified in a way that takes account of responsible critical scholarship.

One of the needed adjustments in understanding has to do with the notion of "institution by Christ" and the closely related notion of *de jure divino*.[28] Really, to see "institution" as something not limited to actions of the historical Jesus would accord quite well with the basic Catholic view that the ongoing historical life of the Church is an essentially positive growth of a community directed by God. The activity of Christ that might be seen as "institution of the Church" pertains more to that postresurrectional period in which, present to the Church through his Spirit, the risen Lord works continuously to bring into being whatever can serve the advance of the kingdom of God. Even if (which, of course, is not the case) the episcopacy had not come into existence until the sixth century, this would not necessarily mean that one could not see its emergence as resulting from divine institution.

Karl Rahner has made this point quite forcibly. Though several diverse patterns of Church order may well have existed side by side in primitive Christianity, and it may have taken some time for the Church to realize what form was most in accord with its nature, this does not mean that a structure such as the episcopacy, after having once emerged as the universal and recognized form, is not thereafter a perennial and necessary element of institutionalized Christianity. The *de jure divino* claim for the episcopacy is not grounded on some explicit establishment by Jesus himself, but on the fact that it is a necessary means of ensuring that the believing community throughout

27. For a review of some of the recent theological study of the relationship of Jesus' life, death, and resurrection to one another, cf. John Galvin, "Jesus' Approach to Death: An Examination of some Recent Studies," *Theological Studies* 41 (1980): 713–44.

28. For a survey and analysis of much of present discussion of *ius divinum*, cf. Avery Dulles, "*Ius divinum* as Ecumenical Problem," *Theological Studies* 38 (1977): 681–708.

history will remain in contact with its origins. Though the circumstances of the hierarchy's origin were historically contingent, this does not mean that the episcopacy is a contingent element of the Church's existence.[29]

Applying this understanding to an episcopacy that historically claimed and exercised jurisdictional authority according to a *monarchical* model,[30] one has to raise a basic question: Is it possible for there to emerge, as an element attributable to the Spirit's influence, something that is contradictory to Jesus' (and primitive Christianity's) understanding of "the kingdom of God"? The question would seem to demand a negative answer: Catholic theology is faced with the need to resolve earliest Christianity's repudiation of dominative authority (starting with Jesus' rejection of a political interpretation of messiahship) and the historical episcopate's claim to monarchical power of rule. Simply put: episcopal fullness of power cannot relate to anything other than that kind of power that is appropriate to the Church as agent of God's kingdom and extension of Jesus' own exercise of power. But what kind of power did Jesus himself claim and exercise, and how did earliest Christianity understand itself and its leadership to be empowered? What emerges in the historical episcopate is at least partially of a different order. The question is, can this *different* element be seen as an organic outgrowth of what begins with Jesus, or can it even be seen as intrinsically reconcilable with Jesus' own establishment of the kingdom? Understanding and justification of episcopal "fullness of orders" and its relationship to the broader reality of Christian ministry presuppose a clearer knowledge of the continuity between Jesus and the bishops than we now possess.

Given this element of uncertainty, what conclusions can one draw in the practical order? Certainly, the ministerial activities of Catholics should be carried on with regard for continuity with

---

29. Karl Rahner, "Reflection on the Concept of 'jus divinum' in Catholic Thought," *Theological Investigations*, ed. Karl H. Kruger, vol. 5 (Baltimore: Helicon, 1966), 226–40; "The Episcopal Office", *Theological Investigations*, ed. Karl H. Kruger, vol. 6 (Baltimore: Helicon, 1969), 313–60.

30. In his "Open Questions in Dogma Considered by the Institutional Church as Definitively Answered," *Journal of Ecumenical Studies* 15 (1978): 211–26, Karl Rahner proposes the possibility that the episcopal office need not be exercised by an individual. It seems that this would move us away from *monarchy*, but still leave us within the political model for understanding the governing power proper to the Church.

the deepest levels of tradition; we should cherish our history and remain constantly open to learning from our present experience. In the overall endeavor of the community, theology has a specific task: not to legitimate or defend either the past or the new, but to examine critically by research and reflection that stream of belief and devotion and life that flows from Jesus himself up to and beyond the present. More specifically, this means a serious study of the *sacramentality* of the episcopal college, a clear analysis of the *authority* intrinsic to the ministers (or ministries), and a candid examination of the kind of *power* that is appropriately exercised in the Church.

Authority of Tradition: Learning with Latino/a Experience

The issue of authority of the ordained hierarchy demanded Cooke's attention as he worked from the 1960s through 1980s to establish theologically the essential—and essentially needed—power of the laity in the Church. This gave rise, as we saw above (see pp. 182–84), to his argument for unity, not uniformity, as the criteria for allowing the plethora of gifts among the entire body of the Church in its members to flourish. While the promotion of unity in diversity likewise included no small amount of ecumenical involvements during that period, Cooke's appreciation for the value of pluralism in a truly universal Christianity found new inspiration within North American Catholicism as he accompanied Pauline in her pastoral ministry among the rapidly growing Latino/a population. The couple's move to the Southwest upon his retirement from Holy Cross provided Cooke's career-long theology of and for the laity with new insights into the authority of Christian tradition borne at the profoundly popular level.

When we decided on San Antonio as the place for "retirement," we had no intention of further teaching. Instead we hoped to work with the Mexican American Acculturation Center (MAAC) in that city, having already made contact with its director. We received a very positive response to our offer of help, especially to our suggestion that we could assist by traveling for a week or so at a time to provide theological and liturgical formation to the numerous *communidades de base* in southern Texas. The leadership at MAAC mentioned, however, that they wished us to enroll in the program they provided to acquaint coworkers with the special characteristics of the Mexican-American apostolate— a very wise and agreeable idea. For a year, the two of us, Pauline full-time and I part-time because of teaching obligations that almost immediately entered the picture, participated in the orientation program.

Even before we reached San Antonio, however, the religious studies department of Incarnate Word College contacted me, asking me to accept a newly established chair in theology, at least for a year or two. As first proposed, it would not interfere with our plans at MAAC, so we agreed. As it turned out, the position was not exactly what one associates with "chair" in most academic institutions. It was really a full-time, nontenured, undergraduate position funded by a new grant. Though very different, the teaching proved both enjoyable and worthwhile.

Incarnate Word College (IWC), now Incarnate Word *University*, had been for many years a select school that catered to the daughters of well-to-do Catholics of the region. It was conducted by the religious of the Incarnate Word Congregation, who had a long history of providing education and health care in that part of the country and Mexico. The sisters are still prominent in both fields and remain an extremely important part of Catholic ministry in these changing times of contentious immigration. Because of the increasing need to confront the developing situation of Mexican immigration, the sisters at Incarnate Word made the decision a few decades ago to shift somewhat the purpose and character of the college. Without abandoning the school's traditional ministries, it would now open its doors to relatively poor Latino/a young people, making higher education available to many who would not ordinarily enjoy a college education. What this meant for me was the student body with which I dealt was heavily Latino/a, young women and men who were bright and eager and hardworking but, in many instances, attempting to overcome deficiencies in their earlier education.

My exposure to *Tejano* culture at IWC was expanded by Pauline's work with Fuerza Unida. About a year before our arrival in San

Antonio, a large Levi Strauss clothing factory closed unexpectedly, moving to Costa Rica. No provision was made for the women who had been employed there, skilled workers whose dismissal now meant that their resources for mortgages, children's education, health care, etc., suddenly disappeared. Instead of simply giving up at that point, many of these women organized into a protest movement, Fuerza Unida (United Power). Although Levi Strauss rebuffed their protests over several years, the company did alter somewhat their closing of plants in other cities in order to avoid the bad publicity that resulted from their behavior in San Antonio. Despite their relative failure with Levi Strauss, the women in Fuerza Unida developed into a potent force for social justice in San Antonio and elsewhere. Pauline became deeply involved with Fuerza Unida, a close friend of the women who were its leaders, accepted by these women as a valued member who provided some of the technical skills that they had not been able to acquire. Needless to say, this gave me the opportunity to enter the world of San Antonio's Latino/a community.

When we moved to San Antonio, the real estate agent recommended our locating in the northern, mostly Anglo section of the city. We were geographically in St. Matthew's parish, the richest in the city, with which we could not identify psychologically. As I've often remarked, if one drove a Buick, it would have been the poorest car in the parish parking lot on Sunday. I've never seen such a collection of Mercedes and Jaguars. When we still lived in that portion of the city, our Latino friends never accepted our invitations to dinner. When, however, we moved to the King William (originally Kaiser Wilhelm) district bordering on the southern Mexican-American neighborhoods, our Latino friends felt comfortable visiting us. "We like your barrio," they told us. This whole experience of the two cities and two dioceses of San Antonio made me question the understanding of "Christian community" that functioned in my ecclesiology....In subtle ways, we were imbibing a culturally different understanding of Christian faith, something that was to change substantially some aspects of my doing theology.

Cooke recounts, however, that after several years in San Antonio, his and Pauline's expectations for working with MAAC failed to materialize. Even as those prospects dwindled, a new opportunity emerged in Southern California. Upon serving as one of the outside examiners for the reaccreditation process of the department of religious studies at the University of San Diego (a Roman Catholic diocesan institution), Cooke accepted a one-year visiting professorship that eventuated in offers of regular teaching positions to both him and Pauline.

Delighted to find himself in a religious studies department striving to become a leading center of Latino/a theology, Cooke joined in a two-year collaborative project studying, discussing, and eventually publishing a book on the theology of tradition. Cooke's contribution to that volume afforded him the opportunity to argue for the multifaceted authority of tradition from the perspective of a particular sociocultural body of the Church, the one comprising the growing base of US Catholicism in the twenty-first century (FOP 23–42):

Authority and/or Tradition

Implicit in all the discussion of tradition in this volume's essays[31] is the issue of *normativity*: in what way(s) do the various agents and forms of tradition provide a guideline or a law for individual and community behavior? To express it differently, what *authority* attaches to a specific element of tradition, to a specific bearer of a tradition, or to the process of traditioning as a whole?[32] Any response to these questions demands a clarification of the kinds of authority that function in the process of traditioning and of the manner in which they apply to the bearers of tradition.

---

31. Cooke's essay here originally appeared as a chapter in the multiauthored, collective volume *Futuring Our Past: Explorations in the Theology of Tradition* (2006). Thus, his multiple references to "this volume" in the body and, especially, the footnotes of this essay are in reference to that book. *(Ed. note.)*

32. Drawing from the group's recognition of the need to nuance use of the term *tradition*, this essay will employ the following usage: (1) When the term *Tradition* is capitalized, it refers to the official use of the term, which for most of the past has pointed to the content of faith formulations. (2) There are any number of traditions (celebrations, texts, practices, etc.) that are handed down in family or ethnic or religious or territorial groups; and such traditions always involve some understandings that can be referred to as content. The tendency is to consider content as objective and unchanging, but in actuality, it is diversified and conditioned by changing circumstances. (3) There is growing recognition that in using the term *tradition*, whether capitalized or not, one is dealing with a process of handing on an entire way of life and belief; groups traditionalize. When the focus is on this process, this essay will use the term *traditioning*, but when tradition is used, the assumption is that one is dealing with a process of traditioning that involves one or another developing content.

Such clarification is the intent of this essay, which, fortunately, can draw from a considerable body of reflection about authority during recent decades.[33]

Authority is a multiform kind of power that functions both to govern relationships in the public sphere and to affect the motivation of individuals. One could also describe authority as the operative influence of a person, text, event, custom, or institution upon the thinking and action of a community or an individual. Much recent explanation of authority has insisted that, in practice, it is a modality of the complex relationships of influence among people, and there is disagreement whether authority can be viewed as a "quality" residing in one or other agent.[34] In an important and provocative essay, Orlando Espin has elaborated the way in which the phenomenon of globalization is fundamentally affecting the way in which traditioning occurs and the resultant perspective that must guide research into tradition. While the essay does not explicitly deal with the element of authority in traditioning, the entire essay can be read as an analysis of the way in which globalization has changed the reality and the theoretical consideration of authority.[35]

Though in some cases authority is made effective by enforcement of one sort or another, authority as such operates by persuasion directed to people's free choices. Dependent upon the function of authority in a particular instance, it is specified by and grounded in a distinctive base; for example, authority in the case of teaching can flow from the knowledge of the teacher, in the political sphere from the office of the office holder, in the case of a charismatic prophet from divine inspiration and commission. From among the many forms of authority that exist, this essay will deal only with those that impinge or depend upon tradition.

---

33. For a more extensive discussion of authority, see Bernard Cooke, *Power and the Spirit of God: Toward an Experience-Based Pneumatology* (New York: Oxford University Press, 2003), chap. 3.

34. See Terrence Tilley, *Inventing Catholic Tradition* (Maryknoll, NY: Orbis Books, 2000), 66–87. In similar fashion, David J. Stagaman writes, "Authority, then, is an attribute of human interaction among human agents and the objects that surround them" (*Authority in the Church* [Collegeville, MN: Liturgical Press, 1999], 39).

35. Orlando O. Espin, "Towards the Construction of an Intercultural Theology of Tradition," *Journal of Hispanic/Latino Theology* 9 (2002): 22–59. Espin's essay provides a complement to what Stagaman describes as the diachronic approach to understanding authority (*Authority in the Church*, 51–55).

Actually, the relation of authority and tradition is very close, almost one of inseparability; traditioning always involves an aspect of authority, and most instances of authority are grounded in and draw from traditioning for their legitimation and their implementation.[36] Tradition is a primary source of authority in thinking and acting; conversely, elements of a people's tradition are embodied in those persons, texts, rituals, and offices that are viewed as bearing authority. Tilley, in his recent study of tradition, criticizes much of the discussion of tradition because "the practices of institutional authority are absent....An understanding of the authority of office is so absent that such theories [of tradition] are simply not adequate to account for the multifaceted reality that is an enduring faith tradition."[37]

The intimate link between authority and tradition is immediately apparent if one examines the broad experiential context of a culture and the role within it of a people's "religious" faith. David Stagaman (following Gadamer) has in his monograph on authority in the Church drawn attention to what he calls the authoritative, that is, the implicit, taken-for-granted evaluation of events, persons, and institutions that implicitly passes judgment as good or evil, appropriate or inappropriate. The normativity of a culture's "hermeneutic of experience" is a fluid, constantly shifting influence on people's outlook and choices—pervasive and for the most part unrecognized.[38] Such an overarching, authoritative influence has in any particular case emerged from the previous experiences and wisdom evaluations of that people, especially from those evaluations that because "religious" are considered in some form to have come from God. This constitutes a broad, lived tradition that guides the activity and ethical judgments of a group, even when scarcely recognized, much less enunciated. It is often seen as simply natural, what has always been done, and therefore acceptable.

It is not a long leap to associate this value-bearing general cultural judgment with the faith notion of *sensus fidelium*.[39] In a

---

36. Stagaman goes so far as to identify authority and Tradition: "Authority considered in the light of the temporal before and after is called tradition" (*Authority in the Church*, 51).

37. Tilley, *Inventing Catholic Tradition*, 154.

38. On the need to include a diachronic consideration in any definition of authority, see Stagaman, *Authority in the Church*, 51–55. This indicates the need to apply such an approach to a study of Tradition.

39. See Orlando O. Espín, *The Faith of the People* (Maryknoll, NY: Orbis Books, 1997), 63–90.

culture such as the Latino/a, in which a presence of the divine is part of the "atmosphere" of experience, a faith perspective is intrinsic to people's awareness of themselves and their world regardless of whether they are "religious" or not. Because life is experienced and carried on *latinamente,* there is a shared assumption of what is appropriate and "true," not only as humans but also as Christians. To some extent, cultural memory extends beyond the influence of faith, but it is impossible to establish any bounds of demarcation. The ongoing process of traditioning provides a fundamental hermeneutic by which the occurrences of daily life are interpreted in the light of faith, and faith is interpreted in the light of *lo cotidiano.*

Authority of Tradition-Bearing Texts

Beyond this amorphous, overarching "authoritative" that accompanies traditioning as it unfolds,[40] there is a number of identifiable agencies that combine to shape and legitimate Tradition. When one thinks of the agents that have carried traditioning, one of the first that comes to mind is the canon of texts, religious or secular, that is recognized as bearing explicitly the ideas, values, hopes, worldview, and identity of a group. For Latino/a cultures, the place of privilege among such texts has been the sacred Scriptures of Israel and Christianity, texts that carry unparalleled authority across a range of differing faith communities because they are regarded as the inspired word of God.[41]

That is not to say that Scripture is authoritative in the same way for all its readers/hearers; instead, it speaks to individuals

---

40. Though Stagaman and others are correct in stressing the importance of studying the development of Tradition, a caution must be kept in mind. It is typical of the modern mentality to consider the historical sequence as a gradual, cumulative gain of insights and wisdom. However, until modern times, it was assumed that the normative *auctores* were figures of the past and that the wisdom of the ancient sages was sometimes dimmed or distorted with the passage of time. It is interesting to compare this older view with recent focus on ressourcement. On the attitude of medieval theologians, like Thomas Aquinas, to the creative use and rethinking of ancient wisdom, see M.-D. Chenu, *Towards Understanding Saint Thomas* (Chicago: University of Chicago Press, 1964), 20–38.

41. In Catholic reflection on the "inspiration" of the Bible, there was an important advance in official teaching at the Second Vatican Council; its document *Dei Verbum* opened up the notion of revelation as an ongoing process in the life of the Church, instead of the previously prevalent understanding that revelation ended with the death of the last of the apostles. This "new" view was linked with mid-twentieth-century advances in understanding the nature of Jesus' resurrection and the continuing presence of God to history in the gift of the Spirit.

and communities in distinctive ways dependent upon their social location and especially the nature and extent of their educational background. For many fundamentalists, the Bible acts as an icon in which they believe they encounter a present revelation of the will of God. For those in a context of Scripture being proclaimed in worship, the word can be heard, dependent upon the expertise of the homilist explaining the text, with more critical understanding. For a trained scripture scholar, the text can constitute a means of uncovering the revelation communicated to people at the origin of the text, revelation communicated through this text during centuries of interpretation by faith communities, revelation that is accepted as faith guidance. In short, a person regards the authority of Scripture according to the tradition(s) of interpretation that he or she has inherited and accepted.[42]

Justo Gonzalez, reflecting on his own evolving experience of reading the Bible, points out the way in which the precise authority of Scripture depends upon the life context of a person and, at any given moment of that experience, can be multiple.[43] Childhood and adolescent confidence in the vision of the biblical word of God can for some individuals fade in adulthood as the Bible no longer seems to speak to life's happenings. Technical study of Scripture can provide the tools for evaluating the text as historical evidence or as source of theological reflection, with a result quite different from the religious authority the text has for the ordinary believer. While the latter person can share the centuries-old traditions of a faith community, the exegete draws as well from the scholarly evaluation of methodology and insights handed down in the academy.

Within academic worlds, for example, biblical scholarship in nineteenth-century German universities, there develop schools of exegesis, each with its traditional interpretation of many texts. The fact that they are handed down relatively unchanged from

---

42. On the influence of an "audience" on the identity and interpretation of a test, see Jorge Gracia, *Texts: Ontological Status, Identity, Author, Audience* (Albany: State University of New York Press, 1996), 141–69.

43. Justo Gonzalez, *Santa Biblia: The Bible through Hispanic Eyes* (Nashville, TN: Abingdon Press, 1996). Gonzalez describes the ways in which popular Latino interpretation of the Bible is influenced by marginalization, poverty, *mestizaje*, and cultural solidarity. While the Bible provides out of the traditions of the people an authoritative interpretation of their life, their experience furnishes the hermeneutic that governs the religious understanding of the sacred text.

one generation to another gives these interpretations an authority that can endure unchallenged for decades.[44] The German scripture scholar Luise Schottroff has drawn attention to the extent to which biblical interpretation had been dominated and truncated because all the interpreters of the Bible until very recently have been men who assumed the validity of an androcentric perspective.[45]

It is not only professional biblical scholars, however, who accept certain meanings of biblical texts as authoritative because those meanings have always been assumed as the true sense of the text. Among the ordinary faithful, many texts are understood the way they are because that has been the meaning passed down from one generation to the next. In evaluating the way in which Scripture operates authoritatively for the bulk of Latino/a Christians, it is good to keep in mind the remark of Jean-Pierre Ruiz in the theological discussion that produced *From the Heart of Our People*:

> A *teologia de conjunto* that seriously engages in critical dialogue with the ancient voices that emerge from the biblical texts, voices that testify to a self-disclosing God, must attend respectfully to voices outside of the academy, to those who bring their own language and their own experience to their dialogue with the biblical text.[46]

Authority of Nonbiblical "Official" Religious Texts

The variation in authority that religious texts bear is even more pronounced when one looks at the actual impact of key historical statements that are considered officially normative, such as the creed of the Council of Chalcedon. Indirectly, through the recognition it receives as dogma, and therefore through preach-

---

44. On the need to reassess the authoritative (traditional) interpretation of Scripture, see Fernando F. Segovia, *Decolonizing Biblical Studies* (Maryknoll, NY: Orbis Books, 2000), reviewed in *Journal of Hispanic/Latino Theology* 9 (2001): 60.

45. Luise Schottroff, *Lydia's Impatient Sisters* (Louisville, KY: Westminster Knox, 1995). Her critique runs throughout the book as she proposes, in contrast to the exclusively androcentric view that has predominated, the feminist perspective on various texts that has been developed by current biblical scholarship by women.

46. Jean-Pierre Ruiz, "The Bible and U.S. Hispanic American Theological Discourse," in *From the Heart of Our People: Latino/a Explorations in Catholic Systematic Theology*, ed. Orlando O. Espin and Miguel H. Diaz (Maryknoll, NY: Orbis Books, 1999), 112.

ing and catechisms and guiding the transmission of faith understandings to those not theologically sophisticated, such a text does
help shape Tradition, but on the level of immediately influencing
people's faith the text is unknown and irrelevant. Such texts function only within professional circles as normative guides in the
community's official transmission of traditional beliefs.

One can attribute to other historical statements of belief,
especially the explanations of Christian faith provided by the
great figures of the patristic period, like Augustine or Ambrose,
an authority because of the intrinsic genius of their insights and
their influential role in shaping Christian thought. Such authority has also been attributed over the centuries to prominent theologians like Aquinas or Alexander of Hales. During the past two
centuries, papal statements have increasingly acquired, whether
justifiably or not, this kind of authority, to some extent supplant-
ing the influence of earlier ecclesiastical statements.[47]

Canonical "Secular" Texts

Biblical or ecclesiastical texts can claim no monopoly in the
transmission of Tradition. Along with canonical religious Scriptures, other literary classics play a canonical or semicanonical
role in a culture's traditions—and in some instances, function
cross-culturally. One need only reflect on the communication of
human insights and values through Shakespeare's *King Lear* or
Sophocles's *Antigone* or Cervantes's *Don Quixote*. Nor need such
sharing in a people's traditions be limited to "great" pieces of
literature; popular songs and nursery rhymes that pass on interpretations of human experience very likely have a broader effect
on popular understanding of what it means to be human.[48] One
can point, for instance, to the immense influence on religious
understandings and attitudes of the hymns of the Wesley brothers in the Methodist movement. Moreover, in many cases it is not

---

47. On the authority of official statements, especially the teaching of the papacy in recent
times, see Francis A. Sullivan, *Magisterium: Teaching Authority in the Catholic Church* (New
York: Paulist Press, 1983). For a discussion of papal teaching's relation to the broader
"ordinary magisterium," see Richard R. Gaillardetz, *Witness to the Faith* (New York: Paulist
Press, 1992).

48. Poetry is a specially powerful instrument for shaping people's religious understandings.
See Horacio Pena, "The Thousand Faces of God in Central American Poetry," *Journal of
Hispanic/Latino Theology* 6 (1999): 35–77.

easy, sometimes impossible, to say when texts carry religious or secular meaning.[49]

Linked with the cultural authority of literary classics is the subtle but widespread impact of the arts. Elusive though it is to define or identify in a given culture, *style* exerts a broad and profound effect on people's decisions and lifestyle. Closely connected though it is with custom and memory, style is a very fluid force in people's perception of the good life and with their judgment of acceptable social behavior. The aesthetic appreciation belonging to those who are genuinely "stylish" is, however, not a natural endowment but a sensibility that must be acquired by education, essentially by exposure to the beautiful. It is in this realm that the arts make an indispensable contribution to a people's culture and in which objects of true quality possess an authority as guides in forming aesthetic judgments.[50]

Schools of artistic production with their distinctive traditions come and go, but they unquestionably shape people's perception of the beautiful in some enduring fashion. Museum exhibits witness the extent to which artists and their work constitute an important influence in a people's traditioning. Despite the overall fickleness of style, truly beautiful artistic creations—whether paintings or symphonies or poems or buildings—transcend time's changes and provide a heritage that is not limited by ethnic or temporal boundaries.

"Texts" can and do acquire an authority of their own, but that authority is generally rooted in the authority (real or presumed[51]) of their authorship. Biblical texts possess unique authority for believers because of their "divine" origin, though (as we saw earlier) this is conditioned by the manner and extent of their

---

49. One of the more intriguing instances of such double meaning is the way in which apparently completely secular texts such as some Shakespearean plays carried encoded elements of the Hermetic religious tradition. See the writings of Frances Yates, especially *Giordano Bruno and the Hermetic Tradition* (Chicago: University of Chicago Press, 1964) and *The Occult Philosophy in the Elizabethan Age* (London: Routledge, 1979).

50. On the resources of cultural traditions in development of a Latino theology of art, see Alejandro Garcia-Rivera, "A Wounded Innocence," *Journal of Hispanic/Latino Theology* 8 (2002): 5–20. Also, Roberto Goizueta's study of the influence of Jose Vasconcelos draws attention to the aesthetic aspect of the overarching "authoritative" dimension of a people's culture ("*La Raza Cosmica?* The Cosmic Vision of Jose Vasconcelos," *Journal of Hispanic/Latino Theology* 2 [1994]: 5–27).

51. The classic case of such presumption is that of Pseudo-Dionysius, whose alleged connection with Saint Paul gave widespread and lasting authority to his writings.

reception. Key dogmatic creeds derive authority because they come from the "infallible" voice of Church councils. Great literary classics reflect the genius of their creators. Subsequently, the attribution of authority to these texts and the authority of any particular exegesis comes because of the personal authority of "teachers." Under this general rubric of teacher, there is a wide range—parents and other family members, credentialed teachers in schools, experts through research, religious pastors and Church authorities, charismatic prophets, saintly models of faith and behavior, well-informed friends.

Most basic, of course, in any person's beginning to share in his or her cultural heritage or religious traditions are the members of the individual's immediate family. Orlando Espin has repeatedly pointed to older women, especially the grandmother, the *abuela*, as key authority figures in the transmission of Latino/a tradition.[52] Teaching authority within the family is, however, a shifting influence and one that is challenged by other social forces such as peer pressures on adolescents. For children in their early years, the authority of parents is unquestioned, but with the onset of adolescence, this authority is often diminished by discovery that the older generation is not infallible, not "in synch" with the surrounding dominant culture, not always honest. Eventually, as persons grow into maturity, their measured "conformity" to tradition grows out of their own understandings and experienced choices. They have been taught by life itself, but shared memories and continued interchange still wield a powerful influence in closely knit families.

Other teachers enter the picture as children go to school. These figures are assumed to "know their stuff" and possess the authority that implies. But their authority is often enhanced by other factors: many of us can remember the religious women who presided over the classroom, women whose authority (symbolized by their garb) came at least as much from their ecclesial and professional role as from their knowledge. In some cases, there is the influence of a charismatic teacher, one who with a unique kind of authority represents what it means to be human as well as learned, one who epitomizes what is best in a cultural tradition.

---

52. See, for instance, his discussion of the role of older women in Espin, *The Faith of the People*, 4–5.

Along with academic teachers there are parish pastors. Within the broader influence of a parish community that embodies people's outlook on life, often as an island in the midst of an alien culture, the symbolic role of the ordained pastor is unique.[53] His (or, in some cases, hers) is a voice of established religious authority. He is the one representing God as well as the official Church, designated by ordination to guide the faith and, in somewhat prophetic fashion, through sermons and teaching, to explain ethical precepts as the will of God. In the realm of "the sacred," his words bear an authority beyond teaching, for they confect the great mystery of eucharistic transformation; his words of confessional absolution are believed to have power over sin. This is true even when the priest is not personally an exemplar of his role.

However, in the concrete context of Christians' lives, the authority of a pastor is conditioned by such factors as his knowledge, his skill in communicating, the authenticity of his faith, and even his personality traits. It is not uncommon for the exhortation given during Sunday worship to be neutralized for children by a parent's criticism of the sermon. Simply put, in addition to the authority that comes with special relation to "the sacred," a pastor must gain human authority by what he himself is and does. Moreover, today, when greater opportunities exist for people to develop an accurate and adult conscience, the authority of a person's own conscience at times conflicts with and overrules the authority of religious leaders.

Authority of Scholarly Historical Research

In the past few centuries, associated with the overall respect for science, critical historical research has exerted increasing authority as a guide to people's memory of their antecedents. The supposed objectivity of this scholarly effort had inescapably been affected by the differing social locations of the researchers, but this influence was not always recognized nor admitted by those historians who have claimed to be and have often been considered to be "mainstream history." Confronting this hegemonic

---

53. On the role of the parish and its pastor in the transmission of tradition, see William B. Taylor, *Magistrates of the Sacred* (Stanford, CA: Stanford University Press, 1996), reviewed in *Journal of Hispanic/Latino Theology* 7 (1999): 72. It is obvious, then, how desirable it is to have as pastors indigenous priests who share the culture of the people.

claim, Gary Macy has rejected the view that Latino/a historical scholarship is marginal to such a mainstream; instead, he details a centuries-long recording of remembered events that provides a rich heritage and resource for Latino/a traditioning.[54]

Authority of Ritual

In families, parishes, schools, and neighborhoods, a key agency in traditioning is ritual. Among Latinos/as this is accentuated because of the cultural prominence of fiestas. In his essay in *From the Heart of Our People*, Roberto Goizueta has provided a penetrating analysis of the central and complex role played by fiestas of various kinds in the life of Hispanic peoples.[55] He has pointed out how fiesta celebration involves much more than the element of play, because the basic forces of ritual present in fiestas work to shape a culture and the individuals within it.

Rituals make clear, as perhaps no other exercise of traditioning, the interplay of authority and power. In the realms of teaching and social administration, authority is at times claimed when it is not truly possessed, and in its place, dominating power is employed. This is accentuated in religious rituals, in which an official leader can claim to be a necessary and irreplaceable mediator between the divine and humans. This implies that the very possibility of human salvation, of humans attaining their destiny, lies in the hands of these designated religious officials. Such a view is, of course, a misconception of the manner in which ritual is meant to function.[56]

Ritual has its own distinctive dynamic, which comes into play in proportion to the authenticity of the ritualizing activity. Recent studies of ritual[57] have highlighted four effects of genuine ritual celebration: (1) it expresses and creates the group's self-identification;

54. See Gary Macy's essay, "The Iberian Heritage of US Latino/a Theology," in FOP, 43–82.

55. Roberto Goizueta, "Fiesta: Life in the Subjunctive," in Espin and Diaz, *From the Heart of Our People*, 84–99.

56. For Roman Catholics, the first major document of Vatican Council II, *Sacrosanctum Concilium* (Constitution on the Sacred Liturgy), constituted a revolution in this regard. By characterizing the Eucharist as a ritual rather than a spectacle, the decree began to reverse centuries of passive congregational attendance by insisting on ritual involvement.

57. See, for example, Raymond Firth, *Symbols, Public and Private* (Ithaca, NY: Cornell University Press, 1978); and Victor Turner, *Dramas, Fields, and Metaphors* (Ithaca, NY: Cornell University Press, 1974). I have found Catherine Bell, *Ritual Theory, Ritual Practice* (New York: Oxford University Press, 1992) particularly helpful, especially the chapter on ritual and power, 171–223.

(2) it shapes the character of the group; (3) it alerts the group to its purpose for existing and demands a commitment to that goal; and (4) it reflects and confirms or challenges the structure of power within the group. Properly conducted ritual achieves these goals, not by dominating control of the participants but by appeal to their free decisions and the communal conversion of their understandings, attitudes, and behavior.

The authority of ritual lies, then, not in a personal prerogative of the presiding leader but in the shared actions and relationships of the persons engaged in the ritual. It is precisely because of this engagement of persons in confronting together the meaning of their lives and the decisions that are needed to shape a shared future that ritual has an inescapable ethical dimension, a distinctive authority in directing people's moral behavior. And it is for this reason that rituals, unofficial as well as official, play a key role in the process of traditioning.

Specific elements of ritual celebration have their own role in passing on understandings and attitudes. There has been a good deal of attention given recently to the cultural impact of the "bloody" crucifixes that are common in Latinos/as' homes and churches,[58] crucifixes where in symbol the religious memory of the suffering of Jesus intertwines with the popular memory of conquest and painful domination. In similar fashion, popular religious music carries from one generation to the next the worldview and outlook, the emotional response to life, that is central to the diachronic process of tradition.[59]

I saw the authoritative teaching influence of these popular rituals illustrated in dramatic fashion in the Good Friday "passion play" in San Antonio. During the years I lived in that city, I had the opportunity not only of observing but also of sharing in that ritual. It began in the Mercado, where, on a raised stage, the condemnation of Jesus by Pilate was reenacted. Because a good-sized crowd had gathered, the actual drama itself was preceded by a long line of greetings delivered by local Mexican American politicians; the present-day relevance of Latino religious roots

58. On the symbolic power of the crucifix in Hispanic devotion and catechesis, see Espin, *The Faith of the People*, 46–48.

59. On the role in transmitting belief that can be played by familiar songs, see Edwin David Aponte, "*Coritos* as Active Symbol in Latino Protestant Popular Religion," *Journal of Hispanic/Latino Theology* 2 (1995): 57–66.

was quite evident. The judgment scene was not simply observed by the crowd; they entered into it, the shared communal memory of Jesus' passion was obviously being reinforced. As I looked around the crowd, I was struck by something that made clear how traditioning was occurring: much of the crowd was made up of children with their grandmothers, these *abuelas* quite obviously using the occasion to catechize. The memory of those passion plays, with the interpretation given them by their grandmothers, will remain for those children in the imagination's storehouse of "exegesis" along with the overtone of reality that will give authority to Christian religious beliefs in later years.

From the Mercado, we processed for several blocks on a way of the cross, along a city street that bears the name *Dolorosa*, to the cathedral. There, in front of the Church, three crosses were raised bearing the "stand-ins" for Jesus and the thieves. Illustrating again the mixture of past and present, a long pole with a microphone was raised to "Jesus," so that the crowd in the cathedral plaza could hear the seven last words. Though that song was not used, experiencing this Good Friday liturgy could not but bring to mind the words of the old Negro spiritual, "Were You There When They Crucified My Lord?"

This folk liturgy exemplified quite clearly the authoritative power of ritual in Tradition as a process of people's culture and faith. It was not accidental to the drama that it began and ended in the two locations in San Antonio, the Mercado and San Fernando Cathedral, that continue to play important roles for the Mexican American populace in celebrating and reinforcing their folk memories in fiesta.

In principle, celebration of Eucharist should be for Roman Catholics (and similarly for other "catholic" communities like the Anglican and Lutheran) the most important ritual to bear the process of traditioning. As the ultimate instance of anamnesis, it carries through history for communities of Christian faith not just the memory and proclamation of Jesus' Passover but the very presence of the risen Christ. Eucharist is, of its essence, however, a ritual, and its effective authority as normative of faith is conditioned by the extent to which it is actually enacted as ritual. For centuries, however, the experience of Christians at Eucharist has not been that of sharing actively in a ritual; instead, it has been basically that of attendance at a sacred spectacle. It is only with

Vatican Council II's Constitution on the Sacred Liturgy (*Sacrosanctum concilium*) that official teaching of the Catholic Church has directed eucharistic celebration back to ritual. Given its traditional understanding and exercise of fiesta, and its frequent linking of fiestas with celebration of the Eucharist, the Latino/a community can be a valuable resource in the US Catholic Church's reassessment and "reconstruction" of its eucharistic activity.

In Protestant denominations that do not have as explicitly eucharistic forms of worship, the basic principles of ritual traditioning still apply.[60] In proportion as those in attendance are actively engaged, individually and communally, in response to the proclaimed word of God, the ceremony creates a lively faith in the saving presence of God and is thereby transformative. This supposes that such gathering for worship relates to and gives a deepened Christian meaning to people's present faith experience at the same time that it draws upon the shared religious memory of the past.

Before leaving this topic of the authoritative function of ritual, we need to stress again the centrality of festive activity within family circles. It is the experience of such folk festivity that will develop the mentality that must flow into larger community liturgies. Authentic liturgy cannot be taught in classrooms; it must be learned by doing.

Authority of Church Structures

Usually when people refer to the exercise of authority within the Church, they are thinking of official structures and those who function in that arena. Even though we are today questioning the monopolistic exercise of authority by ecclesiastical officialdom and becoming more aware of a multitude of other authoritative influences—the discussion shared in *teologia de conjunto* is a leading example of this—there is no question of the abiding importance of official authority and the influence it has had and still has on the process of Tradition. It was only in the mid-twentieth century,

---

60. There is among Catholics a prevalent view that Protestants, especially in the Reformed and Pentecostal traditions, lack a ritual approach to worship. Actually, there has been for some decades an increase of Protestants' interest in their own liturgical history and present practice. A striking example of Protestant scholarly study of ritual is the research and reflection of James White, for twenty-two years professor of liturgy at Perkins School of Theology and more recently at the University of Notre Dame. See particularly his *Sacraments as God's Self Giving* (Nashville, TN: Abingdon Press, 1983).

with the research of Geiselmann and Jungmann in Germany and the *nouvelle theologie* in France, that the static view of Tradition that had prevailed for decades was finally challenged. Many of us who studied theology in the pre–Vatican II years can remember how we resonated with the movement to think about Tradition as more than official ecclesiastical statements, to view it as a process that involved the entire Christian people. This important change was furthered by Vatican II, but continuing monopolistic use of the term *magisterium* to refer to the Vatican (and by extension to the bishops) indicates that the struggle is far from over.

Genuine advance in our understanding of official exercise of authority in the Church and its role in the process of Tradition will not be aided, however, by simply rejecting the authority of officeholders. Rather, it must come by assessing not only the distribution of religious authority in Christianity but also the very nature of the authority that is appropriate to the life and mission of the Church. The standard historical narrative, especially as it developed in academic circles and then trickled down into the post-Reformation polemic theology taught in seminaries, pointed to three basic exercises of authority by Church officials: (1) normative explanation of doctrine, especially through regional or Church-wide gatherings of bishops (in recent centuries this activity has focused increasingly on the authority of papal teaching as the indispensable channel of Tradition); (2) modeling and then gradually controlling the structure of sacramental rituals (while liturgical similarity had gradually been established over the centuries, it was in reaction to the Protestant Reformers that the rubrical approach to ritual unity became absolute); and (3) with increasing monopoly of ministry by the ordained, participation in the active ministry of the Church depended upon permission or mandate of Church officials. Vatican II, of course, helped break this pattern by its recognition of the responsibility and right of ministry for all the baptized, but its theory still needs to be implemented thoroughly.

In all three of these ways, ecclesiastical structures and personnel ruled the public aspects of Tradition, with a clear stress on orthodoxy. The voice and activity of Church officials was for all practical purposes identified in academic ecclesiology with the process of Tradition. While all this was happening, however, there was always an unofficial development that somewhat

221

independently and in supposedly nonauthoritative ways carried on faith and wisdom through channels such as family life and informed conversation of devoted Christians. In evaluating the actual authority of these parallel, sometimes complementary, sometimes conflicting, paths of traditioning, research is needed into the range of authority that extends beyond officialdom. This research is being importantly assisted by recent study of popular Christianity. It is to be hoped that this will not result in opposing authentic official guidance but rather in recognizing and fostering a healthy though tensive relationship between the institutional and prophetic aspects of the Christian community.

Authority of Social Location

Current discussion of authority relationships within society has drawn attention to the influence of an individual's or a group's "social location." Feminist scholars in particular have pointed out the subtle or not so subtle discriminations that occur in power relationships because of gender differences. Significantly, as leading feminist reflection deepened, women realized that within their own ranks, there was such discrimination—study of sexist imbalance had been unconsciously focused on Euro-American women to the neglect of Hispanic and African American women. This awareness led, in turn, to greater appreciation of the extent to which wealth, education, ethnic identity, class, and sexual orientation give hidden but important weight to people's speech and actions. Those who are on the receiving end of such discrimination are naturally more aware of it than are those who profit from it. So, it is not surprising that much of the important research on the impact of social location is currently being done by Latina scholars.[61]

Though one ordinarily thinks of social location as a force within secular society, it functions also within religious circles. It is difficult to find any situation in which there are advantages of social location more traditional and more firmly entrenched than that of clergy in the Catholic Church. While the ordained are generally considered to be set apart as a sacramental reality,

---

61. For summary descriptions of theology from the social location of African American and Hispanic women, see Ada Maria Isasi-Diaz, *Mujerista Theology* (Maryknoll, NY: Orbis Books, 1997); and Stephanie Mitchem, *Introducing Womanist Theology* (Maryknoll, NY: Orbis Books, 2002).

clergy itself is not a sacramental designation but rather refers to a set-apart group whose privileges go back at least as far as Constantine. To an extent, even some who are clearly not ordained, such as vowed women religious, tend to possess some of the "superiority" attached to the clergy. On a less structured level, wealthier members of parishes and dioceses generally have closer links and more influence with Church officials, and therefore a stronger voice in decision making.

Over the centuries, the social location of the wealthy has meant that those with financial ability to provide for publication of their ideas have disproportionately influenced the narrative of history and therefore people's traditions. It has been remarked, somewhat cynically but truly, that history is the story of those who have won. Yet the apparent monopoly of elites in fashioning Tradition has been matched to some extent by the folk-level memories and customs of the poor and powerless.

One aspect of social location providing authority that is distinctive to modern times is the prestige and respect given professionals. We have become accustomed to the importance attached to physicians, lawyers, and clergy, especially in smaller towns—in some countries, teachers can be added to this list. Whenever there are public gatherings of one sort or another, it is common practice to invite some of these professional people in order to give prestige to the gathering. Even when an individual who is, let us say, a physician, steps outside his or her particular domain to become active as a political figure, some of the authority of the profession still clings to the person. It is assumed that one trained as a lawyer is more responsible in the public realm—an assumption not always justified. In many instances, the views of professionals are sought in matters outside their field. A reflection of this esteem for professionals is the desire on the part of many new immigrants to have their children attain the prestige of being a doctor or lawyer.

It is clear that, rightly or wrongly, traditional views within a given culture underpin the authority with which certain individuals or institutions are endowed. Medical practice was for many centuries an activity reserved for men.[62] Then, during the early

---

62. On the rise and then decline of women's role in the healing arts, see Renate Bridenthal, Susan Stuard, and Merry Wiesner, *Becoming Visible: Women in European History* (Boston: Allyn Bacon, 1998), 222–24.

medieval period in the West, it was increasingly associated with the healing practices of women. With the approach of modern times, it again reverted to men, with the accompanying "memory" of women's healing being superstitious and untrustworthy and medical practice by men now considered "scientific."

There is an interesting (and for some people troubling) shift at present in the public identification of imitable professionals. Instead of those presumably dedicated to public service, the models of admiration and imitation are professionals in sports and entertainment. Particularly among young people, it is athletes or movie stars or rock musicians who enjoy a prominent authority as "important" humans, and the level of their monetary income reflects a broader societal evaluation of their role in society. Given this phenomenon, it is interesting to speculate about the basis for the "charismatic" authority they enjoy, whether they do embody the values of the culture and symbolize "success," or whether the attention they receive comes from people's regard for unusual physical or artistic endowments. More traditionally, among Christians, there is still a widespread devotion to those models of faith and virtue referred to as saints, whether formally canonized or not. An interesting instance of this that is prominent in Latin American cultures is the respect, even veneration, paid to some *curanderoslas.*

Authority of Established Structures

It is not only individuals to whom authority is attributed. Institutional structures and processes, both civil and ecclesiastical, can acquire and exercise authority. The US Constitution, for example, grants the Supreme Court the authoritative power to influence decisions made by lower courts and in cases of legal dispute, to be the final authoritative voice. True, individuals—in this case Supreme Court justices—exercise this authority, but it is precisely the authority attached to their office.

Authoritative structures can be directly and explicitly established, as was the case when the government of the United States was brought into being by a representative group selected by the people from whom the authority was ultimately drawn. In other cases, a structure can be set up by an authority-bearing individual who delegates designated authority to it; an example would be an official commission appointed by the president. In the religious sphere, a structure such as the law of Israel can be seen to have its authority because of direct divine establishment.

In other instances, a structure can gradually acquire authority through authoritative actions to which people have acquiesced. This seems to have been the case with the papacy, which, in the course of history, came to be viewed in the West as an arbiter in cases of dispute among "lower-level" authorities.[63] In some such cases, the authority being claimed and exercised is justified by a process of legitimation, a process that attempts to ground authority in historical tradition. Such claims to tradition are not always validated by solid historical evidence. Basing papal primacy as ruling authority on the grant of authority to Peter by Jesus was unquestioned for centuries; today such an exegesis of Matthew 16:14 is regarded as uncertain at best. Some of the most solidly established patterns of institutional authority are today being challenged, historical research indicating that their claimed authority derived from a less than justified grab of power. Perhaps the most drastic such reassessment has to do in many cultures with the long presumed headship of the family by a male patriarch.[64]

Christianity has not escaped this challenge. To an extent considered alarming in many quarters, the traditional authority of Christian churches is being questioned because of the rapidly changing social situations in many "traditional" Catholic or Protestant regions. The structured experience that created the seemingly unchanging outlook of so many, an outlook reflected in religious beliefs and practices, has been fragmented by wars and migration and economic globalization. Life is no longer what it seemed to be, and the explanations of life previously given have lost their authority as interpretations of reality. Not only has the longstanding Catholic religious hegemony in Latin America been confronted with a new prominence of Protestantism, but mainline churches, Protestant and Catholic, have been "threatened" by the explosion of Pentecostal groups. For millions of people, the social situations that fostered the old allegiances no longer exist, and in their new "neighborhoods," they are often drawn to what

---

63. See Richard Southern, *Western Society and the Church in the Middle Ages* (Baltimore: Penguin Books, 1970), 91–169.

64. See Gerda Lerner, *The Creation of Patriarchy* (New York: Oxford University Press, 1986).

seems to be more relevant acknowledgment of the divine. The question is unavoidable: Has "the traditional" lost its authority?[65]

Gradual acquisition of an institution's authority can occur in several ways.[66] Long use of certain practices can give the impression of their intrinsic validity; custom can even be elevated to law on the basis of being what has always been done. Women in the Catholic Church are familiar with this argument because of the appeal in the papal prohibition of women's ordination to the "fact" that women have never been ordained.[67] In other cases, certain structures and processes come to be considered authoritative because in practice they have proved to be successful. Their authority is challenged, of course, when social conditions shift and these formerly profitable ways of doing things are no longer advantageous.

Abuse of Authority

The theory is quite clear regarding legitimate appeal to authority, especially when it is based on religious traditions. Religious authority should be claimed and exercised, not for obtaining or retaining power, but as a means of furthering the reign of God by nurturing the faith of individuals and communities. Still, human nature being what it is, there have been and still are instances of abuse when authority is claimed without foundation or when those in authoritative positions attempt to legitimate unjust activity by appealing to their authority.

To pass fair judgment on any specific instance of abuse would require knowledge and appraisal of many influences bearing on the case, something that the space limitations of this essay do not allow. Suffice it to mention a few of the more common infractions. Those in position of official power can control the information

---

65. For an interesting study of the dynamics of such "conversion"—in this case the religious interaction of a received tradition (Lutheranism) with a changing social context and experience in El Salvador—see Mary Solberg, "Working on the Church: A Contribution to Lutheran Ecclesiology," *Journal of Hispanic/Latino Theology* 2 (1994): 60–77.

66. On the process by which Church structures have come to be considered authoritative, see Manuel Jesús Ejido, "Theoretical Prolegomenon to the Sociology of US Hispanic Popular Religion," *Journal of Hispanic/Latino Theology* 7 (1999): 27–55.

67. For evidence of women's "ordination" to various offices in the course of Church history and of the arguments against this practice, see the essays of Gary Macy and Hilary Martin in *A History of Women's Ordination*, ed. Bernard Cooke and Gary Macy, vol. 1 (Lanham, MD: Scarecrow Press, 2003).

that people need in order to make informed judgments. Again, those occupying positions of official authority can misrepresent the reality of historical happenings so that the distorted account can appear to be a tradition that legitimates their claims to power. Again, those in official positions can claim to speak for God and demand of their "subjects" submission rather than justified obedience, using the threat of divine punishment or socioreligious ostracism to underpin their rule. Finally, there can be the attempt to suppress legitimate dissent from official decrees by characterizing it as disloyal, heterodox, or irrelevant. The basic corrective to such injustices is the careful research that determines what has been the genuine Tradition of the living Church.

Summary

A final word about the relation between Tradition and authority. It is intrinsic to Tradition as the distilled wisdom of a people that it be an authoritative guide to thinking and acting. Conversely, acceptance of Tradition as authentic and normative depends on the authority of the agencies that in the course of traditioning create and transmit it.

Cooke's description and analysis of Christian tradition as an authoritative (or authorizing) process at once historical-cultural, divinely inspired, and significantly, located in people's lives in community, comprised a fitting conclusion to a half-century of publications in service to a theology of and for the laity. Fundamental to that theology remains his insistence on the sacramentality of human experience, of individual believers participating in the ongoing history of divine revelation. That the essay concludes with consideration of the abuse of authority within social bodies, and not least the Church, likewise witnesses to Cooke's valorizing of the prophetic dimension of revelation. This combination of the sacramental with the prophetic may well constitute the distinctive contribution Cooke offers to theology in the evolving postmodern context of the twenty-first-century American Church.

Selected Bibliography of Publications by Bernard Cooke

Bernard Cooke was a prolific author from early in his masters-level studies through the ninth and final decade of his life. The following is a complete list of his books, followed by a list of articles selected for their relevance to the biographical and theological themes treated in this present volume. Cooke also published scores of articles in religious education and catechetical magazines, as well as in such magazines of opinion as Commonweal, The Christian Century, America, *and* The National Catholic Reporter *(including a set of twenty audiocassette lectures on ministry in the 1970s and a pair of three-part series in the 1990s, one on the Eucharist and the other on reform of the papacy). For a curriculum vitae, including a fuller (but incomplete) bibliography through 2003, see "Highlights of Bernard Cooke's Career," in* A Sacramental Life: A Festschrift Honoring Bernard Cooke, *ed. Michael Barnes and William Roberts (Milwaukee: Marquette University Press, 2003), 13–21.*

Books

Christian Sacraments and Christian Personality. New York: Holt, Rinehart and Winston, 1965.
Formation of Faith. Chicago: Loyola University Press, 1965.
The Challenge of Vatican II. Chicago: Argus Communications, 1966.
Christian Involvement. Chicago: Argus Communications, 1966.
Vatican Council II. Seoul, Korea: Sogang College, 1966.

The Essential Writings of Bernard Cooke

New Dimensions of Catholic Life. Wilkes-Barre, PA: Dimension Books, 1968.

Beyond Trinity. Milwaukee: Marquette University Press, 1969.

The Eucharist: Mystery of a Friendship. Dayton, OH: G. A. Pflaum, 1969.

The God of Space and Time. New York: Holt, Rinehart and Winston, 1969.

The Spirit and Power of Christian Secularity. With Albert L. Schlitzer. South Bend, IN: University of Notre Dame Press, 1969.

Christian Community, Response to Reality. New York: Holt, Rinehart and Winston, 1970.

Theology in an Age of Revolution. Wilkes-Barre, PA, Dimension Books, 1971.

Rethinking Your Faith. Chicago: Claretian Publications, 1972.

Ministry to Word and Sacraments: History and Theology. Philadelphia: Fortress Press, 1976.

Sacraments and Sacramentality. Mystic, CT: Twenty-Third Publications, 1983, rev. ed. 1994.

Reconciled Sinners: Healing Human Brokenness. Mystic, CT: Twenty-Third Publications, 1986.

Alternative Futures for Worship. Vol. 5, *Christian Marriage.* Contributing editor. Collegeville, MN: Liturgical Press, 1987.

The Papacy and the Church in the United States. Editor. New York: Paulist Press, 1989.

The Distancing of God: The Ambiguity of Symbol in History and Theology. Minneapolis: Fortress Press, 1990.

God's Beloved: Jesus' Experience of the Transcendent. Philadelphia: Trinity Press International, 1992.

Why Angels? Are They Real...Really Needed? Mystic, CT: Twenty-Third Publications, 1996.

The Future of the Eucharist. New York: Paulist Press, 1997.

A History of Women and Ordination. Vol. 1, *The Ordination of Women in a Medieval Context.* Editor with Gary Macy. Lanham, MD: Scarecrow Press, 2002.

A History of Women and Ordination. Vol. 2, *The Priestly Office of Women: God's Gift to a Renewed Church.* Editor with Gary Macy. Lanham, MD: Scarecrow Press, 2003.

Power and the Spirit of God: Toward an Experience-Based Pneumatology. New York: Oxford University Press, 2004.

Christian Symbol and Ritual: An Introduction. With Gary Macy. New York: Oxford University Press, 2005.

Selected Articles and Book Chapters

"The Mutability-Immutability Principle in St. Augustine's Meta-physics." Pts. 1 and 2. *The Modern Schoolman* 23 (1946): 181–94; 24 (1947): 37–49.

"Developments in Dogma." *Perspectives* 4 (1959): 11–18.

"Synoptic Presentation of the Eucharist as Covenant Sacrifice." *Theological Studies* 21, no. 1 (1960): 1–44.

"Presidential Address." *Proceedings of the Society of Catholic College Teachers of Sacred Doctrine* 7 (1961): 7–13.

"The Sacraments as Continuing Acts of Christ." *Proceedings of the Catholic Theological Society of America* 16 (1961): 41–68. Reprinted in *Readings in Sacramental Theology*, edited by J. Stephen Sullivan, 31–51. Englewood Cliffs, NJ: Prentice Hall, 1964.

"The Core of the Christian Message" and "Some Unifying Themes." In *Sharing the Christian Message: Proceedings of the First Annual Institute 1961*, 77–89, 90–103. Detroit: Midwestern Institute of Pastoral Theology, Sacred Heart Seminary, 1962.

"The Hour of Temptation." *The Way* 2 (1962): 177–87.

"Catechesis of the Church." *Religious Education* 59, no. 2 (1964): 149–61.

"The Task of Ecumenicity." In *Ecumenism and Vatican II*, ed. Charles A. O'Neil, 1–66. Milwaukee: Bruce Publishing Co., 1964.

"Word of God: Scripture and Sacrament." *Proceedings of the Society of Catholic College Teachers of Sacred Doctrine* 10 (1964): 122–38.

"Catechetics and Social Structures." *The Living Light* 2 (1965): 76–81.

"Christian Sacrifice." *The Way* 5 (1965): 118–25.

"Eucharistic Action of the Word." *The Scotist* 21 (1965): 5–16.

"Christ's Eucharistic Action in History." In *Wisdom in Depth: Essays in Honor of Henri Renard*, 51–67. Milwaukee: Bruce, 1966.

"Eucharist: Source or Expression of Community?" *Worship* 40, no. 6 (1966): 339–48.

"Existential Pertinence of Religion." In *Spirituality and the Secular City. Concilium* 19, ed. Christian Duquoc, 32–43. New York: Paulist Press, 1966.

"The Pilgrim Church." *The Way* 6, no. 4 (1966): 284–88.

"Review of Books on Sacraments, 1955–65." *Worship* 40, no. 2 (1966): 73–79.

"The Church Always Undergoing Reformation." *Lutheran Theological Quarterly* 19, no. 3 (1967): 249–56.

"Intercommunion with the Orthodox." *Diakonia* 1 (1967): 256–62.

"The Social Aspects of the Sacrament of Penance." *Proceedings of the Catholic Theological Society of America* 22 (1967): 173–84.

"Essentials in Theological Curriculum." *Theological Education* 5, no. 1 (1968): 15–22.

"Holiness in the Bible." *Worship* 42, no. 2 (1968): 67–76.

"Charity and the Eucharist." *Diakonia* 5, no. 4 (1970): 309–25.

"Theologians as Teachers in the Church." In *Theology in Revolution: Proceedings of the College Theology Society*, ed. George Devine, 267–76. New York: Alba House, 1970.

"The 'War-Myth' in 2nd Century Christian Teaching." In *No Famine in the Land: Studies in Honor of John L. McKenzie*, ed. James W. Flanagan and Anita Weisbrod Robinson, 235–50. Missoula, MT: Scholars Press, 1975.

"Living Liturgy: Life as Liturgy." In *Emerging Issues in Religious Education*, ed. Gloria Durka and Joanmarie Smith, 116–26. New York: Paulist Press, 1976.

"Wie vertragen sich Gemeinschaft und Individualität in der Theologie?" In *Theologie im Entstehen: Beiträge zum ökumenischen Gespräch im Spannungsfeld kirchlicher Situationen*, ed. Lukas Vischer et al., 33–44. Munich: Kaiser, 1976.

"Women and Catholic Priesthood." *Worship* 51, no. 5 (1977): 400–407.

"The Church: Catholic and Ecumenical." *Theology Today* 36, no. 3 (1979): 353–67.

"The Current State of Theological Reflection." *Bulletin of the Council on the Study of Religion* 10, no. 2 (1979): 37–41.

"Horizons on Christology in the Seventies." *Horizons* 6, no. 2 (1979): 193–217.

"The Experiential Word of God." *Journal of Ecumenical Studies* 17, no. 1 (1980): 69–74.

"The Family, Heart of Liturgy." With Pauline Turner. In *Family Ministry*, ed. Gloria Durka and Joanmarie Smith, 182–200. Minneapolis: Winston Press, 1980.

"'Fullness of Orders': Theological Reflections." *The Jurist* 41, no. 2 (1981): 405–21.

"Spiritual Renewal and Professionalism." *Saint Luke's Journal of Theology* 25, no. 2 (1982): 106–21.

"Non-patriarchal Salvation." *Horizons* 10, no. 1 (1983): 23–31.

"Presidential Address: Death and Resurrection of Sacraments." *Proceedings of the Catholic Theological Society of America* 38 (1983): 45–57.

"Feminist Thought and Systematic Theology." With Pauline Turner. *Horizons* 11, no. 1 (1984): 125–35.

"Obstacles to Lay Involvement." In *The Teaching Authority of Believers, Concilium* 180, ed. Johann Baptist Metz and Edward Schillebeeckx, 63–70. Edinburgh: T & T Clark, 1985.

"Historical Reflections on the Meaning of Marriage as Christian Sacrament." In *Alternative Futures for Worship*. Vol. 5, *Christian Marriage*, ed. Bernard Cooke, 33–46. Collegeville, MN: Liturgical Press, 1987.

"History as Revelation." *Philosophy and Theology* 1, no. 4 (1987): 293–304.

"Indissolubility: Guiding Ideal or Existential Reality?" In *Commitment to Partnership: Explorations of the Theology of Marriage*, ed. William P. Roberts, 64–80. New York: Paulist Press, 1987.

"Prophetic Experience as Revelation." *Philosophy and Theology* 1, no. 3 (1987): 214–24.

"Basic Christian Understandings." In *Education for Citizenship and Discipleship*, ed. Mary C. Boys, 79–97. New York: Pilgrim Press, 1989.

"Ecclesiology: Implicit but Influential." In *Tensions between Citizenship and Discipleship*, ed. Nelle Slater, 69–83. New York: Pilgrim Press, 1989.

"Sacramentality of Second Marriages." In *Divorce and Remarriage: Religious and Psychological Perspectives*, ed. William P. Roberts, 70–77. Kansas City, MO: Sheed & Ward, 1990.

"Charism, Power, and Community." In *That They Might Live: Power, Empowerment, and Leadership in the Church*, ed. Michael Downey, 77–88. New York: Crossroad Publishing, 1991.

"Jesus of Nazareth, Norm for the Church." *Proceedings of the Catholic Theological Society of America* 49 (1994): 24–35.

"Body and Mystical Body: The Church as *Communio*." In *Bodies of Worship: Explorations in Theory and Practice*, ed. Bruce T. Morrill, 39–50. Collegeville, MN: Liturgical Press, 1999.

"Progressive Approaches to Ministry" and "Call to Action: Engine of Lay Ministry." In *What's Left? Liberal American Catholics*, ed. Mary Jo Weaver, 135–46, 147–54. Bloomington, IN: Indiana University Press, 1999.

"Worship in the Spirit: A Renewed Vision of Liturgy and Spirituality." With Anne E. Patrick and Diana L. Hayes. In *What's Left? Liberal American Catholics*, ed. Mary Jo Weaver, 155–75. Bloomington, IN: Indiana University Press, 1999.

"*Sacrosanctum Concilium*: Vatican II Time Bomb." *Horizons* 31, no. 1 (2004): 105–12.

"Authority and/or Tradition." In *Futuring Our Past: Explorations in the Theology of Tradition*, ed. Orlando Espin and Gary Macy, 23–42. Maryknoll, NY: Orbis, 2006.

Index

Advance Praise for *The Essential Writings of Bernard Cooke*

"What a gift this volume is to the church and academy! Bruce Morrill skillfully weaves together Bernard Cooke's engaging personal narrative and prophetic contributions to the Catholic theological tradition in an accessible volume. Cooke's writing remains as timely as it is lucid and inspiring, and the context Morrill provides for these essential texts further highlights the importance of this great theologian's thought for our own time and for many years to come. This book is a must-read resource for a new generation of ministers, scholars, and educators who seek to understand their faith better in the postconciliar age."

—Daniel P. Horan, OFM, author, *Postmodernity and Univocity: A Critical Account of Radical Orthodoxy and John Duns Scotus* (Fortress Press, 2014)

"No one has told the Christian story with more persuasion, better scholarship, or greater credibility than Bernie Cooke. This work captures many of his best punchlines—like the sacramentality of friendship."

—Thomas Groome, professor of theology and religious education, and director of the Church in the 21st Century Center, Boston College

"The work of Vatican II was made possible by the pioneers of the theological movements—liturgical, biblical, and ecumenical. The same is true for the work—still in progress—of the reception of Vatican II. Bernard Cooke was one of the pioneers of the post–Vatican II period, and this book of his essential writings helps us rediscover that tumultuous and energizing moment in the life of the Church."

—Massimo Faggioli, author, *Vatican II: The Battle for Meaning*; coeditor, *The Legacy of Vatican II* (both Paulist Press)